Talend Open Studio Cookbook

Over 100 recipes to help you master Talend Open Studio and become a more effective data integration developer

Rick Barton

[PACKT] open source
PUBLISHING
community experience distilled

BIRMINGHAM - MUMBAI

Talend Open Studio Cookbook

First published: October 2013

Production Reference: 2221013

Published by Packt Publishing Ltd.

Livery Place
35 Livery Street
Birmingham B3 2PB, UK.

ISBN 978-1-78216-726-6

www.packtpub.com

Cover Image by Artie Ng (artherng@yahoo.com.au)

Credits

Author
Rick Barton

Reviewers
Robert Baumgartner
Mustapha EL HASSAK
Viral Patel
Stéphane Planquart

Acquisition Editor
James Jones

Lead Technical Editor
Amey Varangaonkar

Technical Editors
Monica John
Mrunmayee Patil
Tarunveer Shetty
Sonali Vernekar

Project Coordinator
Abhijit Suvarna

Proofreader
Clyde Jenkins

Indexer
Tejal R. Soni

Production Coordinator
Adonia Jones

Cover Work
Adonia Jones

About the Author

Rick Barton is a freelance consultant who has specialized in data integration and ETL for the last 13 years as part of an IT career spanning over 25 years.

After gaining a degree in Computer Systems from Cardiff University, he began his career as a firmware programmer before moving into Mainframe data processing and then into ETL tools in 1999.

He has provided technical consultancy to some of the UK's largest companies, including banks and telecommunications companies, and was a founding partner of a "Big Data" integration consultancy.

Four years ago he moved back into freelance development and has been working almost exclusively with Talend Open Studio and Talend Integration Suite, on multiple projects, of various sizes, in UK. It is on these projects that he has learned many of the lessons that can be found in this, his first book.

I would like to thank my wife Ange for support and my children, Alice and Ed for putting up with my weekend writing sessions.

I'd also like to thank the guys at Packt for keeping me motivated and productive and for making it so easy to get started. Their professionalism and most especially their confidence in me, has allowed me to do something I never thought I would.

About the Reviewers

Robert Baumgartner has a degree in Business Informatics from Austria, Europe, where he is living today. He began his career in 2002 as a business intelligence consultant working for different service companies. After this he was working in the paper industry sector as a consultant and project manager for an enterprise resource planning (ERP) system. In 2009 he founded his company "datenpol"—a service integrator specialist in selected open source software products focusing on business intelligence and ERP. Robert is an open source enthusiast who held several speeches at open source events. The products he is working on are OpenERP, Talend Data Integration, and JasperReports. He is contributing to the open source community by sharing his knowledge with blog entries at his company blog `http://www.datenpol.at/blog` and he commits software to github like the OpenERP Talend Connector component which can be found at `https://github.com/baumgaro/OpenERP-Talend-Component`.

Mustapha EL HASSAK is a computer sciences fanatic since many years, he obtained a Bachelor's Degree in Mathematics in 2003 then attended university to study Information Technology. After five years of study, he joined the largest investment bank in Morocco as an IT engineer. After that he worked in EAI, an IT services company specialized in insurance, as a senior developer responsible of data migration. He has always worked with Talend Open Studio and sometimes with Business Objects. This is the first time he is working on a book, but he wrote several articles in French and English about Talend on his personal blog.

I would like to thank my parents, Khadija and Hassan, Said, my brother and Asmae, my sister for their support over the years. And I express my gratitude to Halima, my wife for her continued support and encouragement. Finally, I would like to thank Sirine, my little girl.

Viral Patel holds Masters in Information Technology (Professional) from University of Southern Queensland, Australia. He loves playing with Data. His area of interest and current work includes Data Analytics, Data Mining, and Data warehousing. He holds Certification in Talend Open Studio and Talend Enterprise Data Integration. He has more than four years of experience in Data Analytics, Business Intelligence, and Data warehousing.

He currently works as ETL Consultant for Steria India Limited. It is an European MNC providing consulting services in various sectors. Prior to Steria, he was working as BI Consultant where he has successfully implemented BI/DW cycle and provided consultation to various clients.

I would like to thank my grandfather Vallabhbhai, father Manubhai (who is my role model), mother Geetaben, my wife Hina, my sister Toral and my lovely son Vraj. Without their love and support, I would be incomplete in my life. I thank them all for being in my life and supporting me.

Stéphane Planquart is a Lead Developer with a long expertise in Data Management. He started to program when he was ten years old. In twenty years, he worked on C, C++, Java, Python, Oracle, DB2, MySql, PostgreSQL. From the last ten years, he worked on distinct types of projects like the database of the largest warehouse logistics in Europe where he designed the data-warehouse and new client/server application. He worked also on an ETL for the electric grid of France or 3D program for a web browser. Now he works on the application of a payment system in Europe where he designs database and API.

Table of Contents

Preface

Talend Open Studio is the world's leading open source data integration solution that enables rapid development of data transformation processes using an intuitive drag-and-drop user interface.

Talend Open Studio Cookbook contains a host of techniques, design patterns, and tips and tricks, based on real-life applications, that will help developers to become more effective in their use of Talend Open Studio.

What this book covers

Chapter 1, Introduction and General Principles, introduces some of the key principles for Talend development and explains how to install the provided code examples.

Chapter 2, Metadata and Schemas, shows how to build and make use of Talend data schemas.

Chapter 3, Validating Data, demonstrates different methods of validating input data and handling invalid data.

Chapter 4, Mapping Data, shows how to map, join, and filter data from input to output in both batch and real-time modes.

Chapter 5, Using Java in Talend, introduces the different methods for extending Talend functionality using Java.

Chapter 6, Managing Context Variables, illustrates the different methods for handling context variables and context groups within Talend projects and jobs.

Chapter 7, Working with Databases, provides insight into reading from and writing to a database, generating and managing surrogate keys, and managing database objects.

Chapter 8, Managing Files, covers a mix of techniques for reading and writing different file types including header and trailer processing. It also includes methods for managing files.

Chapter 9, Working with XML, Queues, and Web Services, covers tools and techniques for real-time/web service processing including XML, and reading and writing to services and queues.

Chapter 10, Debugging, Logging, and Testing, demonstrates the different methods for finding problems within Talend code, and how to log status and issues and techniques for generating test data.

Chapter 11, Deployment and Scheduling Talend Code, introduces the Talend executable and parameters, as well as managing job dependencies.

Chapter 12, Common Mistakes and Other Useful Hints and Tips, contains valuable tools and techniques that don't quite fit into any of the other chapters.

Appendix A, Common Type Conversions, is a useful table containing the methods for converting between Talend data types.

Appendix B, Management of Contexts, is a in-depth discussion as to the pros and cons of the various methods for managing project parameters, and what types of projects the different methods are suited to.

What you need for this book

To attempt the exercises in this book, you will need the following software

- The latest version of Talend Studio for ESB. At the time of writing, this was 5.3
- The latest version of MySQL
- Microsoft Office Word & Excel or other compatible office software.

It is also recommended that you find a good text editor, such as Notepad++.

Who this book is for

This book is intended for beginners and intermediate Talend users who have a basic working knowledge of the Talend Open Studio software, but wish to know more.

Conventions

In this book, you will find a number of styles of text that distinguish between different kinds of information. Here are some examples of these styles, and an explanation of their meaning.

Talend component names, variable names, and code snippets that appear in text are shown like this: "open the `tFlowToIterate` component"

A block of code is set as follows:

```
if ((errorCode & (1<<3)) > 0) {
System.out.println("age is null");
}
if ((errorCode & (1<<4)) > 0) {
System.out.println("countryOfBirth is empty");
}
```

When we wish to draw your attention to a particular part of a code block, the relevant lines or items are set in bold:

```
XMLUtils.addChildAtPath(customerXML, "/customer
  /orders/order[orderId = "+((Integer)globalMap.get
    ("order.orderId"))+"]", input_row.itemXML);
```

New terms and **important words** are shown in bold.Words that you see on the screen, in menus or dialog boxes for example, appear in the text like this: " Click on **Finish** to import all the Talend artifacts".

> Warnings or important notes appear in a box like this.

> Tips and tricks appear like this.

Reader feedback

Feedback from our readers is always welcome. Let us know what you think about this book—what you liked or may have disliked. Reader feedback is important for us to develop titles that you really get the most out of.

To send us general feedback, simply send an e-mail to `feedback@packtpub.com`, and mention the book title via the subject of your message.

If there is a topic that you have expertise and you are interested in either writing or contributing to a book, see our author guide on `www.packtpub.com/authors`.

Customer support

Now that you are the proud owner of a Packt book, we have a number of things to help you to get the most from your purchase.

Downloading the example code

You can download the example code files for all Packt books you have purchased from your account at `http://www.packtpub.com`. If you purchased this book elsewhere, you can visit `http://www.packtpub.com/support` and register to have the files e-mailed directly to you.

Errata

Although we have taken every care to ensure the accuracy of our content, mistakes do happen. If you find a mistake in one of our books—maybe a mistake in the text or the code—we would be grateful if you would report this to us. By doing so, you can save other readers from frustration and help us improve subsequent versions of this book. If you find any errata, please report them by visiting `http://www.packtpub.com/submit-errata`, selecting your book, clicking on the **errata submission form** link, and entering the details of your errata. Once your errata are verified, your submission will be accepted and the errata will be uploaded on our website, or added to any list of existing errata, under the Errata section of that title. Any existing errata can be viewed by selecting your title from `http://www.packtpub.com/support`.

Piracy

Piracy of copyright material on the Internet is an ongoing problem across all media. At Packt, we take the protection of our copyright and licenses very seriously. If you come across any illegal copies of our works, in any form, on the Internet, please provide us with the location address or website name immediately so that we can pursue a remedy.

Please contact us at `copyright@packtpub.com` with a link to the suspected pirated material.

We appreciate your help in protecting our authors, and our ability to bring you valuable content.

Questions

You can contact us at `questions@packtpub.com` if you are having a problem with any aspect of the book, and we will do our best to address it.

1

Introduction and General Principles

The aim of this book is to provide you, the Talend developer, with a set of common (and sometimes not so common) tasks and examples that, we hope, will help you in:

- Developing Talend jobs more rapidly
- Solving Talend issues more quickly
- Gaining a wider knowledge of the Talend product
- Gaining a better understanding of the capabilities of Talend

This cookbook is primarily intended as a reference guide, however, the chapters have been organized in such a way that it can also be used as a means of rapidly developing your Talend skills by working through the exercises in sequence from front to back.

For the more experienced developers, some of the recipes in this book may seem very simple, because they describe a feature of Talend that you may already know, but we are hoping that this isn't the case for everyone, and that there will be something in the book for developers of all levels of experience.

Many of the recipes in the book require you to complete sections of a partially built job, so it is assumed that in the real world you would be able to get to the starting point independently. Our thinking behind this is that we wanted to squeeze in as many recipes in the book as possible, so only the relevant steps that need to be performed and understood for a particular point to be made, are described in detail within each recipe.

Many any of the examples will write their output to the Talend log/console window when we could easily have written the data out to files or tables. However, the decision was made to provide an easy means (in most cases) of viewing the results of an exercise without having to leave the studio.

Before you begin

Before you begin the exercises in the book, it is worth becoming familiar with some of the key concepts and best practices.

Keep code changes small and test often

When developing using Talend, as with any other development tool, it is recommended to code in short bursts and test (run) frequently.

By keeping each change small, it is much easier to find where and what has caused problems during compilation and execution.

Chapter 10, Debugging, Logging, and Testing, is dedicated to debugging and logging; however, observing the preceding method will save time having to perform debugging steps that can sometimes take a long time.

Document your code

Talend sub-jobs have the ability to add titles, and every component in Talend has the option to add documentation for the component. Where you use Java, you should use the Java comment structures to document the code. Remember to use all these methods as you go along to ensure that your code is well documented.

Contexts and globalMap

`context` and `globalMap` are global areas used to store data that can be used by all components within a Talend job.

`context variables` are predefined prior to job execution in a `context` group, whereas `globalMap` variables are created on the fly at any point within a job.

Context variables

Context variables are used by Talend to store parameter information, and can be used:

- To pass information into a job from the command line and/or a parent job
- To manage values of parameters between environments
- To store values within a job or set of jobs

Chapter 6, Managing Context Variables, is dedicated to the use and management of context variables within Talend

globalMap

`globalMap` is a very important construct within Talend, in that:

- Almost every component will write information to `globalMap` once it completes execution (for example `NB_LINE` is the number of rows processed in a component).
- Certain components, such as `tFlowToIterate` or `tFileList`, will store data in `globalMap` variables for use by downstream components.
- Developers can read and write to `globalMap` to create global variables in an ad hoc fashion. The use of global variables can often be the best way to ensure code is simple and efficient.

Java

Talend is a Java code generator, so having a little Java knowledge can help when using Talend. There are many Java tutorials for beginners online, and a little time spent learning the basics will help speed up your understanding of Talend.

Other background knowledge

As a data integrator, you will be expected to understand many technologies and how to interface with them, and this book assumes a basic knowledge of many of the most frequent data sources and targets.

Chapter 7, *Working with Databases*, relates to using Talend with databases. We have chosen to use MySQL, because it is quick to install, simple to use, and readily available. Basic knowledge of SQL and MySQL will therefore be required to perform the exercises in this chapter.

Other chapters will also assume knowledge of csv files, MS Excel, XML, and web services.

Installing the software

This cookbook comes with a package of jobs and scripts that you will need to complete the recipes. The instructions for installing the code and scripts are detailed in the following section:

How to do it...

1. All templates, completed code, and data are in the `cookbook.zip` file.
2. Unzip `cookbook.zip` into a folder on your machine.
3. Copy the directory `cookbookData` to a directory on your machine (we recommend `C:\cookbookData` or the `linux/MacOS` equivalent)
4. Download and install the latest version of Talend Open Studio for enterprise service bus (ESB) from `www.talend.com`.

5. Open Talend Open Studio, and you will be prompted to create a new project.
6. Name the new project cookbook.
7. Open the project.
8. Right mouse click on the **Job Designs** folder in the **Repository** panel, and select the option **Import Items**.

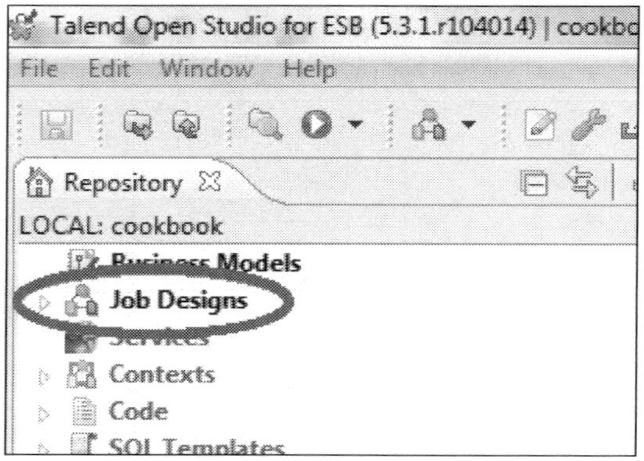

9. This opens the import wizard. Click the **Select archive file** option, and then navigate to your unzipped cookbook directory and select the zip file named `cookbookTalendJobs.zip`.
10. Click on **Finish** to import all the Talend artifacts.
11. If you copied your data to `C:\cookbookData`, then you can ignore the next steps, and you have completed the installation of the cookbook software.
12. Open the cookbook context, as shown in the following screenshot, and click **Next** at the first window.

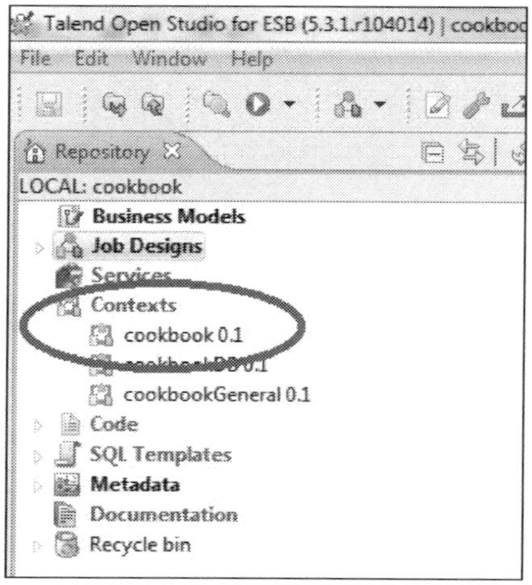

13. Open the **Values as a table** panel and change the value of **cookbookData** to your chosen directory, as shown in the following screenshot:

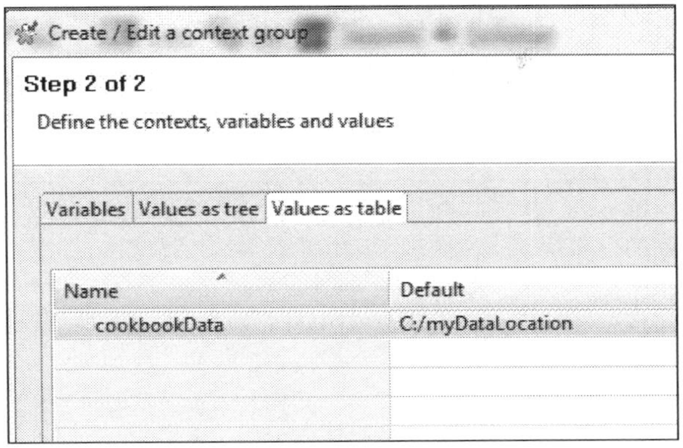

14. Click **Finish** to complete the installation process.

Enabling tHashInput and tHashOutput

Many of the exercises rely on the use of tHashInput and tHashOutput components. Talend 5.2.3 does not automatically enable these components for use in jobs. To enable these components perform the instructions in the following section:

How to do it...

1. On the main menu bar navigate to **File | Edit Project properties** to open the properties dialogue.
2. Select **Designer** then **Palette Settings**.

3. Click on the **Technical** folder and then click on the button shown in the following screenshot to add this folder to the **Show** panel.

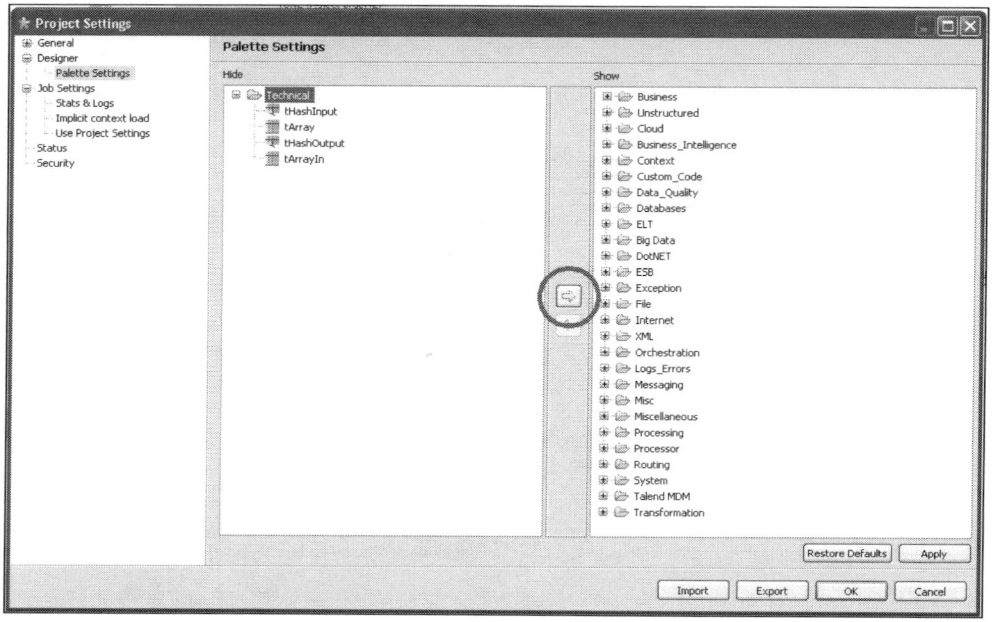

4. Click on **OK** to exit the project settings.

2

Metadata and Schemas

This chapter contains a detailed discussion about **metadata** and Talend **schemas** and recipes that highlight some of the less used / less known features associated with schemas, along with more commonly used features, such as generic and fixed schemas:

- Hand-cranking a built-in schema
- Propagating schema changes
- Creating a generic schema from existing metadata
- Cutting and pasting schema information
- Dropping schemas to empty components
- Creating schemas from lists

Introduction

Managing metadata is one of the most important aspects of developing Talend jobs, and the most common form of metadata used within Talend jobs is the schema.

Schema metadata

For successful development of jobs, it is essential that the metadata defined for a data source accurately describes the format of its underlying data. Failure to correctly define the data will result in numerous errors and waste of time tracking down problems with data formats that could otherwise be avoided.

Talend provides a host of wizards for capturing metadata from a variety of data sources such as database tables, delimited files, and Excel worksheets and stores them within its built-in metadata repository.

Schemas

Talend stores metadata definitions in schemas, which may be built in to individual components or stored in its metadata repository, as shown in the following screenshot:

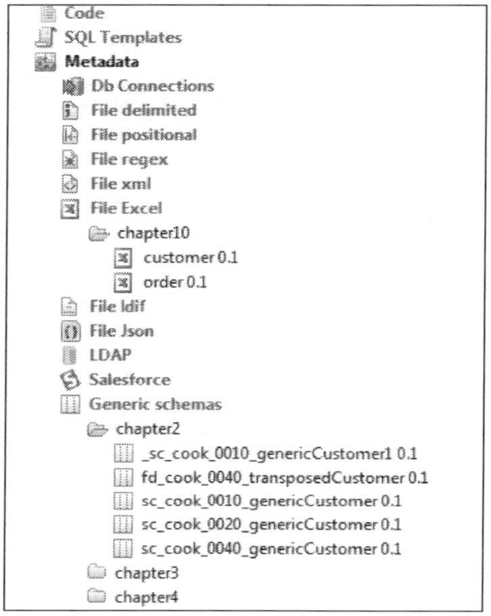

In general, it is best practice to define source and target metadata using a repository schema and mid-flow metadata as a Built-In schema.

The main exception to this rule is when dealing with one-off generated source data, such as a database query. Despite being a data source, it is easier to store the schemas for these custom queries as Built-In rather than cluttering the repository with single-use schemas.

Repository schemas

The benefits of using Repository schemas are:

1. They can be re-used across multiple jobs, thus reducing the amount of re-keying.
2. Talend will ensure that changes made to a Repository schema are cascaded to all jobs that use the schema, thus avoiding the need to scan jobs manually for Built-In schemas that need to be changed.
3. Impact analysis reports can be generated showing where a Repository schema is being used within a project. This enables the impact of changes to be more assessed more accurately when planning changes to any underlying data sources.

Generic schemas

Generic schemas aren't tied to a particular source, so they can be used as a shared resource across multiple types of data source or they can be used to define data sources that are generated, such as the output from custom SQL queries.

Shared schemas

Schemas captured from a particular type of data source are stored in the metadata repository in a folder for that data type (for example, CSV file schemas are stored in the directory for delimited files).

There are however instances where schemas will be shared across multiple types. For example, a CSV file and Excel file could be used to directly load a database table.

If you import the metadata from one of the sources, it will be stored in the folder for that source, which could make it hard to find.

By storing the schema as a Generic schema, it is more obvious that the schema isn't used just for a single source.

Generated data sources

It is often necessary to perform a query against a database and return the result set to the Talend job. It is often the case that the same query is used multiple times in many jobs.

By storing the schema for the result set in a generic schema, it removes the tedious process of having to create the same schema over and over again manually every time the query is used.

> Another very common use for generic schemas is within the `tHashInput` and `tHashOutput` components. If you are using the hash components as lookups, then one `tHashOutput` could be linked to many `tHashInput` components and all will share the same schema. By exporting the output schema to a generic schema, `tHashInputs` can be set up much more quickly in comparison to hand-cranking or cutting and pasting schemas from the output. This also has the benefit of ensuring that changes to the format are cascaded to all related components.

Fixed schemas and columns

Some components, such as `tLogCatcher`, have predefined schemas that are read-only. These can be easily recognized due to the fact that the whole schema is gray.

You may also find that certain flows, for instance the reject flows, have fixed columns that have been added to the original schema. This is because Talend will add the `errorCode` and `errorMessage` fields to the schema to store the error information. These additional fields will be green to distinguish them as Talend fields.

Hand-cranking a built-in schema

In this recipe, we are presented with a CSV file that does not have a heading row and needs to create a schema for the data. This is a basic recipe with which most readers should be familiar: however, it does provide a framework for discussion of some of the more important principles of Talend schemas.

The record we will be defining is as follows:

```
John Smith,27/11/1990,2012-01-10 10:24:54.953
```

As you can see this contains the fields; first name, last name, date of birth, timestamp, and age. Note that age is an empty string.

Getting ready

Open a new Talend Job (`jo_cook_ch02_0000_handCrankedSchema`), so that the right-hand palette becomes available.

How to do it...

1. Drag a `tFileInputDelimited` component from the palette, and open it by double clicking it.
2. Click the **Edit Schema** button (**...**), shown in the following screenshot, to open the schema editor:

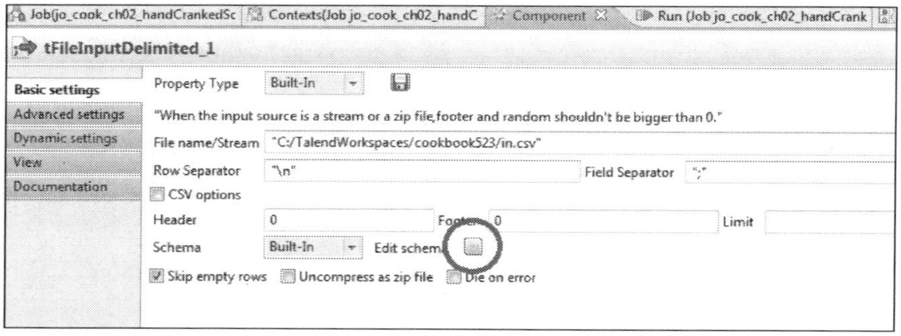

3. Click the **+** button to add a column:

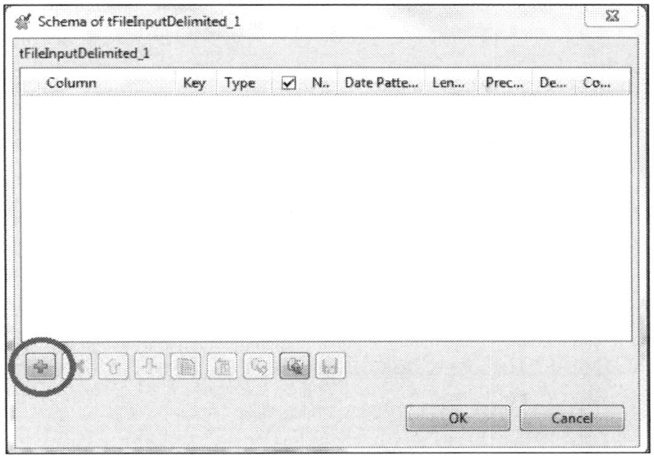

4. Type `name` into the column, and set the length to `50`.
5. Click the **+** button three more times to add three more columns.
6. Type `dateOfBirth` into the second column, select a type of date, and set the date pattern to `dd/MM/yyyy`. Alternatively, press *Ctrl+Space* to open a list of common patterns and select this one.
7. Type `timestamp` into the third column, select a type of date and set the date pattern to `yyyy-MM-dd HH:mm:ss.SSS`.
8. Type `age` into the fourth column, set the type to `Integer`, tick the **Null box**, and set the length to `3`. Your schema should now look like the following screenshot:

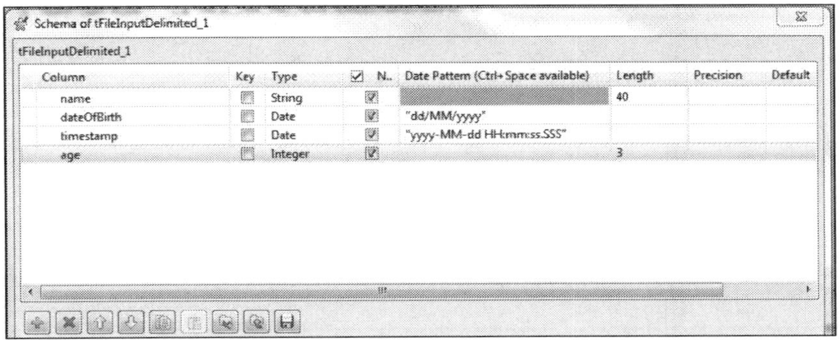

9. Click **OK** to return to the component view.

How it works...

The schema has now been defined for the component, and data may then be read into the job by linking a flow from `tFileInputDelimited` to `tLogRow`, for example.

There's more...

As you saw in the preceding section, Talend can handle many different types of data format. The following sections describe some of the common ones in little more detail.

Date patterns

Date patterns within Talend conform to the Java date format, and full definitions of the possible values to be used can be found at:

`http://docs.oracle.com/javase/7/docs/api/java/text/SimpleDateFormat.html`

Date patterns are case sensitive in Java, and upper and lower case letters often have a very different function.

> In the timestamp, there are `MM` and `mm` characters. These are the month and minute definitions and care should be taken to ensure that they are used correctly in the date and time portions of a date field.
>
> Note also the `ss` and `SSS` fields. These are seconds and milliseconds. Again, care must be taken in their use within the time portion of a date.
>
> `HH` and `hh` are also case sensitive. `HH` is the hour portion of a 24-hour timestamp, whereas `hh` is 12-hour time.

Nullable elements

All Talend data types have the potential to be set to null, but in some cases, this may result in a type change, as described in the following section.

Try removing the tick from the null box for `age`. You will notice that the type changes from `Integer` to `int`. This is because `int` is a primitive Java type that cannot be null, whereas for the Object type `Integer` null is an acceptable value.

A good example of the use of int over Integer is when mandatory values are required for say a database table. If the field is set as `int`, a null value will cause an error to be thrown, highlighting either a data or job error.

> The distinction between primitives and objects becomes more important as you use Talend and Java more frequently, because primitive types do not always act in the same way or have the same range of features as object types.

Field lengths

Talend will generally ignore field lengths in a schema, but that does not mean that they are unimportant. In fact, it is best practice to ensure that field lengths are completed and accurate for all schemas, especially database schemas.

> When creating a temporary table in a database using Talend, **all field lengths** must be present for the DBMS to create the table. Failure to do so will result in job errors.

Keys

Most schemas will not require any keys; however, like field lengths, they become very important for database schemas.

> Key fields are used during database update statements to match records to be updated. If the `insert` or `update` method is used to populate a table, then failure to specify the correct key(s) will result in a record being inserted rather than updated.

Propagating schema changes

Often during development, it is necessary to change schemas by adding, removing, or re-ordering columns. This often is a very onerous task, especially if a schema is used in multiple jobs.

As discussed earlier in this chapter, storing schemas in the metadata enables the schema to be re-used. If a shared schema is changed, then Talend will prompt to find out if the changes should be applied to all jobs.

If the change is performed, then the next time that the job is opened, the component using the schema will normally be highlighted as in error, because the schema no longer matches.

Talend provides mechanisms within the schema dialogues that takes some of the pain away from ensuring that changes are assimilated into all the jobs.

Getting ready

Open the Talend Job `jo_cook_ch02_0010_propagateSchema` so that the right-hand palette becomes available. Then, from the metadata palette, open the Generic schema `sc_cook_0010_genericCustomer`.

How to do it...

1. Add a new field `emailAddress`, as shown in the following screenshot:

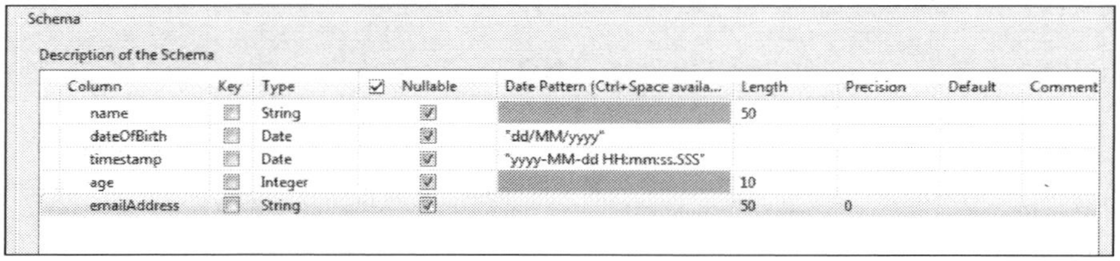

2. Click **Finish** to save the change to the schema. Then, click **Yes** to apply the changes to all jobs when prompted.

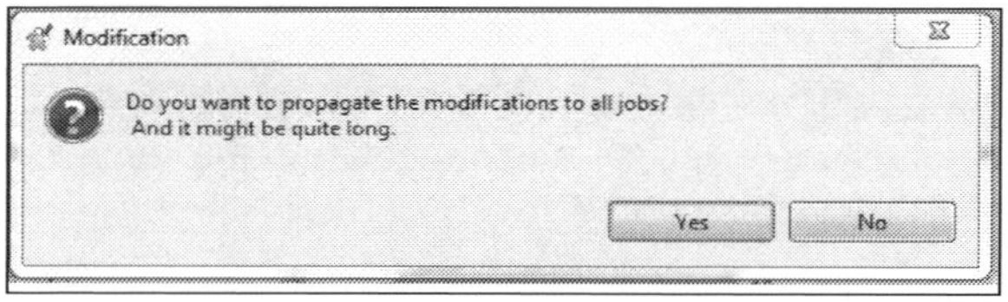

3. Click **Ok** to accept the changes in the next dialogue box. You will now see that the job has an error on the output.

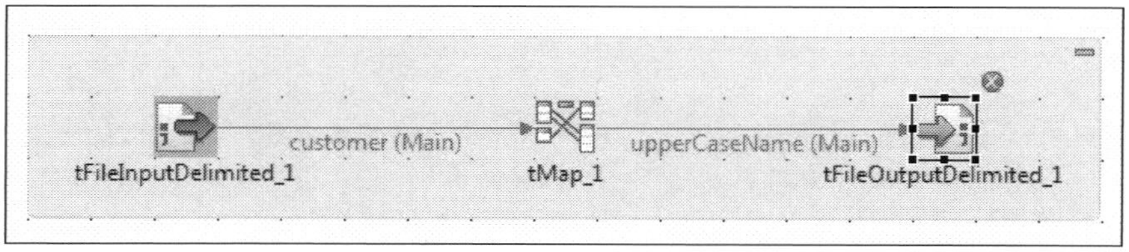

1. Open the `tFileOutputDelimited`, and click the **Edit Schema** button to open the schema and select the **View Schema** option.
2. As you can see in the following screenshot, the table on the left-hand side is different from that on the right-hand side. Click the  to copy the right hand schema into the left-hand panel.

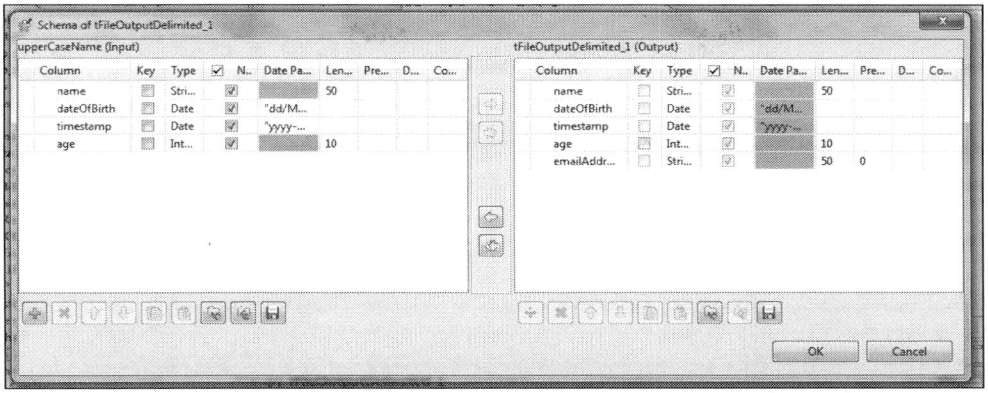

3. Click **Ok** to save the changes.

How it works...

When Talend updates the job schema for an output component, it does not propagate the change to the upstream component. Using the **<<** option allows the developer to copy all the changes from the output schema back into the previous component, ready for a rule to be applied.

There's more...

Using this method also ensures that the link to the Generic schema is maintained. It is possible to make the change in the previous `tMap` output; however, this would cause the output schema to become `Built-in`, which is an undesirable result.

In the preceding example, only one component is changed and the error is removed; however, in many jobs, this will not ensure that the changes are complete. It is a rarity to add fields only to then do nothing with them. Thus it is often necessary to propagate the changed row forward through all components in a job to ensure it is copied to the output correctly or ensure that a field that has been reverse propagated is correctly populated from upstream data.

When adding new fields to an output, it is best to change the schema of the output and reverse propagate the new field, especially when using Repository schemas. The reason for this is that if the schema is changed using `tMap`, then Talend will automatically change the type of schema from repository to Built-In, thus breaking the link to the Repository schema. In most cases, this is not a desirable outcome.

Be careful during reverse propagation that field names have not changed, especially with the `tMap` outputs. If you change the name of a field and reverse propagate to `tMap`, then the rule will disappear and will need to be re-entered.

In these cases, it is worth changing the field names in the `tMap` output schema prior to reverse propagating a schema. Make sure that you choose not to propagate this change from `tMap` to avoid the output being changed to `Built-in`. This will cause the output file to be in error, but when the Repository schema change is applied, the schemas will match, and the error will disappear.

Creating a generic schema from the existing metadata

Any schema can be easily converted into a generic schema to enable it to be re-used. The following recipe shows two methods of creating generic schemas; the first from a pre-existing schema in the metadata repository and the second from a built-in schema.

How to do it...

From repository schema:

1. Open repository schema `fd_cook_0020_customerDelimited` that can be found in the delimited schemas section under **Chapter2**, ensuring that you click the **metadata**, rather than the parent schema.

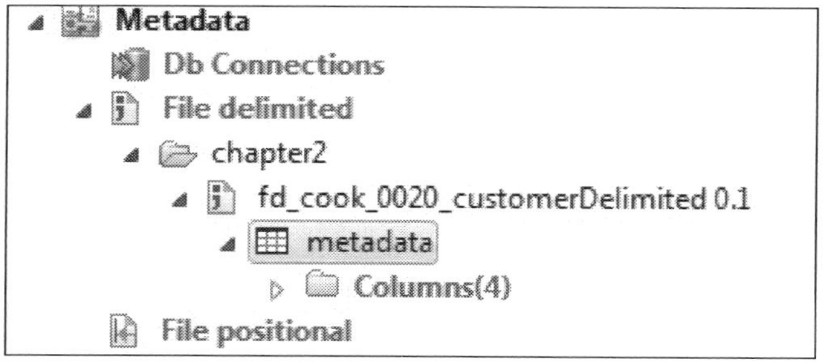

2. Right-click **metadata**, and then select **copy to Generic schema**. This creates a schema `fd_cook_0020_customerDelimited`.
3. Move the new schema to the **chapter 2** folder and double click it to edit it.
4. Change the name to `sc_cook_0020_genericCustomer1`.

From a built-in schema

1. Open the Talend Job `jo_cook_ch02_0020_builtInSchema` and open the `tFileOutput Delimited` component.
2. Click the highlighted button, shown in the following screenshot:

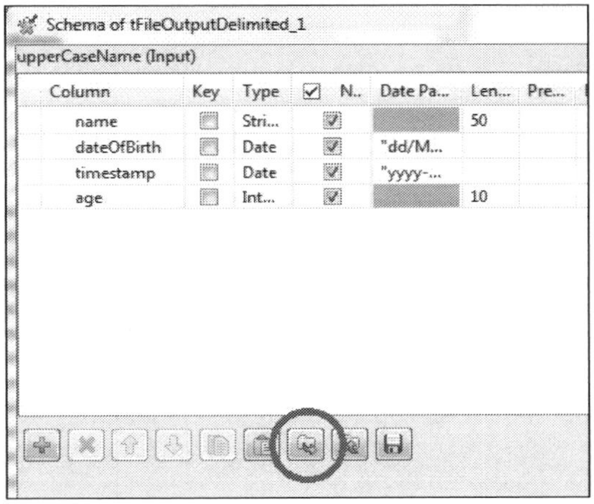

3. This will open a windows file save dialogue. Save the file as `sc_cook_0020_genericCustomer.xml`.
4. Now create a new generic schema from the saved XML file by right-clicking **Generic schemas**, and selecting the option **Create generic schema from xml**:

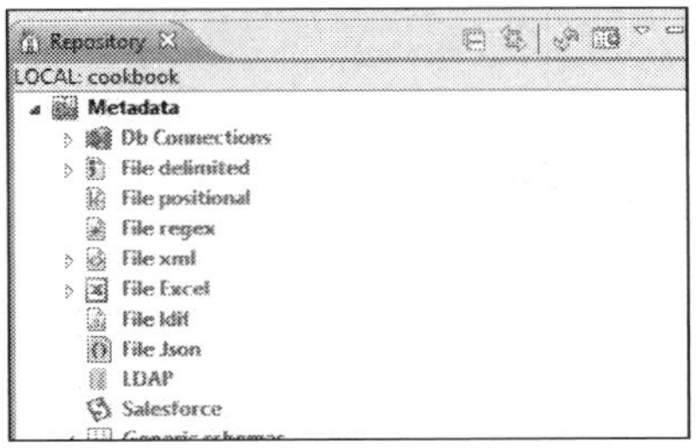

5. Select the XML file that was just saved, and click finish to create the new Generic schema `sc_cook_0020_genericCustomer2`.

How it works...

Under the covers, Talend stores schemas in XML format files, regardless of the type of schema. This means that schemas can be easily converted between types, in this case between built-in and repository.

Cutting and pasting schema information

This technique is a real time saver, but isn't always immediately obvious, because the schema dialogue does not contain a right-click option.

Getting ready

Make a copy of the job `jo_cook_ch02_0020_builtInSchema`, rename it to `jo_cook_ch02_0030_copySchema`, and open the new job.

How to do it...

1. Drag a `tFileOutputExcel` component from the right-hand palette.
2. Open `tFileOutputDelimited`, and then open the schema.
3. Click the left-hand panel and press *Ctrl+A* to select all the columns.
4. Press *Ctrl+C* to copy the highlighted columns.
5. Open the `tFileOutputExcel` component, and then open the schema. It should be blank.
6. Press *CTRL+V* to paste the columns.

How it works...

Talend allows the standard windows shortcut keys to be used to cut and paste column information between schemas.

There's more...

You can also use *Ctrl*+left mouse button to highlight individual columns and *Shift*+left mouse button to highlight a range as per the usual Windows conventions.

> Note that the pasted columns are added to the end of a schema, they do not replace existing columns. This means that in many cases further work will be needed to move the new columns to the correct place in the schema.

Dropping schemas to empty components

This simple tip is a useful time saver, especially when using generic schemas and the `Hash` components.

Getting ready

Open the job `jo_cook_ch02_0040_dragSchema`. If you open the `tHashOutput` components, you will see that they all share the same schema; the schemas are all Built-In.

How to do it...

1. In the left-hand window open the generic schema `sc_cook_0040_genericCustomer` so that you can see the actual metadata.

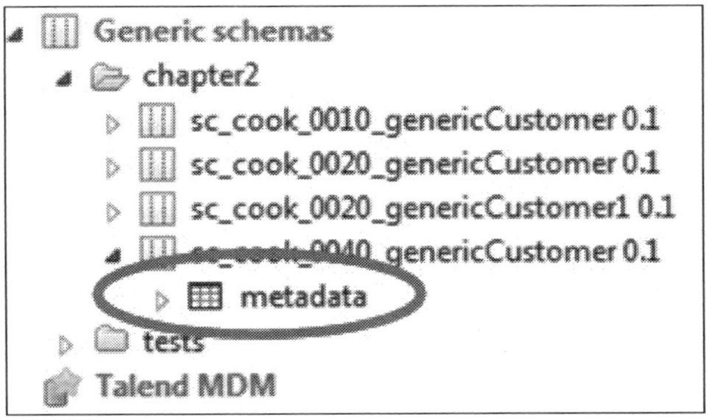

2. Drag the **metadata** icon over each of the `tHashOutput` components.
3. You will now see that all three components share the same generic schema.

How it works...

When you drag a metadata schema onto a component, the component is automatically populated with the new schema.

This is not generally a well-known feature of Talend, but it saves you having to navigate through the schema dialogues when you wish to share a common schema.

There's more...

This method is particularly useful when using `tHashInput` components as re-usable lookups, based upon the schema of an existing `tHashOutput`. Each time you add an additional lookup, the generic schema can simply be dragged from the repository onto the new component, saving time and effort.

Creating schemas from lists

This next recipe doesn't make use of Talend at all. Rather, it is a technique to save lots of tedious typing when creating schemas from documents and/or spreadsheets.

Getting ready

Open the MS Word document `customerFieldList.docx`. As you can see, there are a reasonable number of field descriptions that would take a reasonable amount of time to define individually.

How to do it...

1. Select all the column names from the word document and paste into an Excel spreadsheet:

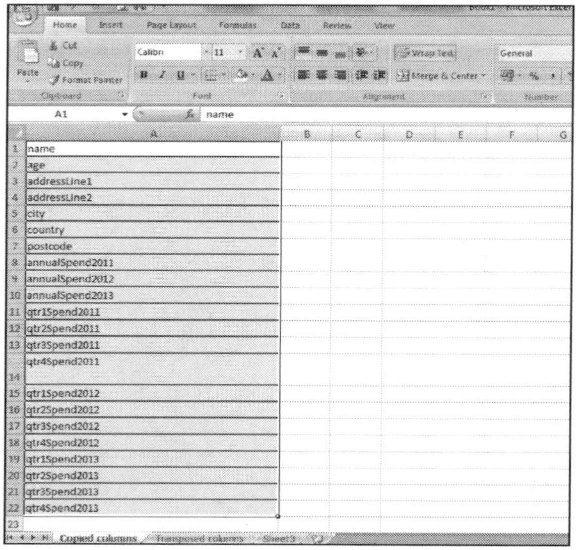

2. Now select all the fields, right click it, and select **Copy**.
3. Go to the second worksheet and click the top-left cell.
4. Then, right-click and select **Paste Special**, and select the option **Transpose**:

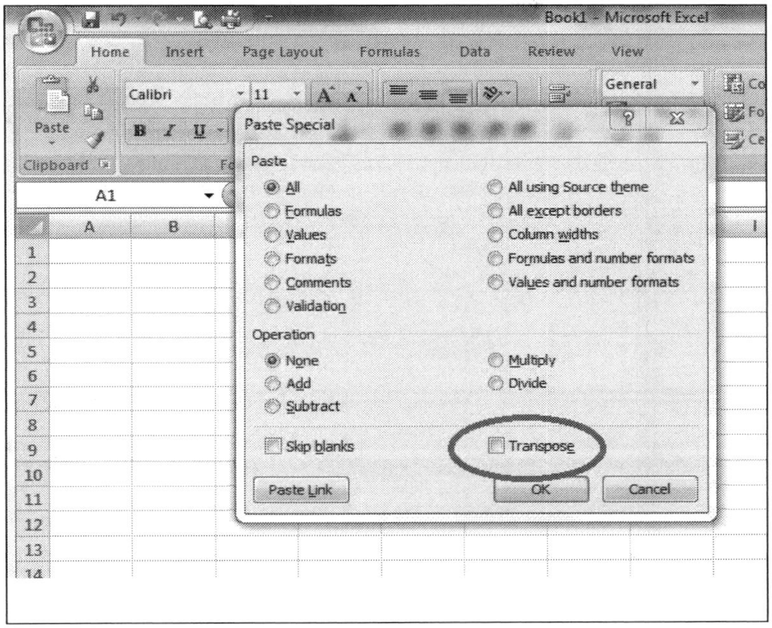

5. This will copy the previous vertical list into a horizontal list.
6. Delete the initial worksheet and save the file as a CSV file named `TransposedCustomer.csv`
7. You can then import the CSV file using the wizard for `File delimited` and stating that the file has a heading row.

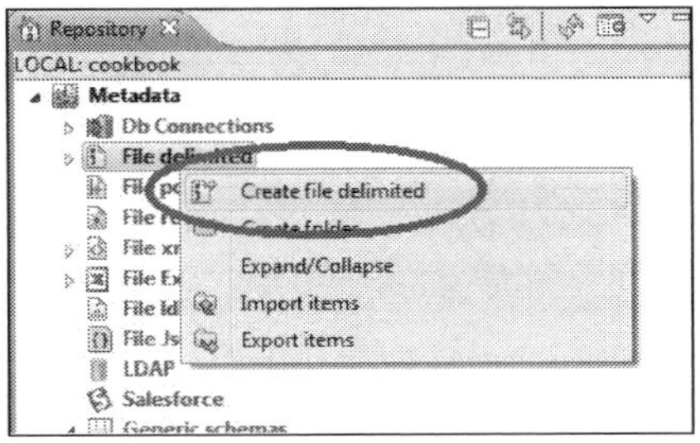

8. Set the field separator as **Comma**, and tick the box **Set heading row as column names**.

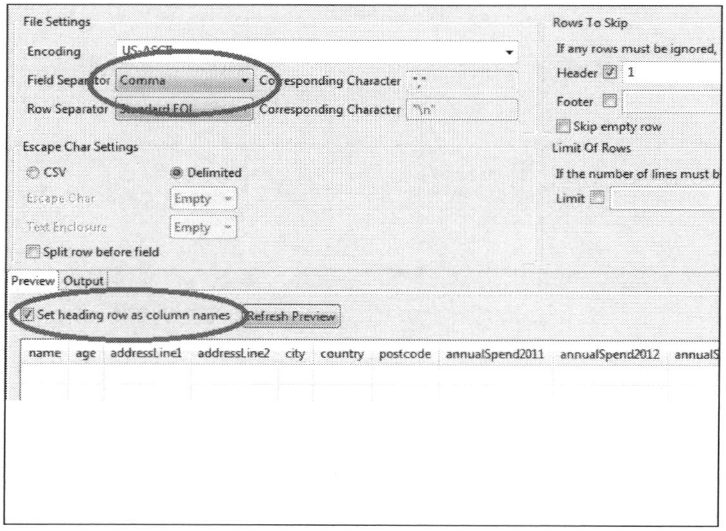

9. Click on **Next**, and you should see the individual fields listed in the schema.You are now able to add the field types and lengths.
10. If you wish, you can then copy the delimited schema to a generic schema.

How it works...

The transpose facility of the spreadsheet enables a vertical list of fields to be converted into a horizontal list. By saving this list as a CSV file, the horizontal field list can be highlighted as a heading row during an import into Talend. This automatically fills in the field names in the schema, thus avoiding the need to type in the names of the columns individually.

There's more...

Even after importing a list using this method, you will still have to ensure that column types and lengths are populated, however, if you also add data to the CSV file prior to importing it, Talend will try to guess the type and length of each column during the import stage

It is possible to force Talend to guess correctly by adding data to the file that matches the type exactly. There are two methods that can be used:

Transpose the data

Starting with the original list, add a second column to the list, and populate it with data values for each of the fields.

When transposing the data in the spreadsheet, copy both the column of field names and the data; and transpose both list columns, so that they become a heading row and a row of data.

Edit the CSV file

The second method is to add a row of data either to excel or CSV files manually prior to importing the metadata.

What data to add? If you take care to add data that is the maximum representative size of the column, then Talend will usually guess the correct types and lengths.

For example, if the field is a ten character string, for example, then ensure that you add ten characters to the data in either the list column or the CSV file. For numbers, ensure that you use numbers to let Talend know that the field is numeric.

In the preceding example, if you only set the number fields to 99999999.999 prior to import, it will save significant time. This is easy to do in Word or Excel and can save time when defining large schemas.

3
Validating Data

This chapter contains recipes that show some of the techniques for validating data and handling invalid rows.

- Enabling and disabling reject flows
- Gathering all rejects prior to killing a job
- Validating against the schema
- Rejecting rows using tMap
- Checking a column against a list of allowed values
- Checking a column against a lookup
- Creating validation rules for more complex requirements
- Creating binary error codes to store multiple test results

Introduction

Clean, timely, and correct data is a business-critical resource for most organizations, because it enables (but is not restricted to) more accurate decision making, compliance, and improved efficiency.

Data integration is often the first point of contact for data arriving into a business (from third parties), and the hub for data held within a business, and as such, plays a key part in ensuring that data is fit for use.

This section concentrates on some of the features and methods within Talend that enable the developer to identify and capture invalid data, so that it can be reported.

Enabling and disabling reject flows

Rejected data is closely coupled to schemas (*Chapter 2, Metadata and Schemas*), as many of the input and output components will validate data according to a schema definition and then pass any incorrect data to a reject flow.

Reject flows thus allow non-conforming data to be collected and handled as per the needs of a project.

In some cases, depending upon the business requirement, rejects are not acceptable. In these cases, reject flows should be disabled and the job allowed to fail.

> Whether a job dies on the first incorrect record, collects rejects in a file, or completely ignores rejects is a design decision that should be based upon the requirements for the process. Where possible, designers and developers should attempt to define how errors and rejects are handled before coding begins.

Getting ready

Open the job `jo_cook_ch03_0000_inputReject`.

How to do it...

1. Run the job and it will fail with an unparseable date error.
2. Open the `tFileInputDelimited` component and in the **Basic settings** tab uncheck the **Die on error** box.
3. Drag a new `tLogRow` to the canvas, open it and set the mode to **Table**.
4. Right-click the `tFileInputDelimited` component, and select **Row,** then **reject**. Connect this row to the new `tLogRow`.Your job should look like the following:

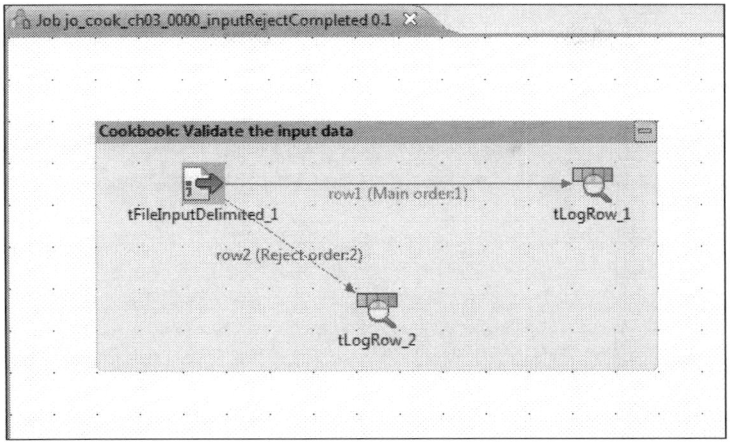

5. Run the job. You should see that two records have now been passed to the **reject** flow.

How it works...

When Talend reads an input data source, it attempts to parse the data into the schema. If it cannot parse the data, then it will fail with a Java error.

When the **die on error** box is unchecked, Talend enables a reject flow to be added to the component and changes the action of the component, so that instead of killing the job, invalid rows are passed to a **reject** flow.

There's more...

You can, if required, ignore any rejects by not attaching a reject flow, but it is wise to double check first if this is a genuine requirement for the process. Most cases of rejects being ignored are down to programmers forgetting to check if there is a **reject** flow for the given component.

In the `tFileInputDelimited` component, there is an **Advanced** tab that enables data to be validated against the schema and for dates to be checked. These options provide an added level of validation for the input data.

> It is always worth checking every input component for the presence of **reject** flow when **die on error** is unchecked, or for additional validation options.
>
> In many cases, these validations will not be explicitly stated in a specification, so it is always worth checking with the customer to see if they require rejects and/or validation rules to be added.

See also

- *Gathering all rejects from an input*, in this chapter.

Gathering all rejects prior to killing a job

As an alternative to collecting incorrect rows up to the point where a job fails (**Die on error**), you may wish to capture all rejects from an input before killing a job.

This has the advantage of enabling support personnel to identify all problems with source data in a single pass, rather than having to re-execute a job continually to find and fix a single error / set of errors at a time.

Getting ready

Open the `job jo_cook_ch03_0010_validationSubjob`. As you can see, the **reject** flow has been attached and the output is being sent to a temporary store (`tHashMap`).

How to do it...

1. Add the `tJava`, `tDie`, `tHashInput`, and `tFileOutputDelimited` components.
2. Add `onSubjobOk` to `tJava` from the `tFileInputDelimited` component.
3. Add a flow from the `tHashInput` component to the `tFileOutputDelimited` component.
4. Right-click the `tJava` component, select **Trigger** and then **Runif**. Link the trigger to the `tDie` component. Click the **if** link, and add the following code

   ```
   ((Integer)globalMap.get("tFileOutputDelimited_1_NB_LINE")) > 0
   ```

5. Right-click the `tJava` component, select **Trigger,** and then **Runif**. Link this trigger to the `tHashInput` component.

   ```
   ((Integer)globalMap.get("tFileOutputDelimited_1_NB_LINE")) == 0
   ```

The job should now look like the following:

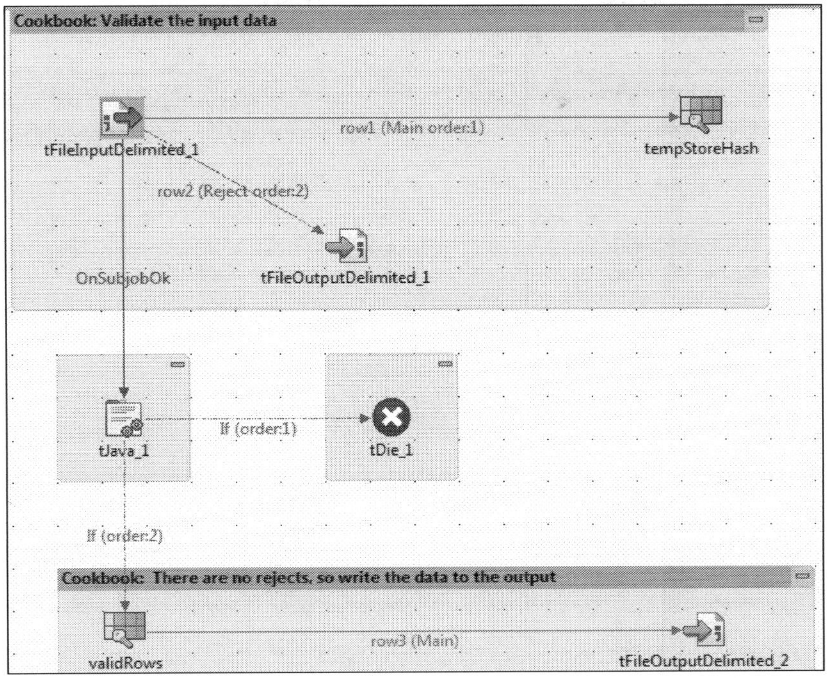

6. Drag the generic schema `sc_cook_ch3_0010_genericCustomer` to both the `tHashInput` and `tFileOutputDelimited`.
7. Run the job. You should see that the `tDie` component is activated, because the file contained two errors.

How it works...

What we have done in this exercise is created a validation stage prior to processing the data.

Valid rows are held in temporary storage (`tHashOutput`) and invalid rows are written to a reject file until all input rows are processed.

The job then checks to see how many records are rejected (using the **RunIf** link). In this instance, there are invalid rows, so the **RunIf** link is triggered, and the job is killed using `tDie`.

> By ensuring that the data is correct **before** we start to process it into a target, we know that the data will be fit for writing to the target, and thus avoiding the need for rollback procedures.
>
> The records captured can then be sent to the support team, who will then have a record of all incorrect rows. These rows can be fixed in situ within the source file and the job simply re-run from the beginning.

There's more...

This recipe is particularly important when rollback/correction of a job may be particularly complex, or where there may be a higher than expected number of errors in an input.

An example would be when there are multiple executions of a job that appends to a target file. If the job fails midway through, then rolling back involves identifying which records were appended to the file by the job before failure, removing them from the file, fixing the offending record, and then re-running. This runs the risk of a second error causing the same thing to happen again.

On the other hand, if the job does not die, but a subsection of the data is rejected, then the rejects must be manipulated into the target file via a second manual execution of the job.

So, this method enables us to be certain that our records will not fail to write due to incorrect data, and therefore saves our target from becoming corrupted.

See also

- The *Validating against the schema* recipe, in this chapter.

Validating against the schema

The `tSchemaComplianceCheck` is a very useful component for ensuring that the data passing downstream is correct with respect to the defined schema.

This simple exercise demonstrates how rows can be rejected using this component.

Getting ready

Open the job `jo_cook_ch03_0020_schemaCompliance`.

How to do it...

1. Run the job. You should see two rows being rejected.
2. Add a `tSchemaComplianceCheck` and two `tLogRow`, right click on `tSchemaComplianceCheck_1` and select **Row** then **Rejects**. Join the flow one of the new tLogRow. Connect the main to the other as shown:

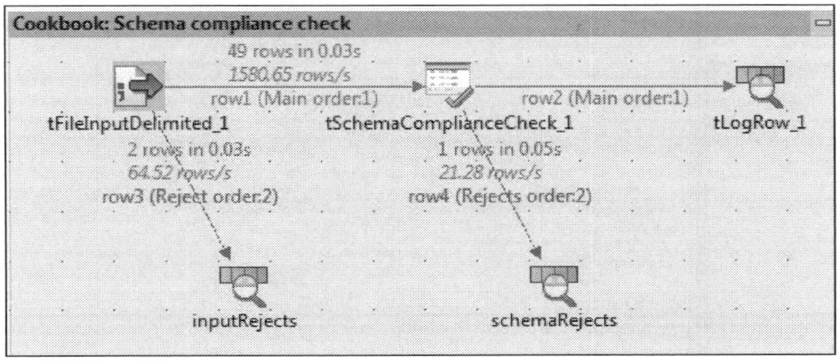

3. Now, when you run the job, you will see an additional reject row being output from the `tSchemaComplianceCheck` component.

How it works...

The `tFileInputDelimited` component will detect only some of the anomalies within the data, whereas the `tSchemaComplianceCheck` component will perform a much more thorough validation of the data.

If you look at the output, you will see the log entry, which shows that the name field has exceeded the maximum for the schema:

```
.--------------------------------------------------------------------------.
|                              #1. schemaRejects                           |
+---------------+----------------------------------------------------------+
| key           | value                                                    |
+---------------+----------------------------------------------------------+
| name          | Johnny Smith asdlaskdjfaslkdffjasldkfjaskdfjlaksdfjl     |
| dateOfBirth   | 27/11/1990                                               |
| timestamp     | 2012-01-10 10:24:54.953                                  |
| age           | null                                                     |
| errorCode     | 8                                                        |
| errorMessage  | name:exceed max length                                   |
+---------------+----------------------------------------------------------+
```

Rejecting rows using tMap

This recipe shows how `tMap` can be used to ensure that unwanted rows are not propagated downstream. This may be as a result of the filter criteria or a validation rule.

Getting ready

Open the job `jo_cook_ch03_0030_tMapRejects`.

How to do it...

1. Open the `tMap` and click the **Activate/unactivate expression filter** button for the **validRows** output.
2. In the **Expression** box add the code `customer.age >= 18`.

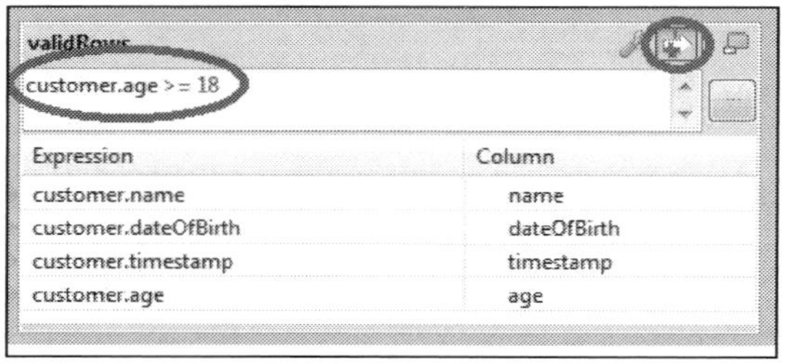

3. Click on the `tMapRejects` output and then on the **tMapSettings** button.
4. Click on **Catch output reject value** column to set it to `true`.

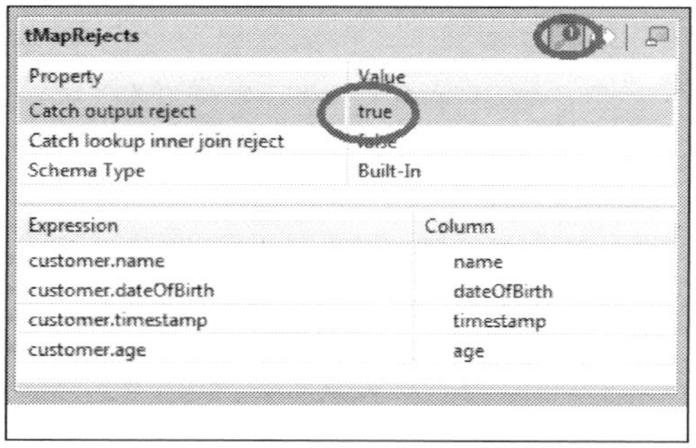

5. Run the job. You should see that one of the rows has been rejected.

How it works...

In this example, `tMap` is working like an if statement. Therefore, if customer's age is greater than eighteen, then write the record to `validRows` or else pass the data to the `tMapRejects`.

There's more...

You can use this method to test for multiple different rejects, by adding additional outputs and adding different filter criteria to each output.

The `tMap` component will process any number of filter criteria from top to bottom, so long as you remember to catch the output rejects for each additional output table.

> Note that if you forget to set catch output rejects to true, then all the input records will be passed to all the outputs. Sometimes, this may be what you want to do, but in the case of the preceding exercise, forgetting to set the catch output rejects would result in rows being duplicated in both of the output streams.

Checking a column against a list of allowed values

Often it is necessary to ensure that a column contains only values as defined in a list. This recipe shows how this can be achieved using a `tMap` expression.

Getting ready

Open the job `jo_cook_ch03_0040_tMapValuesInList`. You will notice that the job is very similar to the previous recipe *Rejecting rows using tMap*.

How to do it...

1. Open `tMap` and click the expression builder button **(...)**, and add the test criteria, as shown in the following screenshot:

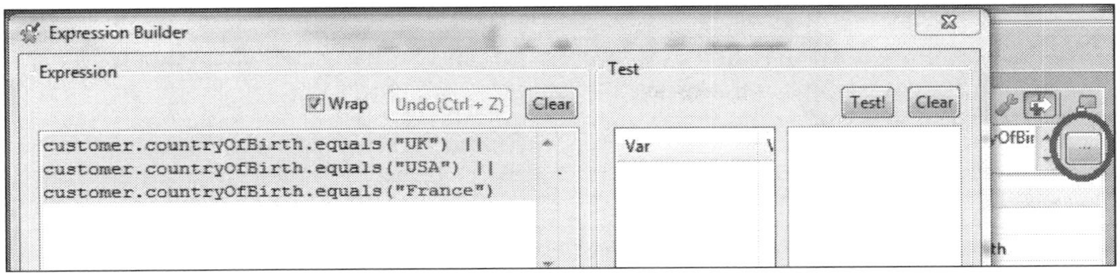

2. Run the job and you should see that one of the rows is rejected.

How it works...

The tMap conditions are the same as Java conditions, so the symbol **||** (pipe pipe) is a logical OR.

Thus, the condition checks for the value being UK or USA or France.

There's more...

This method is fine if the list is quite small and isn't liable to change. If the list is too large or subject to frequent changes, then the code will be hard to maintain and/or will need to be changed often, which will require re-testing of the code. In these cases, refer to the next recipe for a more suitable method.

See also

- *Checking a column against a lookup*, in this chapter.
- *Rejecting rows using tMap*, in this chapter.

Checking a column against a lookup

Another method for validating a column is to refer to a lookup containing a list of allowed values that can be stored in any format (file, table, XML for example).

Getting ready

Open the job `jo_cook_ch03_0050_tMapValuesInLookup`.You will see that there are two inputs to the tMap: customer and country.

How to do it...

1. Open `tMap`, and drag the field `countryOfBirth` from the customer input to the `countryName` field in the country input. This will create a key link, as shown in the following screenshot:

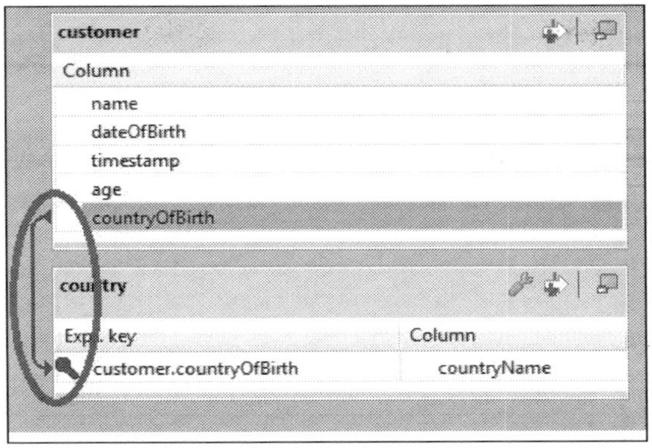

2. Click the button **tMap settings** and set the value for **Join Model** to `Inner Join`.

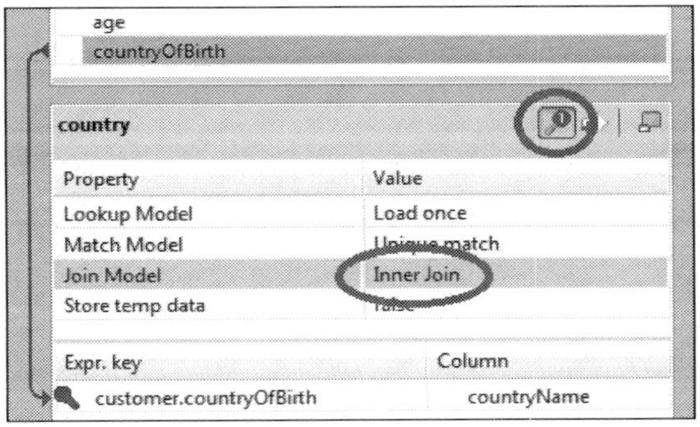

3. In the reject output, click on the button for **tMap settings**, and set the value for **Catch lookup inner join reject** to `true`.

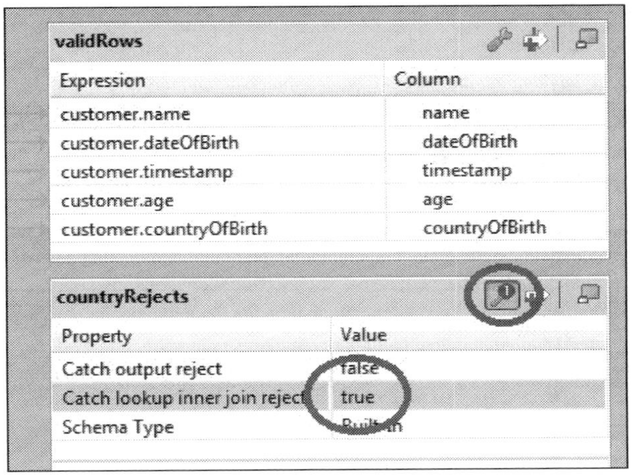

4. Run the job and you will see that three of the records have been rejected.
5. Re-open the `tMap` and change the **Expr.key** on the country to `StringHandling.UPCASE(customer.countryOfBirth)`
6. Re-run the job and you will see that now only one record has been rejected.

How it works...

The `tMap` is performing an inner join between the customer data and the country data using the country name as the key, so any rows that do not join have an invalid `countryOfBirth`.

When a match is found, the record is passed to the valid rows output.

If no match is found, then the customer record is passed to the invalid output, which is set up to catch any row from the main flow that does not fulfill the inner join criteria.

On the first execution of the job, the values being checked were not in upper case, so only 'USA' matched. On the second execution after the customer countries had been converted to upper case, three of the records matched.

Creating validation rules for more complex requirements

Sometimes validation rules require multiple inputs to provide a pass/fail result, so it is often easier to build and understand the code if it is written using Java.

If you aren't familiar with code routines in Talend, it is recommended that you first complete the recipe *Creating custom functions using code routines, Chapter 5, Using Java in Talend* that will take you through the setup of code routines.

Getting ready

Open the job `jo_cook_ch03_0060_validationCodeRoutine`.

How to do it...

1. Create a new **code routine** called `validation`, and copy the following code into it:

```
/**
 * validateCustomerAge: Check customer is 18 or over for UK,
21 or over for rest of world.
 * returns true if valid, false if invalid
 * e.g. validateCustomerAge(23,"UK")
 *
```

```
     * {talendTypes} Boolean
     *
     * {Category} Validation
     *
     * {param} string(age) input: Customer age
     * {param} string(country) input: Customer country
     *
     * {example} validateCustomerAge(23,"UK") # true
     */
    public static Boolean validateCustomerAge(Integer customerAge,
String customerCountry) {
        if (customerAge == null || customerCountry == null) {
           return false;
        }else
        if (customerCountry.equals("UK".toUpperCase()) &&
customerAge >= 18){
                    return true;
             } else {
          if (!(customerCountry.equals("UK".toUpperCase())) &&
customerAge >= 21){
                 return true;
             }else{
                 return false;
             }
          }
        }
```

2. Open the `tMap` component, and in the filter criteria for the `validRows` output, click on the expression button **(...)**
3. Select the function `validateCustomerAge` from the `validation` category and doubleclick to copy the example code to the editor.
4. Change the expression to match the following:

   ```
   validation.validateCustomerAge(customer.age,customer.
   countryOfBirth)
   ```

5. Also, add the same expression to the output column `validationResult` for both outputs.
6. Run the job and you should see that two of the records are rejected and three are valid.

How it works...

The `tMap` expressions are limited to a single line of code, so complex tests on data cannot generally be performed directly within `tMap`.

The `validateCustomerAge` method returns a single Boolean value, so can be easily used within `tMap` expressions and filters was demonstrated in this recipe..

There's more...

Most data processes require validation of some sort or another, so it is a good idea to create a routine just for managing validations.

By collecting all the validation routines together, it makes them easier to find and removes the need for duplicated code.

Because they are stored centrally, a change to a routine is immediately available to all jobs using that particular routine, thus reducing time spent finding and fixing duplicated code in a project.

> While the rule can be created directly using a `tJavarow` component, using a code routine enables the validation to be re-used across multiple jobs in a project as well as allowing the routine to be used within `tMap`. Another downside of the `tJavaRow` method is that a pass/fail flag would need to be added to each row to enable them to be filtered out in a downstream `tMap`.

See also

- *Creating custom functions using code routines* in *Chapter 5, Using Java in Talend*.

Creating binary error codes to store multiple test results

> Prior to doing this exercise, it is recommended that you first jump forward to *Chapter 4, Mapping Data,* and do the exercises related to ternary operators and using variables in `tMap`.

Sometimes, it is desirable to perform multiple checks on a row at the same time, so that when a row is rejected, all of the problems with the data can be identified from a single error message. An excellent method of recording this is to create a binary error code.

A binary error code is a binary number, where each of the digit position represents the result of a validation test: 0 being pass and 1 being fail.

For example, 1101 = failed test 1 (rightmost digit), test 3 and test 4 and passed test 2. This binary value can be held as a decimal integer, in this case 13.

Getting ready

Open the job `jo_cook_ch03_0070_binaryErrorCode`.

How to do it...

1. Open `tMap` and create six new `Integer` type variables: `nameTest`, `dateOfBirthTest`, `timestampTest`, `ageTest`, `countryOfBirthTest` and `errorCode`.
2. Copy the following lines into the Expressions:

```
customer.name.equals("") ? 1 << 0 : 0
customer.dateOfBirth == null ? 1 << 1 : 0
customer.timestamp == null ? 1 << 2 : 0
customer.age == null ? 1 << 3 : 0
customer.countryOfBirth.equals("") ? 1 << 4 : 0
Var.nameTest  + Var.dateOfBirthTest  + Var.
  timestampTest + Var.ageTest + Var.countryOfBirthTest
```

3. Add a condition in the `ValidRows` output

```
Var.errorCode == 0
```

4. Set the `tMap` Settings for the `rejects` output to **Catch output reject**.
5. Your `tMap` should now look like this:

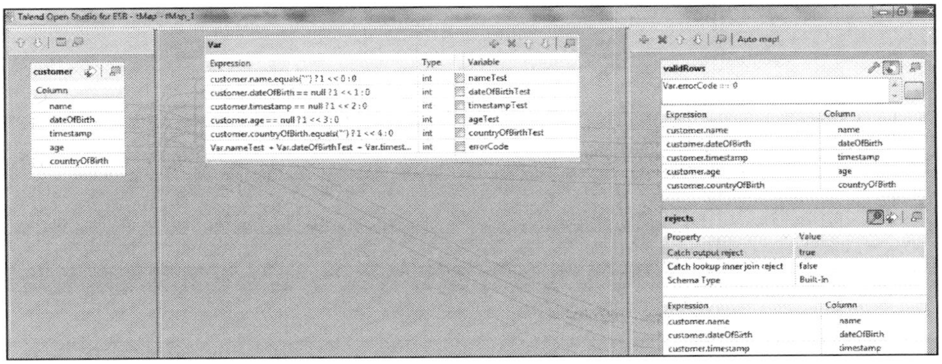

6. Run the job. You should see that the error codes are populated for all the rows where at least one field is null.

How it works...

The operator << performs a bitwise shift of the value by the relevant number of places. For example 1<<3 would place a 1 in the 4th position of a binary number (0 being the first position).

So if the field is null, the variable is assigned a bit-shifted value, otherwise it is set to 0.

By adding the numbers together, we eventually arrive at a decimal value which represents a 1 in each of the positions where a null is found.

This may be simpler to explain using an example. The following is the output from `tLogRow`. In this case, it is one of the rejects where three nulls have been found

```
.-----------------------------.
|         #6. rejects         |
+----------------+------------+
| key            | value      |
+----------------+------------+
| name           | P Jones    |
| dateOfBirth    | null       |
| timestamp      | null       |
| age            | null       |
| countryOfBirth | UK         |
| errorCode      | 14         |
+----------------+------------+
```

So from this output the binary value will be built as shown:

- The `nameTest` variable is assigned 0
- The `dateOfBirthTest` variable is assigned 1 << 1 = 10 (Binary) = 2 (Decimal)
- The `timestampTest` variable is assigned 1 << 2 = 100 (Binary) = 4 (Decimal)
- The `ageTest` variable is assigned 1 << 3 =1000 (Binary) = 8 (Decimal)
- The `countryOfBirthTest` variable is assigned 0

So the decimal total is 0+2+4+8+0 = 14

There's more...

An alternative to using the << operator is to assign the actual decimal values to each position: 1,2,4,8 (2 power 0, 2 power 1, and so on) being positions 0 to 3. Again, adding the values gives us the desired integer result.

Decrypting the error code

Decrypting a binary error message is achieved by testing the individual bits in the integer. This can be achieved by using the shift function to create the binary bit position and performing a bitwise AND against the integer value. If the result is greater than 0, then the position is set.

For instance, if we have the value 0101 (7) in an integer column:

0101 & 1 (where the 1 equates to 1 <<0) = 1 (test 1 failed)

0101 & 10 (where 10 equates to 1<<1) = 0 (test 2 passed)

0101 & 100 (where 100 equates to 1<<2) = 100 (test 3 failed)

0101 & 1000 (where 1000 equates to 1<<3) = 0 (test 4 passed)

So the logic for our errors will look like this:

```
if ((errorCode & (1<<0)) > 0) {
  System.out.println("name is empty");
}
if ((errorCode & (1<<1)) > 0) {
  System.out.println("dateOfBirth is null");
}
if ((errorCode & (1<<2)) > 0) {
  System.out.println("timestamp is null");
}
if ((errorCode & (1<<3)) > 0) {
  System.out.println("age is null");
}
if ((errorCode & (1<<4)) > 0) {
  System.out.println("countryOfBirth is empty");
}
```

Downloading the example code

You can download the example code files for all Packt books you have purchased from your account at `http://www.packtpub.com`. If you purchased this book elsewhere, you can visit `http://www.packtpub.com/support` and register to have the files e-mailed directly to you.

4
Mapping Data

This chapter contains recipes that show some of the techniques used to map input data to the desired output format.

- Simple mapping and tMap time savers
- Creating tMap expressions
- Using the ternary operator for conditional logic
- Using intermediate variables in tMap
- Filtering input rows
- Splitting an input row into multiple outputs based upon input conditions
- Joining data using tMap
- Hierarchical join using tMap
- Using reload at each row to process real-time/near real-time data

Introduction

This chapter mainly deals with the `tMap` component which is usually the main processing component at the heart of any Talend transformation job.

The tMap component

The `tMap` component has extensive transformation capabilities and has thus become the data integration developer's tool of choice. Among the `tMap` component's capabilities are the ability to:

- Add and remove columns
- Apply transformation rules to one or more columns

- Filter input and output data
- Join data from multiple sources into one or many outputs
- Split source data into multiple outputs

Flexibility

The `tMap` component is multipurpose and very flexible and because of this there is often the temptation to do as much as possible in a single `tMap` component. This isn't recommended, since this can raise the complexity to a level where the code becomes difficult to understand and to maintain. It is recommended that multiple `tMap` components be used to manage complex transformations, so that the code is more easily understood.

Single line of code

One of the main limitations of `tMap` is that the output expressions for transformation are limited to just a single line. This can be overcome using code routines that perform complex logic or utilizing tMap variables and the Java ternary operation can be used to perform conditional logic.

All these techniques will be demonstrated in this chapter.

Batch versus real time

The operation of lookups (for joining) can be manipulated in `tMap` to enable efficient joining in both batch and real-time mode. The **reload at each row option** for real-time lookups will be detailed later in the chapter.

Simple mapping and tMap time savers

This recipe will illustrate the most basic mapping options within the `tMap` component and some of the column level tricks that can be used to speed up mapping by removing large amounts of repetitive actions.

Getting ready

Open the job `jo_cook_ch04_0010_basicMapping`.

How to do it...

1. Drag a `tMap` component from the right-hand panel.
2. Connect the `tFileInputDelimited` component to `tMap`.
3. Connect the output, name it as `outputCustomer` and accept the schema of the target component.

4. Open tMap and you will notice that the inputs and outputs are named the same as the flows.

   Rename the flows

5. Close tMap and left-click the input flow so that row1 is highlighted. Take a short pause; click again on the row1 text and the text will be editable. Rename the flow to customer.
6. Open tMap and you will see that the names of the tMap input table have now changed to match the row name of the input flow.

   Manually dragging columns

7. Click the left mouse button on dateOfBirth and drag to dateOfBirth expression in the output. This is the most basic method of copying data from input to output.

   Create new columns by dragging

8. Press *Ctrl* and left mouse click the annualTotal and prevYearTotal columns.
9. Release *Ctrl* and left mouse click annualTotal.
10. Holding down the left mouse button, drag the columns to the very bottom of the output table.
11. Do not release the left mouse button until you see a blue line at the end of the table and an information box that states **Insert all selected entries**.

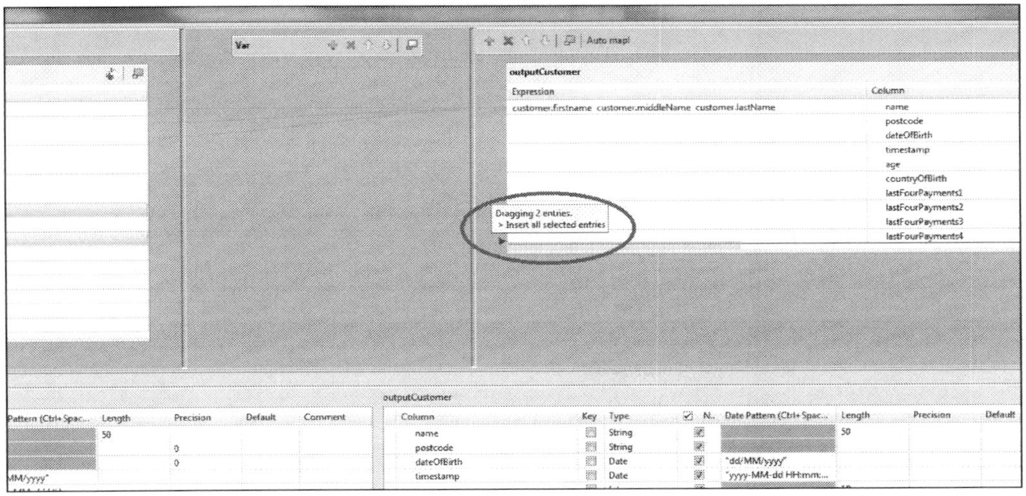

12. You will see that the new columns have been added to the output, and their values automatically mapped from the input.

Reposition a column

13. Use the up and down arrows in the schema tab to move the new columns to the positions below `dateOfBirth`.

Deleting a column

14. Highlight `totalTwoYears` in the output table and then click the **X** button to delete it.

Adding a column manually

15. In the **Schema editor** for the output, left mouse click the `name` field, then click the **+** button to create a new column.
16. Change the name of `newColumn` to `postcode`.

Automapping same named columns

17. Click the output table and then click **Auto map!**, as shown in the following screenshot:

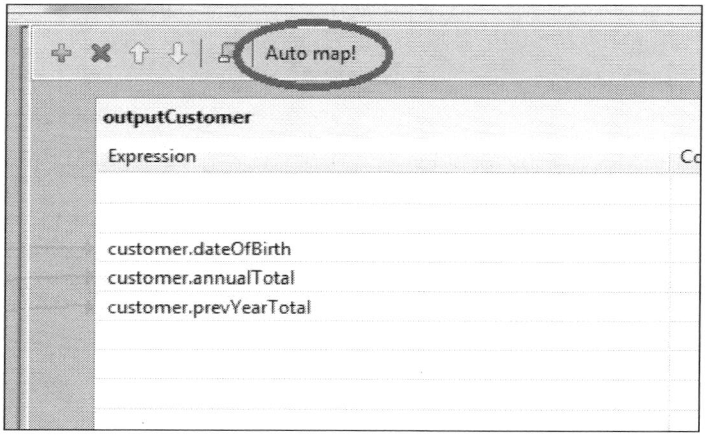

18. You should notice that all the columns that share the same input and output name have been mapped automatically.

Concatenating input columns

19. Highlight the `firstName`, `middleName`, and `lastName` input columns by holding down *Ctrl* and left mouse clicking each one individually.
20. Drag them across to the output `name` column but do not release the left mouse button yet. While hovering over the `name` column, notice the floating information box. This tells us that the **mode** is **append**.
21. Release the left mouse button and notice that the three columns have been copied to the same expression.

22. Repeat steps 10 to 12, and you will see that the columns have been appended yet again. Append is the default mode when dragging and dropping.

Overwriting columns

23. Repeat steps 10 to 12, however before releasing the left mouse button hold down *Ctrl*. You will see that the information box changes to **Overwrite mode**.
24. Release the left mouse button, and you will see that the expression containing six fields has been overwritten by three.
25. Add `+" "+` between each of the columns to complete the expression.

Copy columns by position

26. Highlight the `payment1` column.
27. Hold the *Shift* key and click `payment4`.
28. Release the left mouse button, select the `payment1` column and drag the group across to the `lastFourPayments1` column in the output.
29. Drag the four columns to the output, but do not release the mouse button. Notice that the floating box says that this is the **append** mode.
30. Press *Ctrl* and you will see that the mode changes to overwrite mode
31. Press *Shift* and the mode changes to each source entry to each target expression.
32. This is the mode we want, so release the left mouse button. You will see that the columns have been mapped individually. Note that the copy of multiple columns by position can also be performed with non-sequential columns selected using *Ctrl* and left mouse click.
33. Your `tMap` should now look like the following and you can run the job.

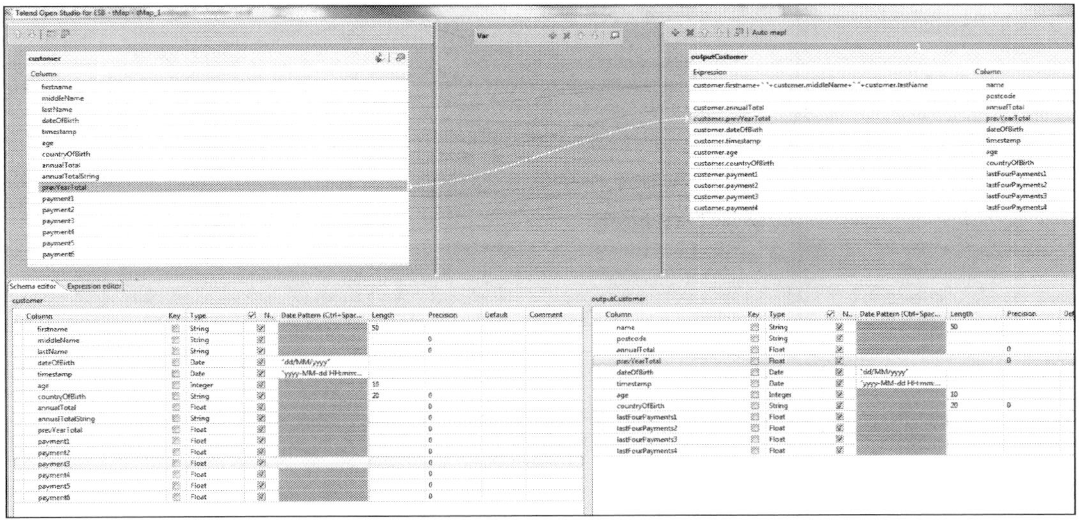

How it works...

`tMap` enables columns to be mapped, ignored, and added to the output very easily to ensure that the correct results are produced.

Shortcuts such as **Auto map!** and the group copies, enable many rows to be copied at once, saving time and effort.

New columns can be created by dragging and dropping from the input, as well as via the schema editor.

There's more...

In this recipe there is just a single input and output, so recognizing the source column in an expression is simple. When multiple inputs and outputs are used, then this is no longer true, unless flows are named sensibly. This is why we have included the renaming of the flows in this, the most basic recipe.

> Always name the inputs to `tMap`. Often, `tMaps` have multiple inputs and outputs. Ensuring that the flow names are consistent helps in identifying from where a data element has been sourced, which will make debugging easier.

Creating tMap expressions

In the previous example, we demonstrated how to manipulate the schemas and basic mapping of input columns to output columns. This recipe will show how to add much more complex rules to `tMap` and how to use the Talend supplied functions.

Expressions are limited to a single line of Java code, but can contain any of the following:

- Constants
- Input variables
- The `globalMap` and `context` variables
- The `tMap` variables (see next recipe)
- Talend supplied functions
- User supplied code routines
- Standard Custom java functions
- Included methods from JAR files

Getting ready

Open the job `jo_cook_ch04_0020_usingExpressions`

How to do it...

1. Open `tMap`.
2. Click the left mouse button on the output `transactionDateTime` column.
3. You will notice that the **expression button** looks like the following:

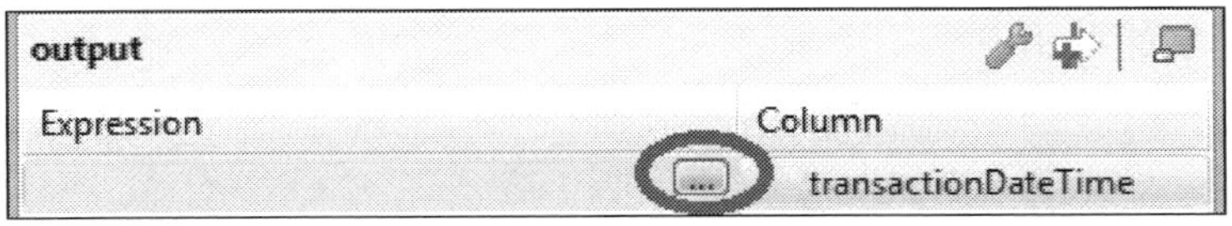

4. Click on the **...** button to open the **Expression Builder** dialogue.

   Adding a Talend function

5. The bottom-left panel lists the **Categories** of Talend functions. Scroll down to the **TalendDate** category and click the left mouse button.
6. You should now see a list of available functions. Scroll down to the **getCurrentDate** function, and double-click the left mouse button.
7. The function has now been added to the Expression panel, as shown in the following screenshot:

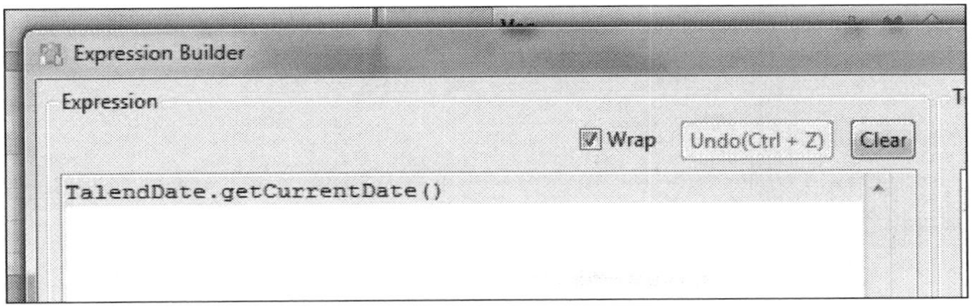

8. Exit **Expression builder** by clicking on **Ok,** and you will now see the function present in the expression column for `transactionDateTime`.

   Transforming input columns

9. Select the output `cleanName` column and open **Expression builder**.
10. Select **Category** of **StringHandling** and the **Function** of **UPCASE** and double-click it to add it to the expression. Delete the text `"Hello"`.

11. In the middle-top panel, you will see the input columns available to add to the expression. From this panel, drag `customer.firstname` into the brackets and add `+" "+`.

12. Double-click `customer.middleName`, add `+" "+` then double-click `customer.lastName`. Your expression should now look like the following:

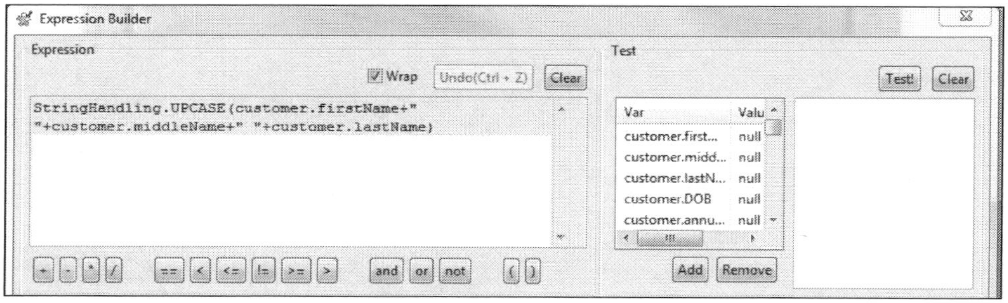

13. Exit **Expression builder** and run the job.

How it works...

The expression editor allows drag-and-drop creation of complex transformation rules. It also includes panels for accessing Talend supplied and user created functions to make building rules much easier.

There's more...

The expression builder also has test functionality, making it a powerful Talend feature, but it isn't the only way to create expressions.

Testing expressions

The expression builder will also allow an expression to be tested by filling in values in the **Value** column and clicking the **Test!** button, as shown:

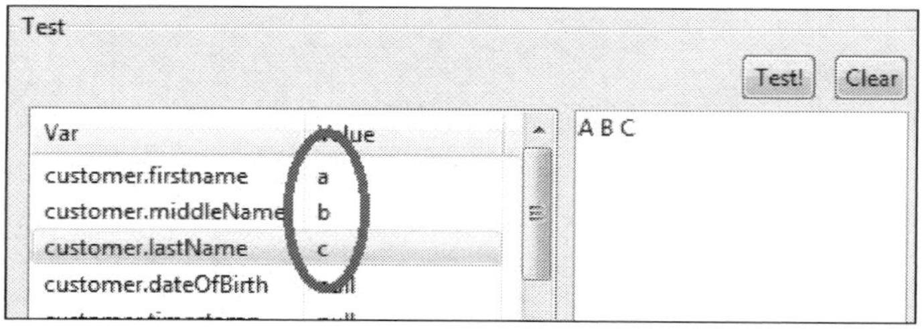

Expression editor

Although the expression builder is useful, it can also be time consuming to open and close the editor continuously. More seasoned Talend developers will often not use the expression builder, preferring instead to edit the line directly in the main `tMap` window expression column or in the expanded expression window, which is an alternative tab of the schema panel, shown in the following screenshot:

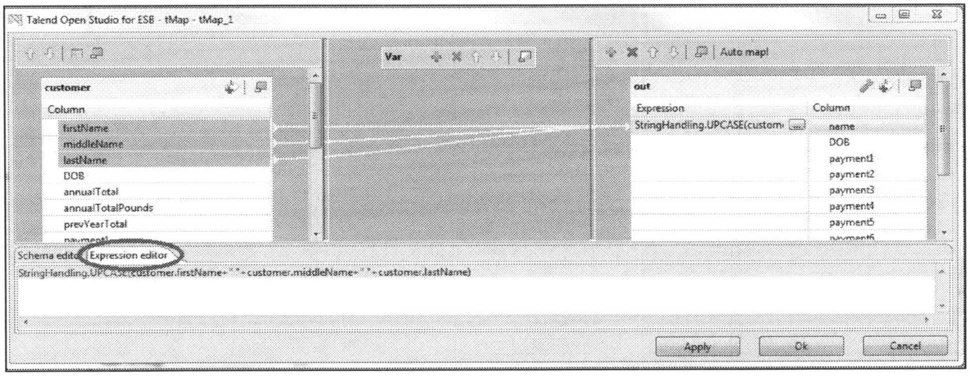

Getting around the 'one line' limitation

Although `tMap` expressions are limited to a single line of code, the use of the `tMap` variables, ternary expressions, and code routines do allow very complex mappings to be handled within a single expression.

See Also

Using the `tMap` variables and ternary expressions are handled later in this chapter. The use of code routines is handled in *Chapter 10, Debugging, Logging, and Testing*.

Using the ternary operator for conditional logic

The previous recipe mentions that a `tMap` expression cannot be more than a single line of Java code. This means that we cannot use the normal if-then-else logic to test for conditions.

Fortunately, Java does provide a mechanism by which we can perform tests on a single line: the ternary expression.

Getting ready

Open the job `jo_cook_ch04_0030_ternaryExpressions`.

How to do it...

We'll be looking at two similar scenarios using the ternary expression.

Single ternary expression: if-then-else

1. Open `tMap` and click the output `singleTernaryLocality` column.
2. Enter the following code:

   ```
   customer.countryOfBirth.equals("UK") ? "UK" : "RestOfWorld"
   ```

3. Run the job. You will see that all countries apart from the UK have a locality of `RestOfWorld`.

Ternary in ternary: if-then-elsif-then-else

1. Open `tMap` and click the output column `multiTernaryLocality`.
2. Enter the following code:

   ```
   customer.countryOfBirth.equals("UK") ? "UK" : customer.
   countryOfBirth.equals("France") ? "Europe" : customer.
   countryOfBirth.equals("Germany") ? "Europe" :"RestOfWorld"
   ```

3. Run the job. You should now see that `France` and `Germany` are now classified as `Europe`.

How it works...

The Java ternary expression is the equivalent to an `if-then-else` statement in Java, but on a single line. If we were coding in Java, the test for locality would look like the following:

```
outputRow.locality = customer.countryOfBirth.equals("UK") ? "UK" :
"RestOfWorld"
```

or we could write it longhand as:

```
if (customer.countryOfBirth.equals("UK")) {
  output_row.locality="UK";
}else{
  output_row.locality="RestOfWorld"
}
```

It also happens that the ternary `else` clause `':'` can also be a ternary expression, thus enabling more complex `if-then-elseif-then-else` type expressions.

There's more...

As with all coding constructs, beware of making them too complex, otherwise they may become un-maintainable. If you have many levels of ternary expressions, then it is probably time to consider using `code routine` or performing the logic in `tJavaRow`.

If you do use multilevel ternary expressions, then they can be broken over many lines and commented appropriately using `/*......*/` comments. This usually makes the code easier to understand. An example is shown in the following screenshot:

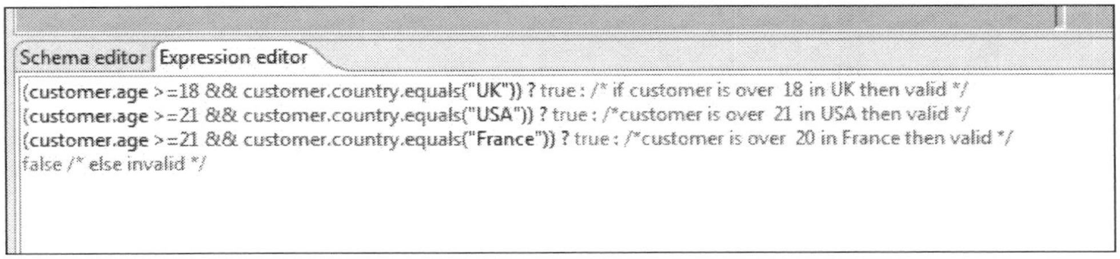

Using intermediate variables in tMap

The `tMap` component is the most flexible and most used component in Talend, despite having the limitation on multiple lines for an expression. In the previous recipe, we saw how ternary expressions can be used to extend the capability of the `tMap` expressions. In this recipe, we will see that the `tMap` variables can also extend the capability of tMap.

Getting ready

Open the job `jo_cook_ch04_0040_tMapVariables`.

How to do it...

1. In the **Var** section, click **+** to add a new variable, set the name to `paymentTotal` and **Type** to `float`, as shown in the following screenshot:

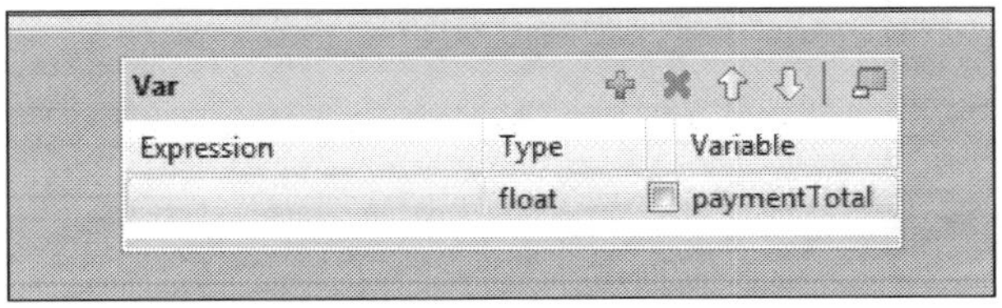

2. Insert the following code into the expression field:

```
customer.payment1+customer.payment2+customer.payment3+customer.
payment4+customer.payment5+customer.payment6
```

3. Repeat step 1 for a variable named `averageLastSixMonths` with **Type** set to `float`, and a variable named `averageAnnual` also with **Type** set to `float`.
4. Select `paymentTotalRow` by clicking the left mouse button.
5. Drag the `paymentTotalRow` variable into the **Expression** column for the new variable `averageLastSixMonths`.
6. Add `/6` to the end of the expression to get:

```
Var.paymentTotal / 6
```

7. Drag the input column `annualTotal` into the **Expression** column for the variable `averageAnnual` and add `/12` to the end of the expression.
8. Add a final `float` variable called `variance`.
9. Drag in the variable `averageLastSixMonths` add - (minus) then drag in the variable `averageAnnual`.
10. Highlight all the four columns using the *Shift* and right mouse click method and add them to the end of the output table.
11. Your `tMap` should now look like the following screenshot:

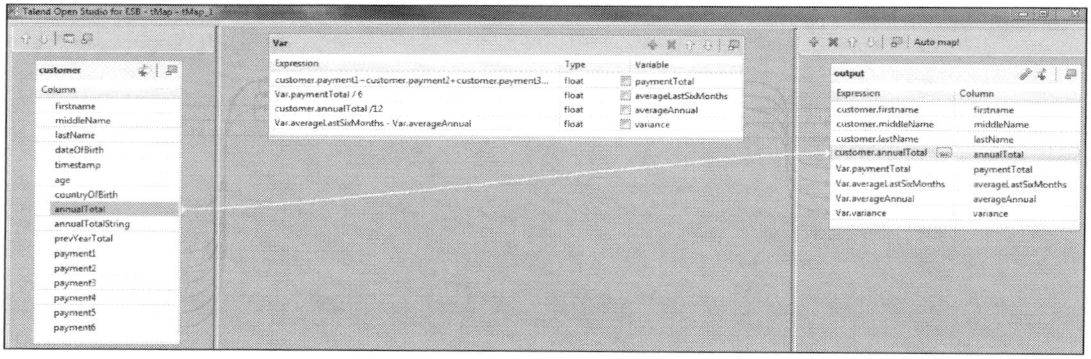

12. Run the job to show the results.

How it works...

The variables are created in a structure called **Var**. New columns can be added to **Var** and can be assigned expressions just like output columns and also copied to output columns, just like input columns.

These variables can also be dragged and dropped in the same way that the input columns can, which means that the methods mentioned in the section *tMap time savers* can also be applied to the `tMap` variables

There's more...

As you can see, the `tMap` variables allow us to create new variables that enable us to build complex mappings using many variables, and then these variables can then be used in later variables, just like in normal Java coding.

As usual though, it is advisable to keep the number of new variables low in `tMap` to avoid maintenance headaches.

> If you find that you are using many variables, and the code is becoming very complex then consider splitting tMap into multiple simpler tMaps or creating one or more code routines or using `tJavaRow`; with the advantage of using code routines or `tJavaRow` being that inline comments can be added to document the code, thus making it easier to debug and maintain.

Filtering input rows

Often, rows can be filtered out of a flow because they do not fulfill the required criteria for processing. This example shows how this can be achieved within the `tMap` component, so as to avoid costly join logic.

> Note that you should not concern yourself too much with the complexity of `tMap` in this recipe; rather you should concentrate on the filters. Joining is covered in later recipes in this chapter.

Getting ready

Open the job `jo_cook_ch04_0050_tMapInputFilter`.

How to do it...

1. Run the job. You will see that there are many records read from `orderItemFile` and all are being output.
2. Kill the job and view the output. You will see many order items being displayed, all of which are duplicates. These are the ones we will need to remove.

3. Open `tMap` and click the **Activate/unactivate expression** button  for the customer input table.
4. Add the filter expression `customer.customerId == 2 || customer.customerId == 3` into the input expression filter, as shown in the following screenshot:

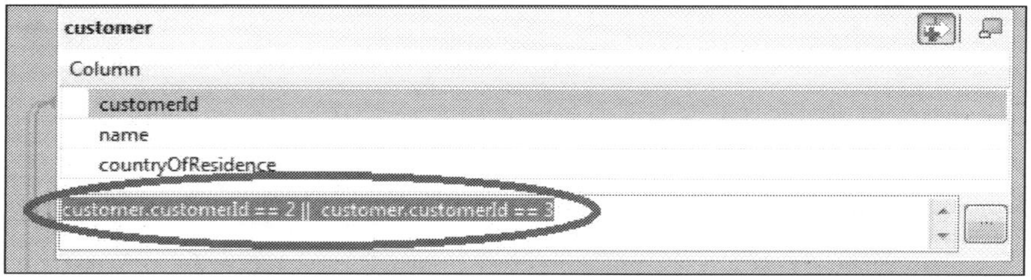

5. Run the job and you will see that only two records have been output.

How it works...

Adding the filter enabled us to reduce the number of customers to two; either the customer with an ID of 2 or the customer with an ID of 3.

There's more...

Talend does provide a separate component for filtering (`tFilterRow`) and it is generally a matter of personal style or development standards as to which method you use for filtering data prior to processing in tMap.

Note that when input filtering is used, the rows are simply discarded. Whether the rows should be discarded is a design decision, and the developer should be clear on the fact that it is ok to discard the rows.

> If the requirement states that rejects must be recorded, then do not use an input filter in `tMap`. Instead, use `tFilterRow` prior to `tMap` to enable the rejected rows to be captured or, if `tFilterRow` cannot be used on the input, then the rows will have to be processed and then filtered at the output.

When using database inputs, it is usually better and more efficient to filter within the SQL query, rather than within the Talend job.

Splitting an input row into multiple outputs based on input conditions

Often, it is required to filter input data into multiple outputs depending upon given criteria, for instance, splitting customer data by region, as in this example, or by team. Another very common example is to split the input data into validated records and records that have been rejected due to having failed a quality check (see *Checking a column against a list of allowed values* in *Chapter 3, Validating Data* for examples of using tMap to filter invalid rows).

This recipe shows how the `tMap` output **Expression filters** are used to perform filtering of the nature described precedingly.

Getting ready

Open the job `jo_cook_ch04_0060_multipleOutputs`.

How to do it...

1. When you open `tMap` you will see three identical output tables
2. Click the **Expression filter** button for the table **UK** to open an expression field, as shown in the next screenshot.
3. Drag the input column `countryOfBirth` into this box.
4. Add `.equals("UK")` to the end of the expression to give the expression:

   `customer.countryOfBirth.equals("UK")`
5. Your table should now look like the following:

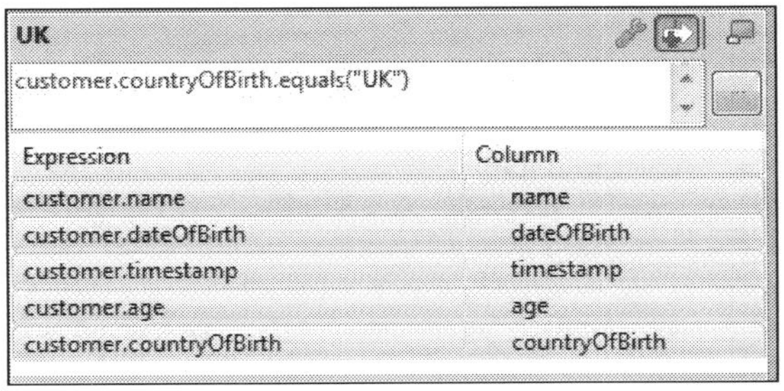

6. Repeat the same for the **USA** table to give the expression:

   `customer.countryOfBirth.equals("USA")`

7. Click the **tMapSettings** button  for the final table, restOfWorld, to open the table properties.
8. Set **Catch output reject** to **true**, as shown in the following screenshot:

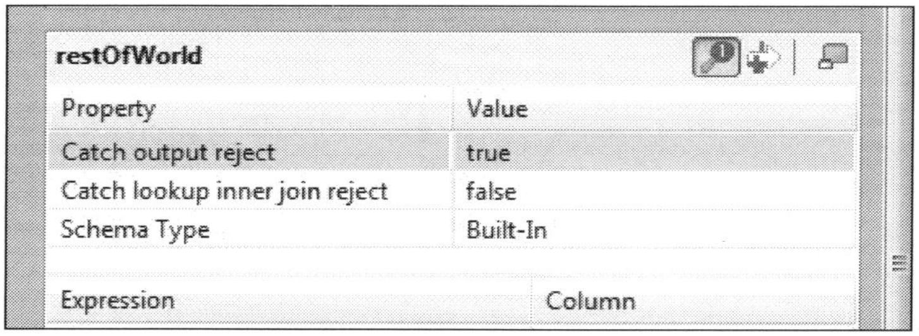

restOfWorld

Property	Value
Catch output reject	true
Catch lookup inner join reject	false
Schema Type	Built-In

Expression	Column

9. Exit `tMap` and run the job to see the results.

How it works...

`tMap` will pass an input row to the output from the top of the output table list downwards, depending upon their settings.

`tMap` will only pass data to an output if:

- It has no filter expression and is not a catch output reject
- It has a filter expression and is not a catch output reject the condition is met
- It is a catch output reject with a filter expression and the row has been rejected from previous output and the condition is met
- If it is a catch output reject with no filter expression

It is sometimes easy to think of this list as a set of if-then-else criteria.

> It is recommended that lists of outputs be ordered like if-then-else to make understanding easier. It is also recommended that multiple `tMaps` be used in the scenario where many outputs are created, depending upon complex conditions. It is not that `tMap` cannot handle a high level of complexity, rather the impact of changes may be difficult to calculate if there are many inputs, outputs, joins, and conditions.

There's more...

In this recipe, we have multiple copies of the input being created using input criteria. It is worth noting that the outputs do not need to be copies of each other.

It is also worth noting that if no criteria is specified for any output, then `tMap` will copy every input row to every output. What's more is that each of the output can be of a different format and have different rules for the same input row. In this instance, `tMap` becomes a means of creating multiple different views of the same output data.

What is also possible is that multiple outputs can be specified with catch output reject specified. This means that multiple views of rejected data can also be created.

Joining data using tMap

So far, we have seen how `tMap` can be used to transform and filter input data. But this is only a part of the `tMap` functionality. The `tMap` component is also the main component used to perform join logic between multiple input sources. This recipe demonstrates the basics of using `tMap` to join multiple data sources.

Getting ready

Open the job `jo_cook_ch04_0070_tMapJoin`.

How to do it...

1. Right-click `tFileInputDelimited`. Go to **Row** | **Main** and connect it to `tMap_1`. Change the name of the flow to `order`.
2. Open `tMap`, and you should see two input tables: customer and order.
3. Select the `customerId` field from the `customer` table and drag it to the `customerId Expr. key` in the `order` table.
4. You will see a purple key icon and a flow showing the linked fields.
5. Type `"Card"` into the `Expr. key` field for `orderType`.

6. Drag all the order fields apart from `customerId` to the output. Your `tMap` should now look like the following screenshot:

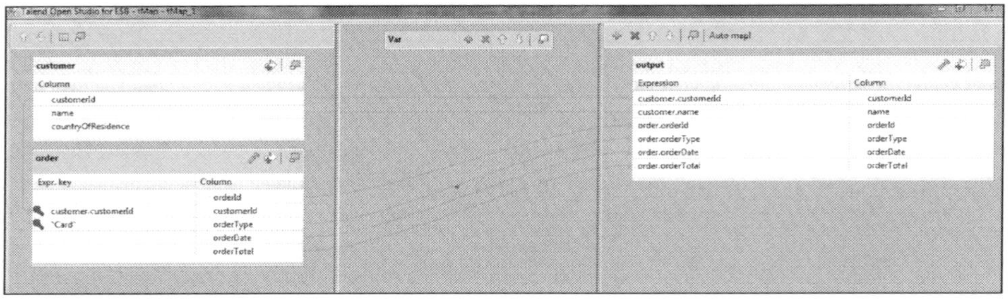

7. Close `tMap` and run the job.
8. You will see that there is a single row for each `customer`, and many of the fields are null.
9. Re-open the `tMap`, and click **tMap settings** 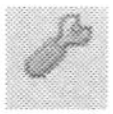 for the input flow order.
10. Change **Match Model** to **All matches** and **Join Model** to **Inner Join**.
11. Close `tMap` and run the job.You will see that only the rows that have an `orderType` of card have been output, but there are now multiple records per customer.
12. Add a new output to `tMap` and rename it to `notMatched`.
13. Drag all the customer fields into the new output.
14. Click `tMap` settings, and set **Catch lookup inner join reject** to **true**.
15. Close `tMap` and add another `tLogRow`. Select `tLogRow` mode of **Table (print values in cells of a table)**.
16. Join the `notMatched` flow from `tMap` to the new `tLogRow` and run the job.
17. You should now see two tables: one containing all Card transactions for customers and another showing all customers who have no Card transactions.

How it works...

`tMap` allows for different join types to be defined using expressions as keys. In this example, we used a variable from the main flow plus a constant (`"Card"`) as our join keys.

The first execution of the job performed a left outer join, so all input records are output and non-matched fields are set to null (or default value if they are Java primitives). In addition, the first execution also specified to use only a unique match, thus printing out only one row per customer.

The second execution, however, specified that we wanted to do an inner join with all matches, so the output contained all orders where the customer paid with a credit card.

In the second execution, we also defined a second output that caught all the rows from the **main** flow that did not have any matches to the lookup.

There's more...

This recipe illustrates the main features of joining using `tMap`, but only joins one table to another. It is also possible to join the same table to many others of a variety of different keys from many lookups in a single `tMap`.

The next two recipes will show some examples of this.

The eagle-eyed among you may have noticed that the lookups are processed slightly earlier than the main flow. Due to the small volumes of data in this recipe, it isn't apparent, but if you replace the file for `tFileInputDelimited_2` with `chapter04_jo_0080_orderData_large.csv`, then this will become very apparent (unless you have a very fast hard disk!).

What you will see is that `tMap` loads the lookup data into memory tables at the start of the job before it begins processing the main data flow.

For batch data integration jobs this is an efficient method, since it reduces the lookup time per transaction on the main flow, however, in the recipe *Using reload at each row to process real-time/near real-time data*, we will see how this method is not appropriate for small volume, real-time or near real-time data.

Also, be aware that in order to process large lookups, you will need to ensure that you have enough memory available and allocated to hold all the lookup data. If not, then the process will return `out of memory` errors. The recipe *Stopping memory errors* in *Chapter 12, Common Mistakes and Other Useful Hints and Tips,* describes the techniques that can help mitigate against `out of memory` errors in Talend.

See Also

- *Hierarchical join using tMap* in this chapter.
- *Using reload at each row to process real-time/near real-time data* in this chapter.
- *Stopping memory errors in Talend* in *Chapter 12, Common Mistakes and Other Useful Hints and Tips*.

Hierarchical joins using tMap

The previous recipe covered the basics of `tMap` joining, but `tMap` has another level of joining capability, in that it can join together data in a hierarchical fashion. This simple example shows how easily this can be achieved using `tMap`.

Getting ready

Open the job `jo_cook_ch04_0080_hierarchicaltMapJoin`.

How to do it...

1. Open the `tMap` component. You will see three input tables.
2. Select **customerId** from the `customer` table and drag it into **Expr. key** of the `customerId` in the order table.
3. You will see that a join link, a purple key symbol has been added to the column.
4. Change the **tMap settings** for the `order` table to **Inner Join** and **All Matches** (see previous recipe if you are not sure how to do this)
5. Now, select `orderId` from the `order` table and drag it to `orderId` in the `orderItem` table.
6. Change the **tMap settings** for the `orderItem` table to **Inner Join** and **All Matches**. Exit `tMap` and run the job.
7. You should see a printed table containing denormalized customer/order/order item rows.

How it works...

This job works on the hierarchy that exists between customer, order, and order item. A customer has many orders and an order has many order items.

The key for orders is customer, and the key for order items is order. Thus, to get all the order items for a customer, it is necessary to first find the keys for all the orders, and then find all the order items that match the order keys.

As you can see. `tMap` allows this relationship to be defined easily simply by dragging the relevant parent key to the child structure.

Using reload at each row to process real-time / near real-time data

Prior to attempting this recipe, you will need to ensure that you have an active MySQL database and have updated the context variables within the context MySQL to contain your database and login details. See the recipe *Setting up a database connection* in *Chapter 7, Working with databases*, for details on how to do this.

As we mentioned in the recipe *Joining using tMap,* `tMap` will load the join data into memory prior to processing the main input rows. This works fine for a batch processing model, because the overhead of loading large lookups in memory is offset against the efficiency in processing the joins against the data held in memory.

This paradigm does not however work in a real-time situation. In a real-time process, it would be unacceptable to wait for say 5 minutes to unload a large database table prior to processing a single record.

This recipe shows how the `tMap` 'reload at each row' feature can be used to process small volumes of real-time information in an efficient manner.

Getting ready

Open the job `jo_cook_ch04_0090_prepTheDatabase` and run it. Once the database has been loaded, open the job `jo_cook_ch04_0090_reloadAtEachRow`.

How to do it...

Run the job. You will see that over 500,000 records are read from the order table into memory prior to the single customer record being processed and the job will take a number of seconds to process.

1. Open `tMap` and change the **tMap option** for the input `order` table to **Reload at each row**. You will see a new header bar appear.

2. Click the **+** button and enter `generatedCustomer.customerId` into the **Expr.** field. Enter `"generatedCustomer.customerId"` (including quotes) into the **globalMap Key** column. Your order table should now look as the following screenshot:

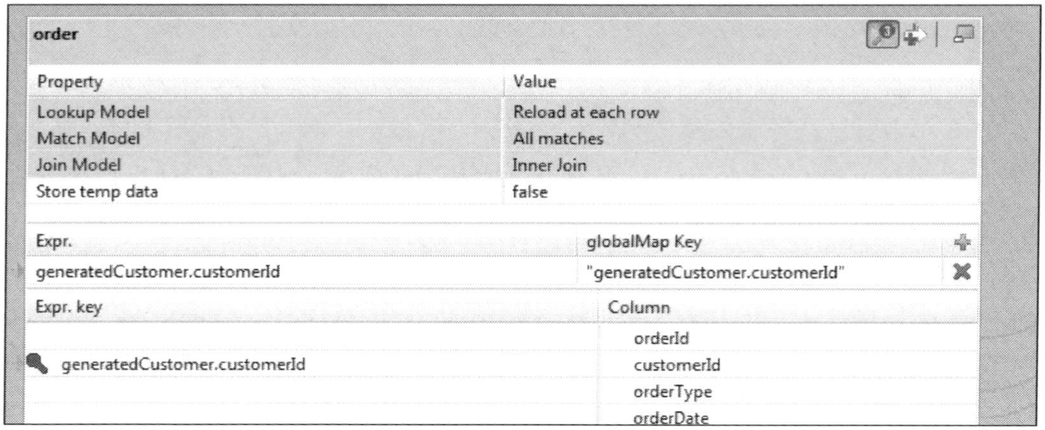

3. Close `tMap` and enter the `MySQLInput` component for order.
4. Remove the trailing double quote and add a WHERE clause to the query so that it looks like the query shown:

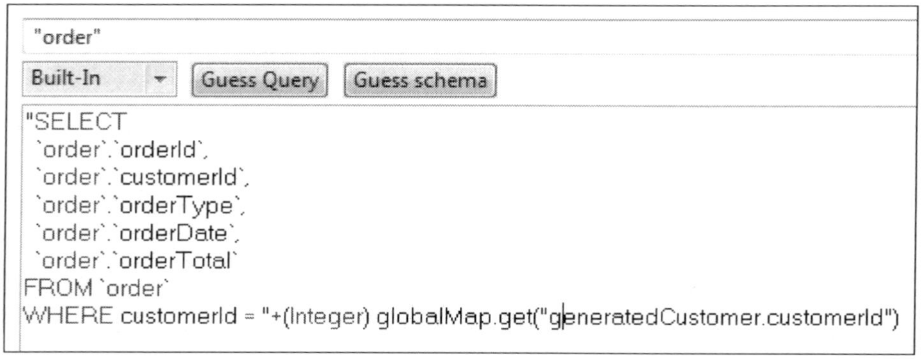

5. Run the job again. You will see that only 84 rows have been returned from the order table.

How it works...

There are four key elements to making this technique work.

Loading the data into memory

The normal tMap join process is to load all the lookup data into memory once, prior to processing the main flow data.

The `reload at each row` option, however, forces the lookup to reload its data many times; once for each row that is read from the main flow. In this example, it therefore forces `tMySqlInput` for the `order` to re-execute its query as each row from the main flow (`generatedCustomer`) arrives at the `tMap`.

The globalMap key

The inclusion of a `globalMap` key value in `tMap` forces `tMap` to populate the `globalMap` value for `customerId` with the `customerId` value of the `generatedCustomer` row. This means that the `globalMap customerId` is changed every time a new customer record arrives
at the `tMap`.

The WHERE clause

The addition of the `WHERE` clause containing the `globalMap customerId` in the query forces the `WHERE` clause to change every time the `customerId` changes. Because we are using reload at each row, this has the effect of changing the query for each record that arrives at `tMap`.

The result

The net effect is therefore that the query is executed for each row from the main flow and that the result set returned from the database for a given input will only contain rows that match on `customerId`.

This action therefore minimizes the number of rows to be loaded into memory, as you can see when you execute the job. The number of rows for the order lookup is 84, even though there are over 500,000 rows on the database.

So, this means that the load of the lookup is very small in comparison to a complete dump of the whole table, which would happen without reload at each row being used.

There's more...

This method will only work efficiently if the number of input rows is small, or the lookup is massive in comparison to the main flow. This is because the number of individual reads to the database is minimal in comparison to the amount of time taken to unload the whole table. As the number of input rows rises, the overhead associated with processing many individual queries will rise significantly, and will eventually overtake the time taken to process a single query and unload the whole table.

> For small lookups in this scenario, it is often more efficient to load the whole lookup into memory, rather than process them using reload at each row. Whether or not to load whole or reload at each row is best determined during volume testing.

5
Using Java in Talend

Java is a hugely popular and incredibly rich programming language. Talend is a Java code generator which makes use of many open source Java libraries, so this means that Talend functionality can easily be extended by integrating Java code into Talend jobs.

This chapter contains recipes that show some of the techniques for making use of Java within Talend jobs.

- Performing one-off pieces of logic using `tJava`
- Setting the `context` and `globalMap` variables using `tJava`
- Adding complex logic into a flow using `tJavaRow`
- Creating pseudo components using `tJavaFlex`
- Creating custom functions using code routines
- Importing JAR files to allow use of external Java classes

Introduction

For many data integration requirements, the standard Talend components provides the means to process the data from start to end without needing to use Java code apart from in `tMap`.

For more complex requirements, it is often necessary to add additional Java logic to a job, and in other cases it may be that adding custom Java code will provide a simpler or more elegant or more efficient code than using the standard components.

Performing one-off pieces of logic using tJava

The `tJava` component allows one-off logic to be added to a job. Common uses of `tJava` include setting global or context variables prior to the main data processing stages and printing logging messages.

Getting ready

Open the job `jo_cook_ch05_0000_tJava`.

How to do it...

1. Open the `tJava` component.
2. Type in the following code:

   ```
   System.out.println("Executing job "+jobName+" at "+TalendDate.
   getDate("CCYY-MM-dd HH:mm:ss"));
   ```

3. Run the job. You will see that message is printed showing the job name and the date and time of execution.

How it works...

If you examine the code, you will see that the Java code is simply added to the generated code as is. This is why you must remember to add `;` to the end of the line to avoid compilation errors.

See also

- *Setting context variables and globalMap variables using tJava*, in this chapter.

Setting the context and globalMap variables using tJava

Although this recipe is centered on the use of `tJava`, it also acts as a convenient means of illustrating how the `context` and `globalMap` variables can be directly referenced from within the majority of Talend components.

Getting ready

Open `jo_cook_ch05_0010_tJavaContextGlobalMap`, then open the context panel, and you should see a variable named `testValue`.

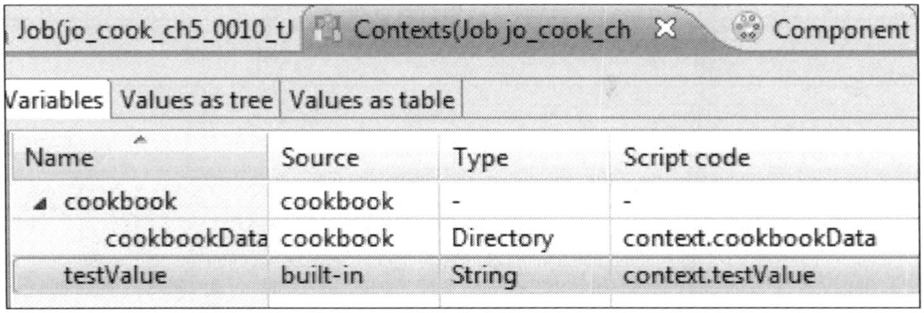

How to do it...

1. Open `tMap_1` and type in the following code:

```
System.out.println("tJava_1");
context.testValue ="testValue is now initialized";
globalMap.put("gmTestValue", "gmTestValue is now initialized");
```

2. Open `tMap_2` and type in the following code:

```
System.out.println("tJava_2");
System.out.println("context.testValue is: "+context.testValue);
System.out.println("gmTestValue is: "+(String) globalMap.
get("gmTestValue"));
```

3. Run the job. You will see that the variables initialized in the first `tJava` are printed correctly in the second.

How it works...

The `context` and `globalMap` variables are stored as globally available Java **hashMaps**, meaning that they are keyed values. This enables these values to be referenced within any of the other components, such as `tMap`, `tFixedFlowInput`, and `tFileInputDelimited`.

There's more...

This recipe shows variables being set in a one-off fashion using `tJava`. It is worth noting that the same principles apply to `tJavaRow`. Because `tJavaRow` is called for every row processed, it is possible to create a global variable for a row that can be referenced by all components in a flow. This can be useful when pre and post field values are required for comparison purposes later in the flow. Storing in the `globalMap` variables avoids the need to create additional schema columns.

See also

- *Managing contexts*

Adding complex logic into a flow using tJavaRow

The `tJavaRow` component allows Java logic to be performed for every record within a flow.

Getting ready

Open the job `jo_cook_ch05_0020_tJavaRow`.

How to do it...

1. Add the `tJavaRow` and `tLogRow` components.
2. Link the flows as shown in the following screenshot:

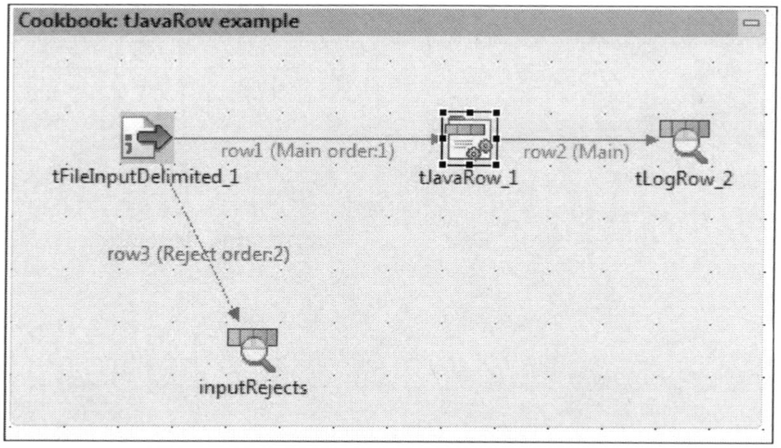

3. Open the schema and you will see that there are no fields in the output. Highlight `name`, `dateOfBirth`, and `age`, and click on the single arrow.
4. Use the **+** button to add new columns `cleansedName` (String) and `rowCount` (Integer), so that the schema looks like the following:

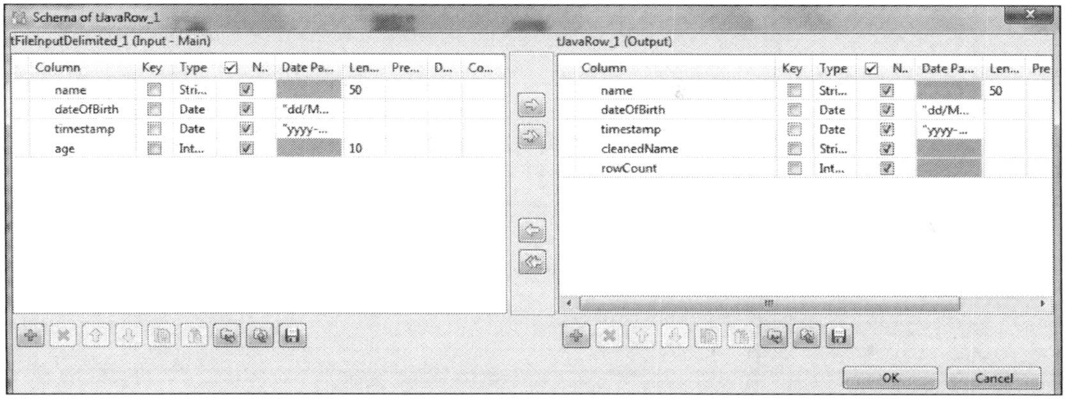

5. Close the schema by pressing ok and then press the **Generate code** button in the main `tJavaRow` screen. The generated code will be as follows:

```
//Code generated according to input schema and output schema
output_row.name = input_row.name;
output_row.dateOfBirth = input_row.dateOfBirth;
output_row.age = input_row.timestamp;
output_row.cleanedName = input_row.age;
output_row.rowCount = input_row.age;
```

6. Change the row `output_row.age = input_row.timestamp` from the code to read `output_row.age = input_row.age`.
7. Remove the rows for `output_row.cleanedName` and `output_row.rowCount`, and replace with the following code:

```
if (input_row.name.startsWith("J ")) {
      output_row.cleanedName = StringHandling.EREPLACE(input_row.
name, "J ", "James ");
}
if (input_row.name.startsWith("Jo ")) {
      output_row.cleanedName = StringHandling.EREPLACE(input_row.
name, "Jo ", "Joanne ");
}
output_row.rowCount=Numeric.sequence("s1",1,1);
output_row.rowCount=Numeric.sequence("s1",1,1);
```

8. Run the job. You will see that `"J  "` and `"Jo  "` have been replaced, and each row now has a `rowCount` value

How it works...

The `tJavaRow` component is much like a 1 input to 1 output `tMap`, in that input columns can be ignored and new columns can be added to the output.

Once the output fields have been defined the **Generate code** button will create a Java mapping for every output field. If the names are the same, then it will map correctly. If input fields are not found or are named differently, then it will automatically map the field in the same position in the input or the last known input field, so be careful when using this option if you have removed fields. In some cases, it is best to propagate all fields, generate the mappings and then remove unwanted fields and mappings.

> Also, be aware that the **Generate Code** option will remove all code in the window. If you have code that you wish to keep, then ensure that you copy it into a text editor before regenerating the code.

As you can also see from the code that was added it is possible to use Talend's own functions (`StringHandling.EREPLACE, Numeric.sequence`) in the Java components along with any other normal Java syntax, like the `if` statement and `startsWith` String method.

Creating pseudo components using tJavaFlex

The `tJavaFlex` component is similar to the `tJavaRow` component, in that it is included into a flow. The difference between the two components is that the `tJavaFlex` component has pre and post processes that are performed before and after the individual rows are processed, so it is similar to a pre-built Talend component.

Getting ready

Open the job `jo_cook_ch05_0030_tJavaFlex`.

How to do it...

1. Open the `tJavaFlex` component.
2. In the **Start Code** section, enter the following:

```
String allNames = "";
Integer NB_LINE = 0;
```

3. In the **Main Code** section enter the following:

```
allNames = allNames + row1.name + "|";
NB_LINE += 1;
```

4. In the **End Code** section, enter the following:

```
globalMap.put("allNames", allNames);
globalMap.put("tJavaFlex_1_NB_LINE", NB_LINE);
```

5. Open `tJava` and enter the following:

```
System.out.println("All names concatenated: "+(String) globalMap.
get("allNames"));
System.out.println("Count of rows: "+(Integer) globalMap.
get("tJavaFlex_1_NB_LINE"));
```

6. Run the job. You will see that the concatenated names and `NB_LINE` have both been printed by the `tJava` component.

How it works...

The **Start** code is executed prior to any rows being processed, so it is used to initialize the variables.

The **Main** code is executed for every row, so the name is added to the concatenated name string, and number of lines is incremented.

The **End** code is executed after all the rows have finished processing, so the completed name string and counters can be copied to `globalMap`, so that it is available to other components.

There's more...

If you examine the `globalMap` variables published by most of the components, you will see that most will have a variable `NB_LINE`. This is because the pre-built Talend components perform a beginning, main, and end routine like `tJavaFlex`, and publish a count of lines at the end.

> Because `tJavaFlex` has the start and end procedures it makes it ideal for complex aggregations or loading of structures such as arrays or lists that can then be accessed downstream after they publishing to `globalMap`.

Creating custom functions using code routines

Code routines enable the developer to create re-usable Java classes that can be integrated into Talend jobs, and in particular within `tMap`.

In the validation chapter, there is an example of a simple code routine. This recipe is a fuller explanation of creating and using code routines within Talend.

Getting ready

Open the job `jo_cook_ch05_0040_codeRoutine`.

How to do it...

1. In the metadata section, open the `Code` folder and right-click on **Routines**. Select **Create routine**.

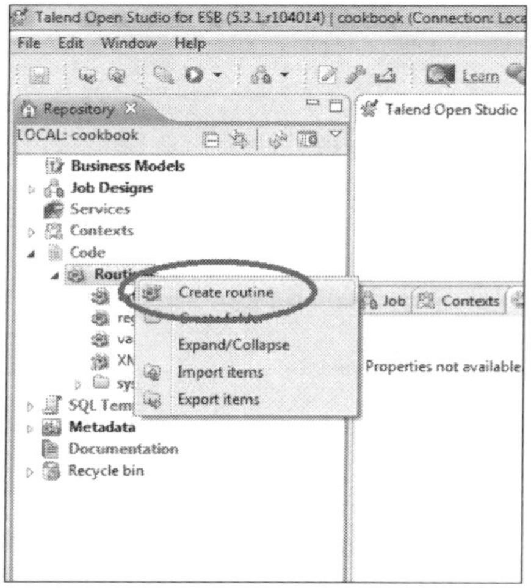

2. Name the routine `regexUtilities` and click on **Finish**. This will open a Java package and create a new class called regexUtilities, and a test method called `helloExample`.
3. Copy the following code immediately after the end of the `helloExample` method.

```
/**
   * regexData: return the first instance of regex pattern in a
string.
   * Returns null if there is no text matching the pattern.
   * e.g. regexData(".*r", "world") # returns "wor"
```

```
      *
      * {talendTypes} String
      *
      * {Category} regexUtilities
      *
      * {param} string("regex Pattern") input: The regex pattern to
find
      * {param} string("string") input: The string to search
      *
      * {example} regexData(".*r", "world") # returns "wor"
      */
     public static String regexData(String inputPattern, String
inputString) {
      java.util.regex.Pattern p =  java.util.regex.Pattern.
compile(inputPattern);
      java.util.regex.Matcher m = p.matcher(inputString);
         if (m.find()) {
             return m.group(0);
         } else {
             return null;
         }
     }
```

4. Save and close the code routine.
5. Open `tMap`.
6. Click on expression builder button for the output field result.
7. Note that the category of `regexUtilities` is now present; click on it.
8. Then, click on the Function `regexData`. This will copy the example function call into the **Expression** panel, as shown in the following screenshot:

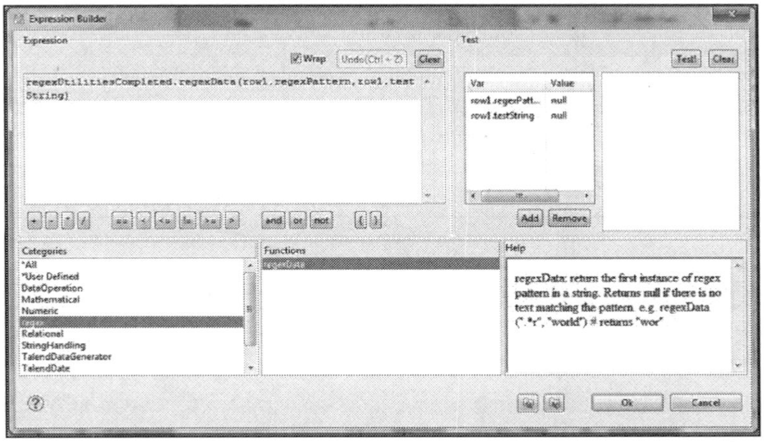

9. Run the job. You will see in the log output the results of the `regexData` calls using the data defined in the `tFixedFlowInput`.

How it works...

Code routines are Java classes whose static methods are made available to all jobs in a project.

Talend uses the comments for the method to define the category and show the help information in the expression builder.

Once defined, the new method can be used anywhere in the Talend project that allows Java code to be entered.

> Always ensure that you complete the comment block for a new method fully and accurately. This ensures that the method is correctly categorized and provides all the required documentation for the expression builder.

There's more...

If you view the underlying code for a `tMap` expression you will see that it is of the form:

```
<output variable> = <expression>;
```

This means that a `tMap` expression is limited to a single line of code, so more complex logic becomes impossible.

This is why the most common use of code routines is to provide a method returning a single value that can be used within `tMap`, as demonstrated within this example.

> If you open the system folder under code routines, you will see the Talend provided routines that are available. It is always worth referring to these if you get stuck with a code routine or wish to understand fully how the talend function works.

See also

- *Creating validation routines* in *Chapter 3, Validating Data*.
- *I can't find my code routine* in *Chapter 12, Common Mistakes and Other Useful Hints and Tips*.

Importing JAR files to allow use of external Java classes

Occasionally, during development it is necessary (or simpler) to make use of Java classes that aren't already included within Talend. These may be pre-existing Java code such as financial calculations or open source libraries, which are provided by *The Apache Software Foundation* (`www.apache.org`).

In this example, we will make use of a simple Java class `ExternalValidations` and its `ExternalValidateCustomerName` method. This class performs the following simple validation:

```
if (customerName.startsWith("J ")) {
  return customerName.replace("J ", "James ");
} else {
  if (customerName.startsWith("Jo ")) {
    return customerName.replace("Jo ", "Joanne ");
    } else {
    return customerName;
  }
}
```

Getting ready

Open job `jo_cook_ch05_0050_externalClasses`.

How to do it...

1. Create a code routine called `externalValidation`.
2. Right-click and select the option **Edit routine Libraries**.

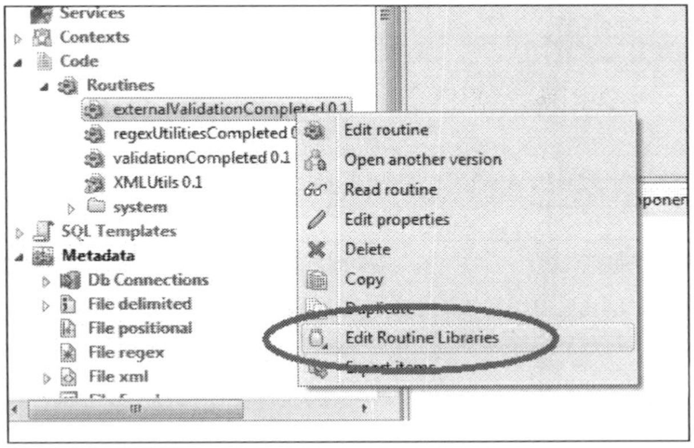

3. In the next dialogue, click on **New**.
4. Select the option **Browse a library file**, and browse to the `cookbookData` folder which contains a sub-folder named `externalJar`. Click on `talendExternalJar.jar`, then click **Ok** to confirm. The import dialogue should now look as the following:

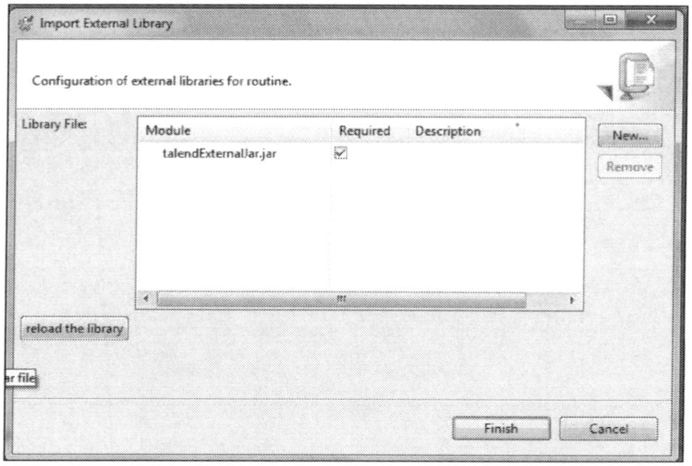

5. Return to the job and open `tJavaRow`, and click on the **Advanced** settings tab.
6. Add the following code:

```
import talendExternalClass.ExternalValidations;
```

7. Return to the **Basic** tab and add the following code:

```
output_row.validatedName =ExternalValidations.
ExternalValidateCustomerName
  (input_row.name);
```

8. Run the job. You will see that the validations have taken place, and the customer names have been changed.

[If you get an error when running this job then it is possibly because the new class has not been set up as a dependency automatically. Check the *Finding code routine* recipe in *Chapter 12, Common Mistakes and Other Useful Hints and Tips* for details on how to fix this.]

How it works...

The code routine `externalValidations` is a dummy routine used to attach the external `jar` file and make it available to all jobs in the project.

In order to use the classes in the JAR file, it is necessary to add an import statement within the `tJavaRow` so that the code knows where to find the methods.

There's more...

An alternate method of achieving this for just a single job is to use the `tLibraryLoad` components at the start of the job to define the location of the external libraries and the JAR files required.

6
Managing Context Variables

This chapter contains exercises that illustrate some of the methods for managing context variables within projects and jobs.

- Creating a context group
- Adding a context group to your job
- Adding contexts to a context group
- Using tContextLoad to load contexts
- Using implicit context load to load contexts
- Turning implicit context load on and off in a job
- Setting the context file location in the operating system

Introduction

In this chapter, we will perform fairly simple tasks for performing basic operations on context variables, but do not take this as a reflection of the unimportance of context variables.

The use of context variables is a fundamental requirement for creating production quality Talend applications. *Appendix B, Management of Contexts*, deals with some of the implications of the different methods of managing context variables within a project.

Transportable code

For code to be of production quality, it must be transportable between environments. This means that, when we move code from the development environment to the test environment, it should execute properly even if we are using different file paths, file names, database names, database user IDs, and so on.

Context variables

Context variables are parameters that Talend uses, that can be set to different values in different environments.

Assuming that the Talend code has been built to use these parameters and they have been set correctly for each environment, a job will execute happily using one set of resources in development, and a completely different set of resources in test.

Common values in contexts

Another use of context variables is to define values that are commonly used within a project, such as data inbox directory, staging area directory, and constants.

Passing command line parameters

Context variables are also used to pass parameters to a job, either via the command line or from a calling a (parent) job. See the *Deploying and Scheduling* recipe of *Chapter 11, Deploying and Scheduling Talend Code* for more information regarding this.

Setting context variables in the code

The ability to manipulate context variables within the code is covered in the *Setting context variables and globalMap variables using tJava* recipe in *Chapter 5, Using Java in Talend*.

Database context variables

Creating a context group for database connections is covered in *Chapter 7, Working with Databases*.

Creating a context group

A context group is a set of (usually) related context variables for use within a project. This recipe shows how to create a new context group.

How to do it...

The steps for creating a context group are as follows:

1. Open the metadata panel, and right-click on the context section.
2. Select the **Create context group** option.
3. Name the new group `cookbookGeneral`.
4. Click on the **Next** button, and you will see the main context variable panel.
5. Click on **+** to add a new variable and type in `cookbookDirectory`.
6. Set the type to **Directory**.
7. Now, click on the **Values as a table** tab, and click on the Default column for cookbookDirectory. Click on the **...** icon.
8. This will open a directory navigation window, so navigate to the cookbook data directory, and click on **Finish**.

How it works...

The context group is created in the metadata panel, and the individual context variables can then be added, along with their default values. Because we chose the type as **Directory**, Talend gives us the option of using a windows dialogue to simplify the mechanism for selecting the directory we wish to use.

There's more...

In this recipe, we have created a basic context, but there are more features that you can explore.

Context types

The context dialogue allows many different types of context variables to be defined, and in some cases, as in this recipe, it will provide a dialogue to make definition easier.

Prompt for variable values using the tree mode

Updating values in the context group can also be done in the tree mode. This is an alternative method that differs in one important way.

The tree mode provides an option that will prompt for a value to be displayed at runtime, by checking the prompt box for a variable.

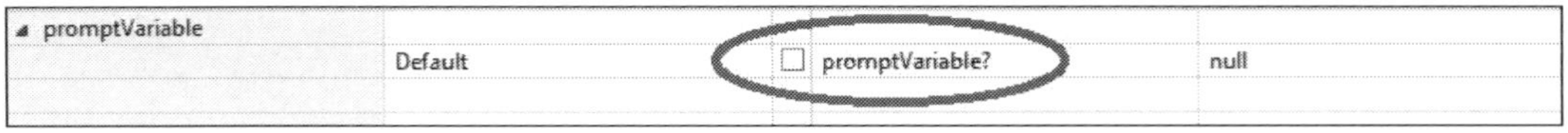

The prompt will appear at runtime, as shown in the following screenshot, and is a useful means for providing test values when developing a job:

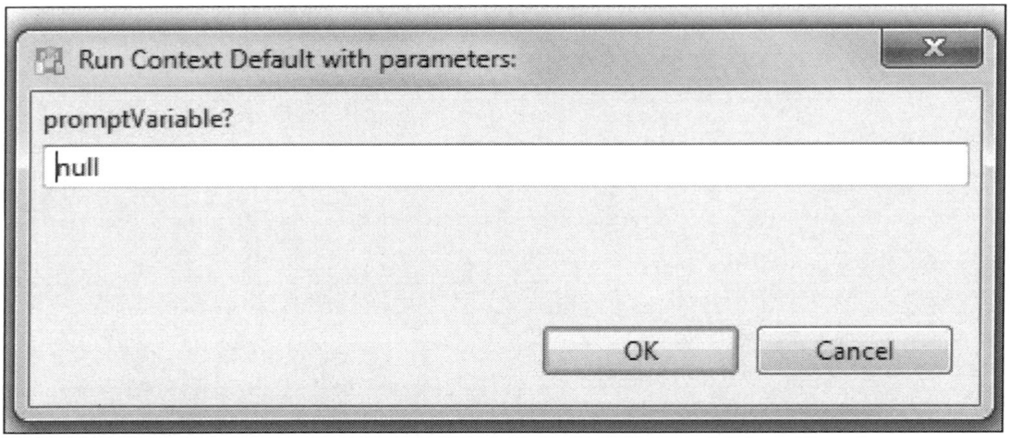

Adding a context group to your job

A job will not automatically use a context group. This exercise shows how to add a context group to a job.

Getting ready

Open the `jo_cook_ch06_0010_addContextGroup` job.

How to do it...

The steps for adding a context group to your job are as follows:

1. Open the context panel, and click on the context icon shown as follows:

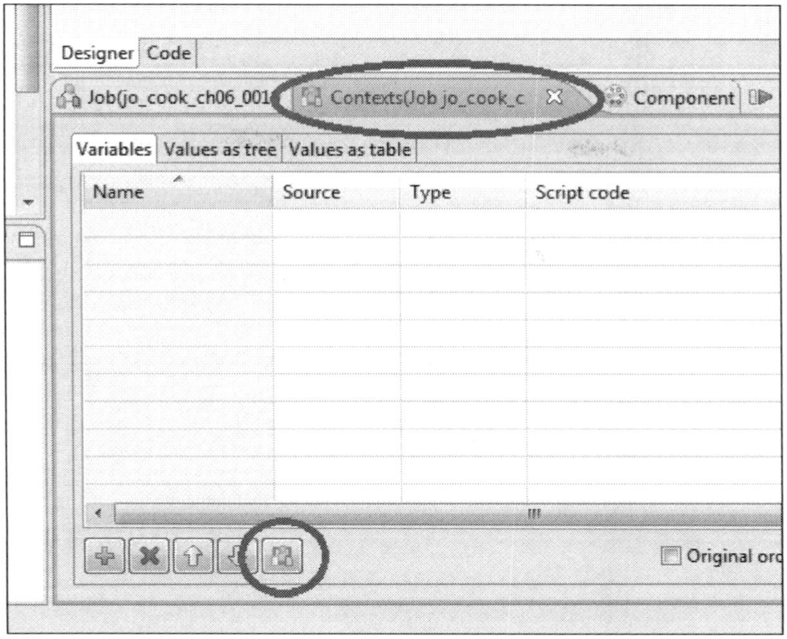

2. You will then be presented with the list of available context groups.
3. Select **cookbookDB**, and then **Ok**.
4. You will now see that the `cookbookDB` context variables have been added as read-only variables into the job.

How it works...

The context dialogue within a job allows single (in job) contexts, as well as context groups, to be added to a job.

There's more...

The preceding method shows how to add all context variables into a job. There is also an option to add only a subset of the variables within the group, if you drill down into the context group when selecting, demonstrated as follows:

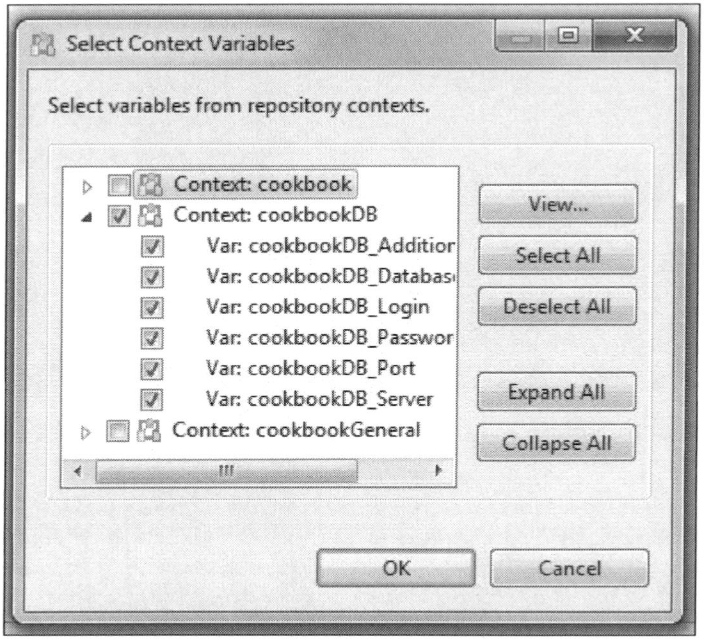

Another method of adding the context to the job from the metadata is to drag the context metadata icon into the **Contexts** panel.

Adding contexts to a context group

Talend provides a means for defining multiple different sets of values for the parameters in a group, one for each environment (or context).

Getting ready

Open the `jo_cook_ch06_0010_addContextGroup` job, and open the context group cookbookGeneral.

How to do it...

The steps for adding contexts to a context group are as follows:

1. Open the context panel, and click on the context icon shown as follows:

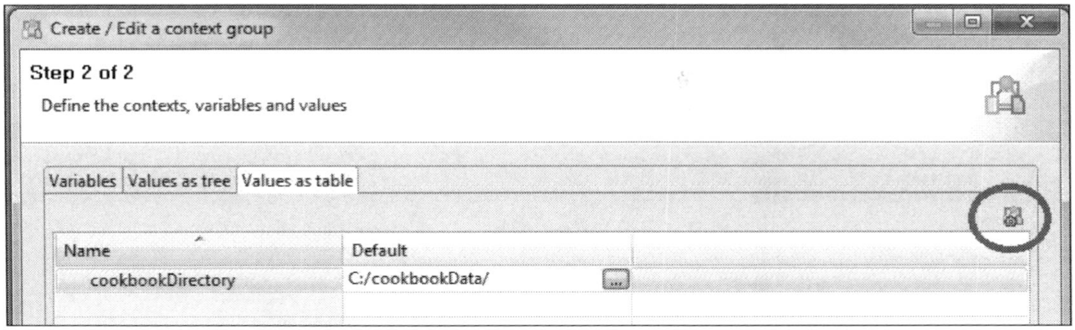

2. Click on **Default**, click on the **Edit** button, and then change the name to `development`.
3. Click on the **New** button, and add a context named `test`.
4. Click on the **New** button, and add a context named `production`.
5. Click on **Ok** to exit the dialogue.
6. Now you will see that there are now additional columns for the new contexts.

There's more...

The additional columns will define the values of a context variable in each context, and these will most likely contain different values, depending upon the environment illustrated as follows:

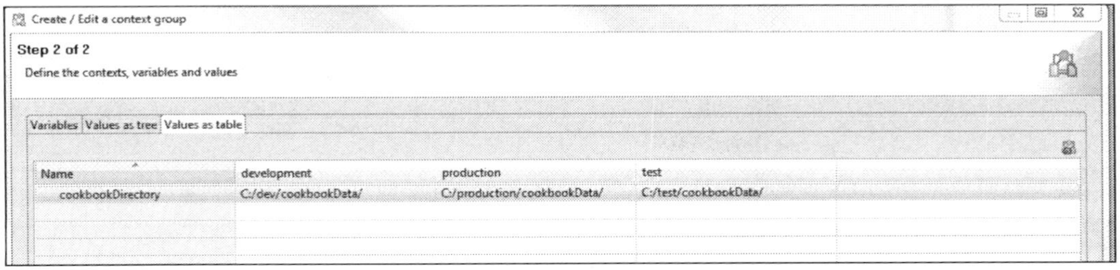

These contexts can then be selected at runtime via the shell launcher, thus ensuring that the correct values are used in the correct environment.

Using tContextLoad to load contexts

A second method for defining context variables in different environment is to store them in a file or database external to Talend, and then load them as part of a job.

Getting ready

Open the `jo_cook_ch06_0020_loadContextData` job.

How to do it...

The steps for using `tContextLoad` to load contexts are as follows:

1. Open the `tFileInputDelimited` component and change the delimiter to, so that it matches the format in the file.
2. Drag a `tContextLoad` component onto the canvas and link it to `tFileInputDelimited`.
3. Open `tContextLoad`, and click on the option **Print operations**.
4. Unclick **Disable warnings**.
5. Run the job.

How it works...

The context file contains name/value pairs in the form of key=value, so setting the delimiter to = means that we can identify each as columns in the Talend schema.

When we click on the print operations, it causes Talend to print out what is happening with the context.

There's more...

The `tContextLoad` does have some additional features that you may wish to use. They are described in the following sections.

Print operations

It is usually only necessary to set print operations when debugging code, since it isn't usually good practice to print the values of say passwords in a log file. It is better, if you wish to log the values, to use the `tContextDump` component.

Warnings

The tContextLoad component allows different variations of warnings and error conditions to be specified, depending upon your requirements. It is therefore possible to check for context variables being correctly set, prior to a job running, and to fail the job if they are not.

> However, you have to take care with this approach, because job-specific context variables can cause errors and warnings if you do not set them in the file, despite the fact that they may not need a value to be set at the start of the job.

Context file location

The downside of this method as shown is that the context file must reside in the same location on every machine. To get around this limitation, see the later *Setting the context file location in the operating system* recipe.

Using implicit context loading to load contexts

This method is very similar to the one discussed previously, that the context data is external to Talend, but differs in the fact that the context data is loaded automatically for every job in a project.

Getting ready

Open the jo_cook_ch06_0030_implicitContextLoad job.

How to do it...

The steps for using implicit context load to load contexts are as follows:

1. Click on **File** then **Edit project properties**.
2. From the dialogue box, expand **Job Settings** and select the option for Implicit context load.
3. Check the option for **Implicit tContextLoad**.
4. Check the option **From File**.
5. Set the **From File** name to C:/cookbookData/chapter6/chapter6_jo_0020_cookbookContextFile.txt.
6. Set the **Field Separator** to =.

7. Click on the **Print operations** box.
8. Click on **Ok** to finish.
9. Run the job, and you will see the context data being loaded and the warnings being produced.

How it works...

The implicit context load functionality reproduces the code in the previous exercise for all jobs in the project.

As with the previous exercise, the context file, the delimiter, and the actions to be taken while loading the contexts are all specified, just that with this method, it is global for every job.

There's more...

This method suffers from the same shortcomings as the method in the previous exercise, but is easier to maintain and implement, because the values are set centrally.

> Remember to set the project properties back to normal once you have completed this exercise, unless you plan to perform the next one.

Turning implicit context loading on and off in a job

Implicit context load can sometimes be annoying, especially when you have many variables, and you are running test jobs. It can sometimes be hard to see the wood from the trees. This exercise show how you can turn off implicit context load if you wish to do so.

Getting ready

Open the `jo_cook_ch06_0040_turnOffImplicit` job.

How to do it...

The steps for turning implicit context load on and off in a job are as follows:

1. Open the **Job** tab.
2. Select the **Extra** tab.
3. Uncheck **Use Project Settings**.

4. Uncheck **Implicit tContextLoad**. Your **Job** tab should look like the one shown as follows:

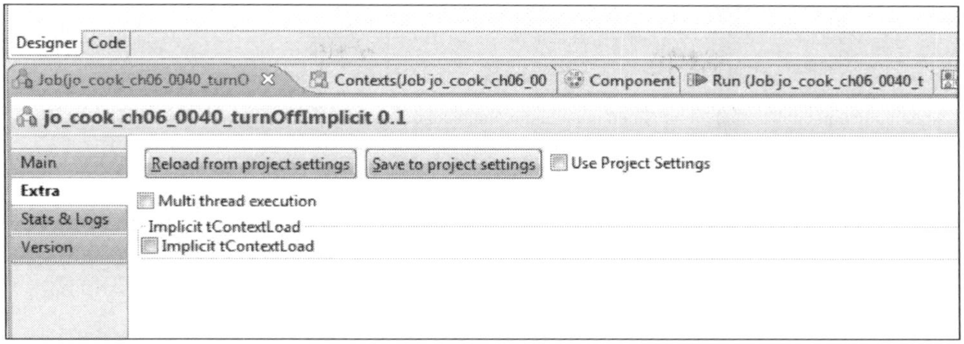

5. Run the job, and you will see that the initial context load is no longer performed.

How it works...

Talend allows the option to perform an implicit `tContextLoad` to be turned off for individual jobs within a project.

Setting the context file location in the operating system

The initial context load method and the `tContextLoad` methods do suffer from having to use a predetermined file location. This exercise shows how it is possible to overcome this via the use of system variables.

Note that this exercise is demonstrated on Microsoft Windows 7; however, it is possible to set and use global environment variables in Talend in any version of Windows, Linux, or Mac OS.

Getting ready

Copy the `systemValueContext.txt` file from the `cookbook directory/chapter6` to `C:\TalendContextDirectory`.

How to do it...

The steps for setting the context file location in the operating system are as follows:

1. Run the job, and you will notice that the value of the context variable is set to `In the job`.

2. Go to **Start** | **Control Panel** | **System and Security**.
3. Select **System**, then click the right-hand side **Advanced system settings**.
4. Click on the **Environment Variables** button.

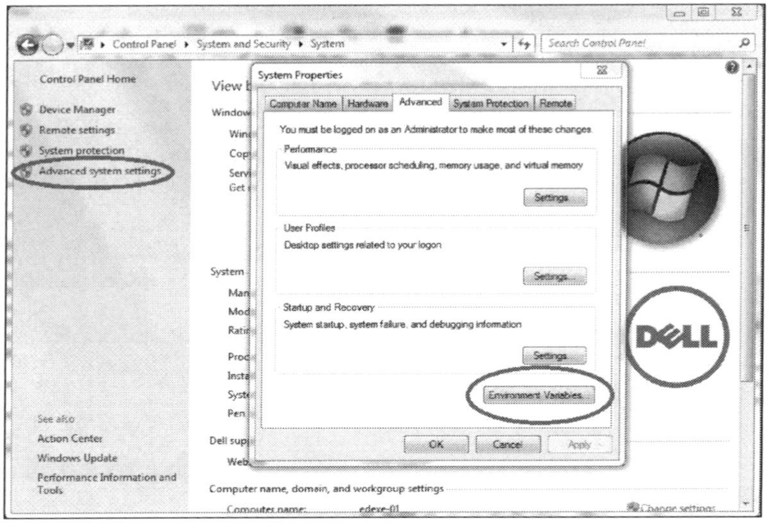

5. Under the System variables, click on **New**.
6. Enter **Variable name** as `TALEND_CONTEXT_DIRECTORY`.
7. Enter value as `C:\TalendContextDirectory\`.

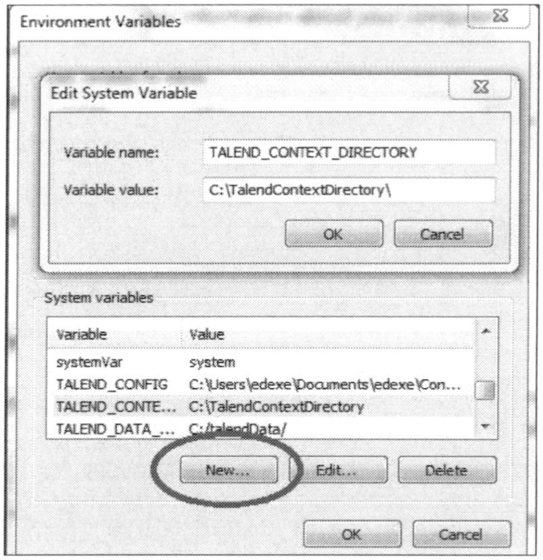

8. Click on **OK** to save.
9. Restart Talend Open Studio.
10. Open the `jo_cook_ch06_0050_systemVariableContext` job.
11. Open `tContextLoad` and change the file location to `System.getenv("TALEND_CONTEXT_DIRECTORY")+ "systemValueContext.txt"`.
12. Run the job, and you will see that the context variable is now displaying context file in Talend directory.

How it works...

As with most fields in Talend, the text can be replaced with a variable or snippet of Java code, and `tContextLoad` is no different.

By replacing the cookbook context variable with a command to read the system variable, we are able to redirect the component to pick up the data from a directory that can be altered at runtime.

There's more...

There are a couple of other things that we will need to consider when using this method. They are discussed next.

Variable not present

Note that we had to stop and start Talend Studio to enable the new variable to be picked up. This is because the variable is included as a part of the Eclipse build, so was not recognized until we restarted the job.

Implicit context load

This method can also be used for the implicit context load method, and is recommended over setting a fixed file location.

7
Working with Databases

This chapter contains recipes that show some of the techniques used to read and write data to databases. It also contains recipes that show techniques to manage tables within a database. In this chapter we will learn:

- Setting up a database connection
- Importing the table schemas
- Reading from database tables
- Using context and globalMap variables in SQL queries
- Printing your input query
- Writing to a database table
- Printing your output query
- Managing database sessions
- Passing a session to a child job
- Selecting different fields for insert, update, and delete
- Capturing individual rejects and errors
- Database and table management
- Managing surrogate keys for parent and child tables
- Rewritable lookups using an in-process database

Introduction

Many applications and organizations rely on databases to store their corporate data. These can be application databases to support operational systems, data warehouses, data marts, or ODS (Operational Data Store), and any data integration developer must understand how to manipulate the database objects and the data held within the database.

Talend usually connects to a database using JDBC, so it can connect to any datasource for which there is a JDBC driver, which means that Talend can connect to all of the most popular databases and a host of less well-known ones too.

In order to perform the recipes in this chapter, you need to ensure that you have a database installed. This book uses MySQL, a popular open source database that is freely downloadable. In addition, some of the recipes will make use of the HSQL database driver as a means of creating transient in-memory tables.

You will also need a general working knowledge of databases and have a reasonable understanding of SQL.

It's worth noting that there are many flavors of databases and while all act generally in the same manner, there are nuances and extensions that may exist in say, Oracle, but not in MySQL.

In this chapter we shall attempt to cover functionality common to the majority of databases supported within Talend, but there may be some functionality not supported by your database of choice (for example, not all of the supported databases have a slowly changing dimension or SCD component).

> Prior to attempting any of the exercises in this chapter, you will need to open a MySQL window and execute the command: `CREATE SCHEMA COOKBOOKDB`. You then need to perform the following recipe, *Setting up a database connection*, and then run `job jo_cook_ch07_setUpDBForExercises`, to create the tables and data required for the rest of the exercises.

Setting up a database connection

This recipe shows how a database connection can be easily created using the Talend supplied wizard. Note that this recipe and the next use the connection `cookbookDB_myCopy`. This version of the database metadata is used for demonstration only. All the other jobs in this chapter use the connection `cookbookDB` unless explicitly stated otherwise.

Getting ready

Ensure that MySQL is running and you have executed the command mentioned in the *Introduction* section.

How to do it...

The steps to be performed are as follows:

1. Navigate to **Metadata** | **Db Connections**. Right-click on it and select **Create connection**.
2. Set the name as `cookbookDB_myCopy` and click on **Next**.
3. Select the database as **MySQL** from the drop-down list and then enter the details as shown in the following screenshot: Note that I have set up a `talend` login on MySQL, so I use this. You will need to set up the information to match your database credentials.

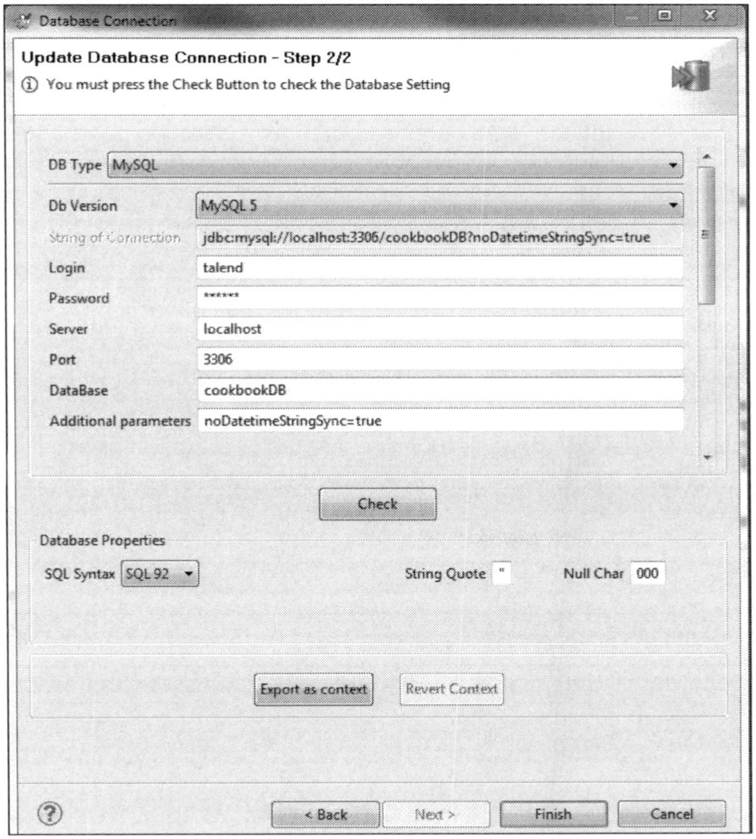

4. Click on the **Check** button and you should see the message: `cookbookDB_myCopy` **connection successful**.
5. Next, click on the button **Export as context**.
6. The context dialogue will appear.
7. Change the name to `CookbookDB_myCopy`, click on **Next** then **Finish**.
8. Click on **Finish**, then **Yes to the modifications**, then **Ok** to complete the setup.

> Now that you have the required parameters for connection, you will need to update the context information in the databases `cookbookDB` and `cookbookDBCompleted` to ensure that the recipes in this section will complete successfully. You can do this by amending the details in the contexts for both connections.
>
> Once you have changed the context variables. Go back to the metadata and check connections for both.

How it works...

This wizard allows you to easily build up the JDBC connection string for your MySQL database and check that you can connect to it.

The database information is then exported to a context of the same name.

There's more...

Database connections are very important within Talend and can be a great time-saver.

Using the connection

If you drag the connection to an open job, you will be presented with a list of options to create components that are pre-populated with the job information.

If, however, you decide to use a component from the palette, then the database information can be populated in the component by dragging the connection and dropping it on the component. This should work for most of the components, but for those where it doesn't, for example, `tCreateTable`, you need to open the component, change the **Property Type** to repository, and then select the connection.

Always create database connections

While you can work with all the database components without using a metadata connection, it is highly recommended that you set one up for every database you use. The short time taken to do this is easily recovered later on.

Connection names

As with all Talend artifacts, careful naming can make life easier in the long term, so do check to see if you have naming standards regarding connections already defined.

If not, then it is recommended that database connections be named exactly the same as the database/schema (including case) for easy identification. If you are using schema within database then include both, separated by underscore, for example, FINANCE_SALES.

Context

You will notice that immediately after checking the connection, we exported the settings to a context. This is a good practice and worth doing immediately after the connection has been tested and is working, since it will allow the database settings to be defined as context parameters; a must when the code is promoted between environments.

Importing the table schemas

Once we have the connection set up, it is very easy to grab table metadata from the database for use in our jobs. The following example shows how simple this is.

Getting ready

If you have set up the database correctly, then you should be able to see three tables in the database; `customer`, `order`, and `order_item`.

How to do it...

The steps to be performed are as follows:

1. Right-click on the `cookbookDB_myCopy` database connection and select **Retrieve Schema**.
2. This opens up a dialogue that will enable you to define filters. We do not need to filter, so click on **Next**.
3. View the list of tables in the **cookbookDB** database by clicking on **>**. This dialogue also enables us to filter the tables that we are interested in.
4. Since we want all the tables, click on **Select All**. You will see that Talend generates the schemas.
5. Once all the selected tables have been generated successfully, click on **Next**.
6. You can now examine and make changes to each of the schemas by clicking on the table in the left-hand side panel.
7. We do not want to make any changes, so click on **Finish**.

8. In the `cookbookDB_myCopy` metadata, you will now see that the tables have been added to the **Table schemas** folder as shown in the following screenshot:

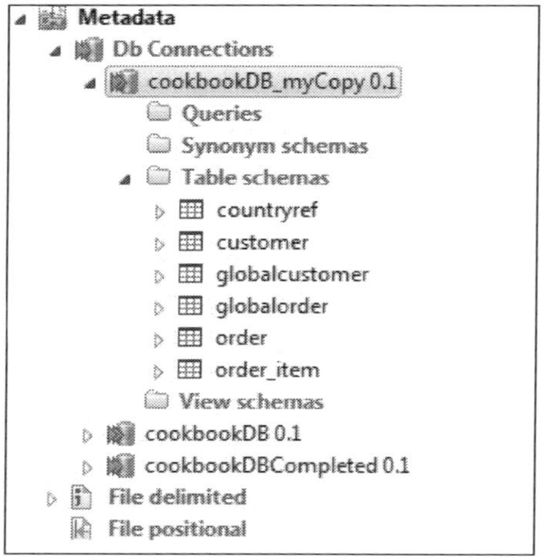

How it works...

Talend uses the connection information to gather schema and table information from the database for presenting to the wizard. When we selected the tables, Talend used the information to create Talend schemas for use in our jobs.

There's more...

As with database connections, schemas, when dragged onto the canvas, will provide us a host of options as to how we wish to use the schema; for example, as an input table or output table.

> It is quicker and easier to work with schemas via the metadata panel than to try to hand-crank them from the palette, so do get into the habit of using the metadata panel for data sources and targets. It will save you time.

Reading from database tables

Now that we have the Talend schemas available, we can start to use them to access the data in the database.

Getting ready

Create a job `jo_cook_ch07_0010_readTables`.

How to do it...

The default mode of reading a table in Talend is to read all the rows and columns of a table:

1. Drag the `customer` table from the left-hand side panel. This will open up a list of options.
2. Select **tMysqlInput**.
3. Add a `tLogRow` component and create a flow between `tMysqlInput` and `tLogRow`. Change the **Mode** of `tLogRow` to **table**.
4. Run the job and you will see that the complete table has been read.

Selected rows and columns

In many cases we do not want the whole table, so it is more efficient to filter the data in the database via a query:

1. Open `tMysqlInput` and change the query to:

```
"
SELECT
  `customer`.`name`,
  `customer`.`countryOfResidence`
FROM `customer`
WHERE `customer`.`countryOfResidence` = 'USA'
"
```

2. Open the schema, change the type to built-in, and remove the `customerId` field.
3. Click on the **guess schema** button to remove the `customerId` field. This will save you from making the change manually.
4. Run the job and you will see that the rows and columns have been filtered to match the query.

Multiple tables and complex queries

Sometimes it is easier or more efficient to let the database do some of the heavy lifting with regards to the data prior to processing:

1. Open `tMysqlInput` and change the query to:

```
"
SELECT
  c.name,
  SUM(o.orderTotal)
FROM customer c
INNER JOIN `order`  o ON c.customerId = o.customerId
GROUP BY c.name
HAVING SUM(o.orderTotal) > 50
"
```

2. Click on the **guess schema** button to refresh the built-in schema.
3. Run the job and you will see the list of customers that have total orders over `50`.

How it works...

Talend will execute the SQL query defined in the component and will allocate the fields in the order they occur in the schema.

Thus, we can develop queries that span multiple tables within a database and we can make use of the rich functionality of SQL to create the result set that we need for downstream processing.

There's more...

There are some additional things worth considering when using Talend with databases.

Efficiency versus readability

This book is about Talend, which is a visual tool. This therefore makes it simpler to understand what the code is doing just by viewing the job in the studio.

The SQL in the input component, however, hides many of the true input sources from the viewer, as we could see in the preceding complex example.

Thus, we are faced with an issue of efficiency versus transparency.

In the main, efficiency should win. Databases are designed to perform joins internally very efficiently, so do make use of this.

On the flip side, however, do not be tempted to create massive and super complex queries unless it is absolutely unavoidable. Breaking down a complex problem into smaller and simpler chunks aids understanding and maintainability.

SQL string

You may have noticed that `tMysqlInput` requires the SQL to be defined as a string and that the SQL defined previously is formatted like:

```
"
...... SQL in here
"
```

This is deliberate and a small time-saver. It means that a query can easily and simply be cut and pasted from and to a database client (such as, MySQL Workbench and TOAD) without having to remember to add the quotes or remove them.

It's a small detail, but it does help.

SQL style

You may have also noticed that the SQL generated by Talend is as per the correct standards for the database and is thus a little more long-winded than the SQL that most developers would write. For instance, if the database connection has a database and schema defined, then you do not need to include the schema name in the SQL.

In addition, you do not need to include the ` characters around every object unless the database absolutely requires it.

> Feel free to change the SQL to be more readable, add comments (/*......*/ type only) and shorten it, but be aware that unless you save the query, it will be lost should you ever decide to replace the component from metadata or regenerate it from the schema.

Using context and globalMap variables in SQL queries

It is possible to use parameters passed or created in a job to drive the results of a SQL query. This short recipe shows how.

Getting ready

Open the job `jo_cook_ch07_0020_contextInQuery`, which is a copy of the job from the previous recipe.

How to do it...

The steps to be performed are as follows:

1. Open the `tMysqlInput` component.
2. Change the final line to `HAVING SUM(o.`orderTotal`) > "+context.minOrderValue`.
3. Run the job and you will be prompted for a value.
4. Enter `10` and click on **Ok**.
5. You should see that the result set contains orders where the sum of the lines is > 10.

How it works...

The SQL statement used by `tMysqlInput` is held in a string, so can be manipulated just as any other string in Java. Thus, we can alter the value of the string using normal Java conventions; in this case a concatenate (+).

The statement is thus translated at runtime and the value of the context substituted into the SQL query, which returns the customized resultset.

There's more...

Following are some additional points to be noted regarding the use of parameterized queries.

The globalMap variables

globalMap variables can be used in exactly the same way as the context variable.

Developing the query

In most cases, it is better to test a query using fixed values in the database client and then substitute these for variables once the query has been proven.

Following are some other notes on developing queries with parameters:

- Be careful of spacing. If the query needs a space in place between items, then the space needs to exist in the query.
- String values need to be quoted in the query for example, the code `where name = 'Fred'`, would be parameterized as `where name = '"+context.selectedName+"'"`.
- As usual, make small changes then test, especially with SQL strings. In fact, it is wise to make changes to SQL that use parameters in isolation, since missed quotation marks will often result in a large number of compile-time errors.

Reloading at each row

This technique is absolutely essential for the reload at each row processing used in realtime scenarios that is described in detail in *Chapter 4, Mapping Data*.

Printing your input query

If your result set isn't as expected and you are struggling to understand why, then it is really useful to be able to see the query that was executed to give you the result. This recipe shows how this can be done.

Getting ready

Open the job `jo_cook_ch07_0030_printInputQuery`, which is a copy of the job from the previous recipe.

How to do it...

The steps to be performed are as follows:

1. Add a `tJava` component.
2. Add `OnSubjobOk` from `tMysqlInput` to `tJava`.
3. Open `tJava` and add the following line:

   ```
   System.out.println("\nExecuted query:
     \n"+((String)globalMap.get("tMysqlInput_1_QUERY")));
   ```

4. Run the job and you will see the query as it was sent to the database.

How it works...

As we have seen in other recipes, many of the Talend components will drop information to `globalMap`, for use by downstream components/subjobs.

In the case of `tMysqlInput`, one of the values written to `globalMap` is the query that was used to produce the result set, which is what we printed in the `tJava` component.

There's more...

Knowing what query was actually used in a database component is the key to debugging database related jobs, so this technique is invaluable.

It becomes particularly useful, as in this example, when parts of the query are parameterized, because you can see the fully completed query with the parameters inserted.

Writing to a database table

Writing to tables using Talend can seem very simple, but in fact is a very big topic, since different databases have multiple modes of writing to tables. In this simple recipe, we'll perform a basic write of data to a table as a basis for a much deeper conversation regarding this very important database requirement.

Getting ready

Open the job `jo_cook_ch07_0040_writingTable`.

How to do it...

The steps to be performed are as follows:

1. Open the **cookbookDB** connection and drag the schema for the table `customer` to the canvas.
2. Select the Component `tMysqlOutput`.
3. Open `tMysqlOutput` and change **Table** to `customerWriteTest`.
4. Connect it to `tFileInputDelimited`.
5. Run the job and you will get the message **Table'cookbookdb.customer_write_test' doesn't exist**.
6. Open `tMysqlOutput` and change **Action on table** to **Create table if not exists**.
7. Run the job again and you will see that the table `customer_write_test` has been created.
8. Run the job again and you will see that the job fails with the message **Duplicate entry '1' for key 'PRIMARY'**.
9. Open `tMysqlOutput` and change **Action on data** to **Insert or update**.
10. Open `tFileInputDelimited` and change the input file name to `chapter07_jo_0040_customerData_update.csv`.
11. Run the job again and you will see that the records with primary keys `1` and `2`, now have updated `countryOfResidence`.
12. Open `tMysqlOutput` and change **Action on data** to **Delete**.
13. Open `tFileInputDelimited` and change the input file name to `chapter07_jo_0040_customerData_delete.csv`.
14. Run the job again and you will see that the records with primary keys `5` and `8` have been deleted.

How it works...

Dragging the metadata for the table allows us to quickly set up an output component for the table. When we first execute the job, the table does not exist, so it failed. Changing **Action on Table**, allowed us to create the table automatically, so the second execution inserted the data.

When we tried to write to the table again, the job failed because the record we were trying to write to was already present. Since we wanted to do an update, changing **Action on Data** to **Insert** or **Update** allowed us to successfully update a couple of the records.

Finally, we have seen that using **Action on data** set to **Delete** can allow us to delete records from a table.

There's more...

As you have seen, the `tMysqlOutput` component is very powerful and flexible and we have only touched on the basic functions of this component. The following sections contain some additional notes regarding its use.

Creating tables

In most organizations, responsibility for defining and creating database tables will rest with a database administrator (DBA) or the data analysts. The exception is usually when temporary tables are required. Usually these are created and deleted by the developer and in Talend this can be achieved using the `tMysqlOutput` component.

By changing the value of **Action on table**, it is possible to create tables from the Talend job.

> In order for the `tMysqlOutput` component to create a table, it must know the primary keys and the column lengths, so these must be defined in the schema. Failure to define these will lead to runtime errors.

Update and delete keys

Always ensure that when you are updating or deleting rows from a table, the fields that you wish to use as keys are defined in the schema or in the field options as keys.

Batches

Many of the database output components enable records to be processed in batches (see the advanced tab for `tMysqlOutput`) and this is often the default method for the component. MySQL has a function called extended insert to perform batch inserts and other databases have other methods.

> You should, however, be aware of the fact that when you are updating and committing using batches, if one record fails, then the whole batch is rejected.
>
> It is therefore important to ensure that processes are in place for identifying batches of records and for fixing rejected batches when an error occurs.

Thus, it is important when designing and building your job that you decide on a strategy with respect to batching of writes before building, since the write strategy can and often will result in a very different code.

Bulk loading

Most databases provide a bulk loading facility to enable rapid insertion of data into the database. Talend does support bulk loading facilities for many databases by wrapping a component around the native bulk loaders supplied by the database manufacturer. This means that the options for bulk loading differ between the Talend components across the different database bulk load components.

It is worth noting though, that only some of the databases and some of the Talend bulk loader components will provide a reject file option. An example is Oracle's bad file option, where rejected records can be routed to a named file.

Most databases will have some documented method for reject handling when using bulk insertion; however, it will usually differ between databases, so is not covered here.

Bulk loading to temp table

If you cannot route bulk error data to a reject file, or capture some file reject information, then it is worth considering inserting to an empty temporary table, where errors are unlikely. After checking row counts, you can then merge the temporary table into the main table. Even though there is the overhead of multiple stages, it will often be quicker than non-bulk updates when dealing with large number of inserts.

Printing your output query

In one of the previous recipes, we saw how we can print the input and select query for debugging. This recipe shows how this can be achieved for an update, delete, or insert, which are all functions available through `tMysqlOutput`.

Getting ready

Open the job `jo_cook_ch07_0050_printOutputSQL`, which is a copy of the job from the previous recipe.

How to do it...

The steps to be performed are as follows:

1. Add `tJavaRow` and link it to `tMysqlOutput`.
2. Add the following code:

```
System.out.println(((String)globalMap.get("tMysqlOutput_1_
QUERY")));
```

3. Run the job. You will see that the output is all null.
4. Open the `tMysqlOutput` component and click on the **Advanced settings** tab.
5. Click the field **Enable debug mode** as shown in the following screenshot:

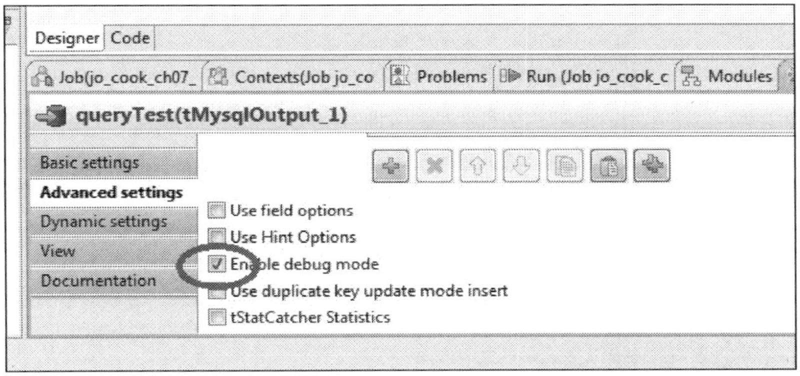

6. Run the job and you will see the individual SQL statements that were executed.

How it works...

Before using a `tMysqlOutput` component, you must first set the **Mode** to **Debug** in the **Advanced** tab for the component. This will allow you to capture the query for every row written to the table.

There's more...

Debug mode is expensive; every row written to the database will have the SQL statement returned to the job, which is why the feature is initially turned off. So you should ensure that when you no longer need to debug it, you turn it off.

Managing database sessions

Database sessions allow the developer to control how and when the data is committed to a database. This recipe shows how this is achieved in Talend.

Getting ready

Open the job `jo_cook_ch07_0060_databaseSession`. On inspection, you will see that the job has been set up to commit after each record has been written.

How to do it...

The steps to be performed are as follows:

1. Run the job. You will see that it is very slowly adding the records to the database.
2. Kill the job. If you inspect the database table `testSession`, you will see that the records have been added to the database.
3. Drag `tMysqlConnection` from the metadata panel and `tMysqlCommit` from the palette (note that this isn't available from the **Repository** panel) and wire up as shown in the following screenshot:

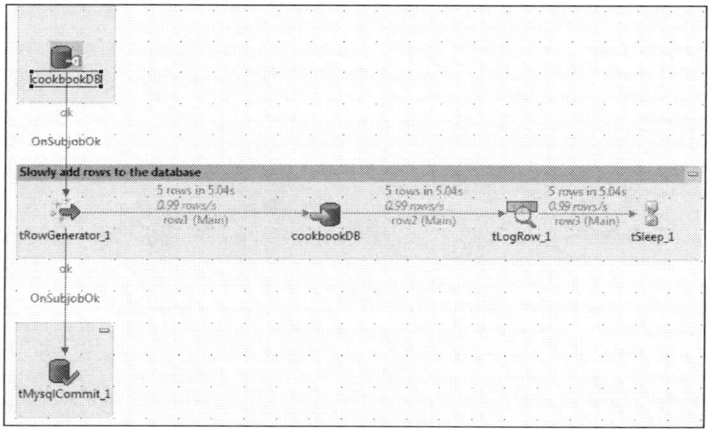

4. Open `tMysqlOutput` and tick the option for **Use an existing connection**. You will see that all the connection information is now hidden.
5. Run the job and **Kill it** before all ten records have been processed. If you examine the table you will see that it has no data in it.
6. Run the job and allow it to complete. The data has now been written to the table.

How it works...

The `tMysqlConnection` component establishes a connection and begins a session. When you select **Use an existing connection** in an output component, it adds the component to the session, thus ensuring that the records written require an explicit commit. The `commit` component will commit the writes to the database and close the session.

Executions

The first execution of the job shows how each record is committed as an atomic transaction.

The second execution shows that records output without a commit will not be added to the database when attached to a connection.

The final execution shows that all the records are committed as a single transaction.

There's more...

When to use sessions and when not to use them are defined by requirements, so it is good to confirm the commit strategy with the process designer during development.

Multiple outputs

Multiple output components can be added to a session in order for a transaction to include multiple tables. For example, we may wish to abort the writing of customer and order if the write for an order item fails.

By ensuring that all three output tables use the same connection, we ensure that they are either committed all together as a single transaction or none are written if any other dependent rows fail.

Don't forget the commit

A common beginner's error is to assume that the connection simply shortcuts the need for manually setting up a component, which is true, but it also begins a database session. So, if you do not add a commit component, you will not get any data written to the database.

Committing but not closing

The commit component is automatically set to close a session. If you wish to commit but keep a session open, then the `tMysqlCommit` component has an option to enable the session to be kept open after the commit.

Passing a session to a child job

Following on from the previous task, this recipe shows how a common connection can be passed from a parent job to a child job.

Getting ready

Open the job `jo_cook_ch07_0070_databaseSessionParent`, which is the same as the completed version from the previous recipe, but with the main process replaced with a child job. On inspection you should see that the child job has a connection set up and it is the same connection as the parent job.

How to do it...

The steps to be performed are as follows:

1. Run the job. If you inspect the database table `testSessionChild`, you will see that no records have been added to the database.
2. Open `tMysqlConnection` in the parent job.
3. Tick the box **Use or register a shared DB Connection**, and set the **Shared DB Connection Name** to `"cookbook"`, as shown in the following screenshot:

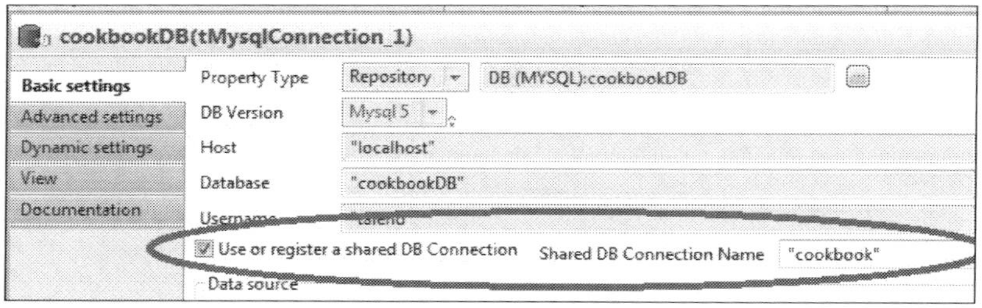

4. Repeat the same for the connection in the child job.
5. Run the job. When you now inspect the database table `testSessionChild`, you will see that the records have been added to the database.

How it works...

The `tMysqlConnection` component establishes a connection and begins a session in the parent job, as does `tMysqlConnection` in the child job. The problem in this scenario is that they both create individual sessions, so that when we run the parent, no records are committed to the database despite records being written by the child (we can see this in the console output).

When we define a shared connection in the parent of "cookbook", the session information then becomes available as a session in the child if we choose to use it, and in this example we do so by using the shared connection registered by the parent.

So the connection for the parent and child are now using the same session and when the commit is executed, the records added by the child are committed.

Selecting different fields and keys for insert, update, and delete

Many applications will write to/delete from the same table in many different ways, using different fields as keys and often updating different fields at different times. This recipe shows how this can be achieved without having to create new schemas each time.

Getting ready

Open the job `jo_cook_ch07_0080_fieldSelection`.

How to do it...

The steps to be performed are as follows:

1. Open the `tMysqlOutput` component and change the field **Action on data** from **Insert** to **Insert or update**.
2. Now click on the **Advanced settings** tab.
3. Tick the box **Use field options** to reveal the **Field Options** panel. You should see that all the fields are set as **Insertable** and **Updatable**.
4. Uncheck **createdDate** and **createdBy** in the column **Updatable**.
5. Uncheck **updatedDate** and **updatedBy** in the column **Insertable**.
6. Finally check the Update Key column for the column id. Your **Field options** should now look as shown in the following screenshot:

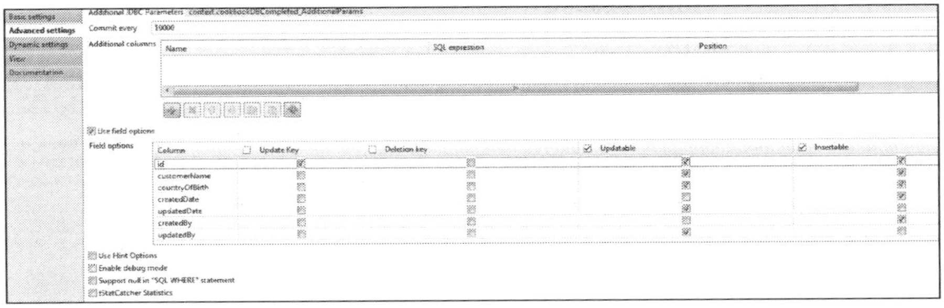

7. Run the job and inspect the table. You will see that the record has been created and that the **updatedDate** and **updatedBy** fields are blank.
8. Open `tFixedFlowInput`, and remove the values for **insertedDate** and **insertedBy**.
9. Add a value to **updatedDate** of `TalendDate.parseDate("yyyy-MM-dd","2012-05-22")`.
10. Add a value of **updatedBy** of `"ZZ"`.
11. Change the **customerName** value to `"testCustomerNewName"`.
12. Run the job and inspect the table. You will see that the name has been changed and the **updatedDate** and **updatedBy** fields have been written.

How it works...

First, we set the insert method to **Insert** or **update**. This allows us to write to new and existing records using the same component.

The first execution is an insert, so that the **createdDate** and **createdBy** columns are populated for the record in the table and the **updatedDate** and **updatedBy** columns are null.

Any subsequent write to this table for the given key is an update, so this will leave the **createdDate** and **createdDate** fields as they were set when first inserted and now populates the **updatedDate** and **updatedBy** columns and the new value of **customerName**.

There's more...

This is a great method for ensuring that pre-defined schemas are used within the jobs, thus encouraging re-usability and traceability, and also allows us to update rows using a different set of key values depending upon the data we have at hand.

Updating

Any key may be used to perform an update, not just the primary key for the table, since Talend will create a SQL `WHERE` clause under the covers. You simply need to select the fields that you wish to use as the key in the column, **Update key** within the **Field options** section.

Deleting

You should also notice that there is a column in the list of fields for defining the deletion key. The same method applies to deleting rows as for update; however, the column **Deletion key** should be used instead in the **Advanced** settings tab and the **Action on data** set to **Delete** in the **Basic** settings.

Capturing individual rejects and errors

Many database applications require a log of rejects and errors to be kept to enable erroneous records to be identified, so that manual repairs can take place. This recipe shows how to capture errors for individual rows using the reject row facility.

Getting ready

Open the job `jo_cook_ch07_0090_rejectsAndErrors`.

How to do it...

The steps to be performed are as follows:

1. Copy the `customer` table from metadata and create a `tMysqlOutput` component.
2. Change the **Table** to `"customer_reject_test"`, and change **Action on table** to **Drop table if exists and create**.
3. Right-click the `tMysqlOutput` component and you will see that the only **Row** option is **Main**.
4. Run the job. You will see that there are errors in the console and that the table is empty.
5. Open `tMysqlOutput`, and click on `Advanced` settings.
6. Uncheck **Extend Insert**.
7. Right-click on the `tMysqlOutput` component and you will now see a flow labeled **Rejects**.
8. Send this flow to a `tLogRow` component which has **Mode** set to **Vertical**.
9. Run the job. You will now see a reject row printed in the console with a duplicate key error.
10. You should also see that, apart from the reject row, the rest of the input rows have been written to the database.

How it works...

In its default mode, `tMysqlOutput` is inserting in bulk mode known as extended insert. This allows many rows to be written as a single SQL statement.

Our data contains a problem row and this means that when we tried to insert this row it is rejected along with all of the rows in the same group (see later in this section for additional details on this).

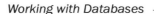

When batch insert methods are turned off, the `tMysqlOutput` component will allow a **Reject** flow to be created. Like other **Reject** flows in Talend it contains a copy of the input record plus a reason for rejection.

Thus, when we first examined the row output from `tMysqlOutput`, we could only see the **Main** row. After turning off the **Extend Insert** option, we were then allowed to connect a rejects flow.

With the bulk insert option turned off, we can now reject individual rows, so the second execution of the job completes successfully, the valid records are written to the table and the rejects are captured and printed in the console.

There's more...

There are some more points which we will cover in this recipe.

Die on error

In addition to having any bulk insert methods deactivated, the option to **Die on error** must also be deactivated in order for rejects to be captured using this method.

Efficiency

The ability to reject rows without killing the job is incredibly useful and does make for simpler code and error management, but does come at a cost; namely the rows must be inserted one at a time.

Inserting rows one at a time is nowhere near as efficient as using bulk insertion methods or by specifying block sizes, so you may find that for some databases there is a trade-off between loading speeds and error reporting and management.

Error management

Having individual rows being rejected makes fixing a problem much simpler, since we have a one-to-one match between the error for a single reject row.

In contrast, the use of batch insert methods, such as the MySQL extended insert method will return one error, but reject a whole batch of rows, both good and bad.

So this gives us slightly more of a headache, as when one row fails, the whole batch is rejected, giving us a situation of having good and bad records in a batch of rejects, which in turn forces us to create more complex methods of fixing than for a single reject.

Database and table management

This simple recipe shows how to execute database management and table related commands.

Getting ready

Create a new job `jo_cook_ch07_0100_tableManagement`.

How to do it...

The steps to be performed are as follows:

1. Drag the `cookbookDB` connection onto the canvas and select the component `tMysqlRow`.
2. In the **Query** area add the following code:

   ```
   "
   CREATE TABLE `test_mysqlrow` (
     `id` int(11) NOT NULL,
     `data` varchar(45) DEFAULT NULL,
     PRIMARY KEY (`id`)
   )
   "
   ```

3. Run the job and you will see that the table `testMysqlRow` has been created.

How it works...

The `tMysqlRow` component is the database equivalent of both `tJava` and `tJavaRow`, it can be used within a flow like `tJavaRow` or standalone like `tJava`.

That said, the `tMysqlRow` component is most commonly used standalone, like `tJava`, as in this case, where we create a table.

There's more...

This simple example shows a single, isolated use of `tMysqlRow`. On most occasions it is used prior to processing to create temporary tables or to drop constraints or indexes prior to bulk loading, and also after processing to remove temporary tables and restore constraints or indexes.

tMysqlRow can also be used on a row-by-row basis to perform say inserts, but this is usually simpler to do using tMySQLOutput, as demonstrated in the previous examples.

Managing surrogate keys for parent and child tables

Many application databases will use surrogate keys as a means of uniquely identifying rows in a table. As a result of this, it is often necessary to capture the surrogate key for the record after writing a record, so that any associated child elements will be able to reference the parent's surrogate as a foreign key. This recipe shows one method of creating surrogate keys in a relation and later discusses few more methods.

Many aspects of this job should be familiar, especially if you have completed the previous recipes in this chapter, so only a few key points have been highlighted.

Getting ready

Open the job jo_cook_ch07_0110_surrogateKeys.

How to do it...

The steps to be performed are as follows:

1. Open the tMysqlInput component labeled globalCustomer, and add the following query:

   ```
   "
   SELECT COALESCE(MAX(customerId),0) FROM globalCustomer
   "
   ```

2. Open tJavaRow_1, and add the following code:

   ```
   globalMap.put("maxCustomerId",input_row.maxCustomerId);
   System.out.println("Max customer id = " +
     globalMap.get("maxCustomerId"));
   ```

3. Open tMap_1, and add the following code into the **Expression** field for **customerId**:

   ```
   Numeric.sequence("customer",((Integer)

     globalMap.get("maxCustomerId"))+1,1)
   ```

4. Open tMap_2, and add the customerURN and source as join keys for the globalCustomer lookup.

5. Add the following code into the **Expression** field for the `orderId`:

```
Numeric.sequence("order",((Integer)
  globalMap.get("maxOrderId"))+1,1)
```

6. `tMap_2` should now look like the following screenshot:

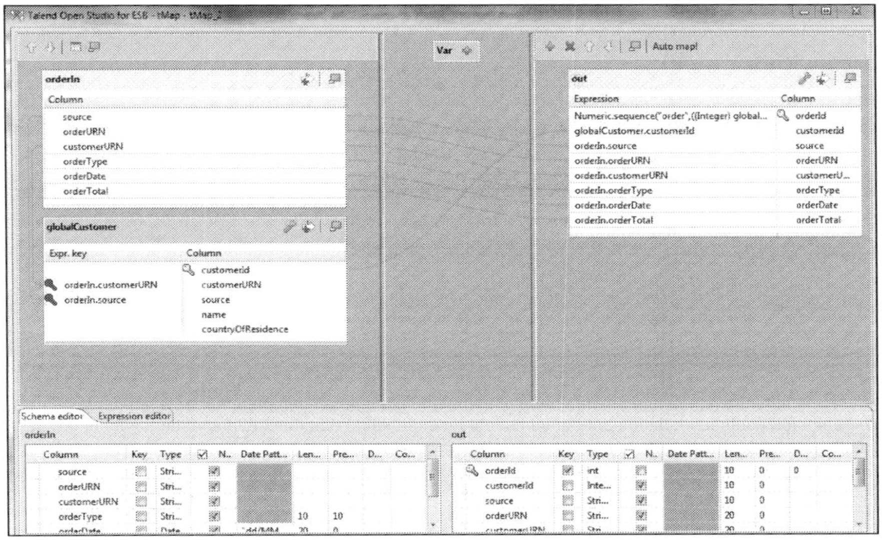

7. Run the job. You will see that the customer and order records have been added, the surrogate keys have been generated correctly, and foreign key references between customer and order are correct.

How it works...

The unique keys are created through the following two stages:

- The first stage is performed in `tMysqlInput`, and that is to capture the maximum value for the key in the `customer3NF` and `order3NF` table. These values are then written to the `globalMap` variables for later use.
- Now that we know the highest key value in the `customer3NF` table, the second stage is to create a sequence that starts at the maximum value plus one and use the result of the sequence as the surrogate key for each input in the customer row.

We then write the customer data to the `customer3NF` table, then read the order data and in `tMap`, join to the `customer` table on the natural key(`customerURN` and `source`), so that we can get the customer surrogate for use as the foreign key for the order data.

In `tMap`, we also generate the order surrogate and then write the completed order row to the database.

There's more...

The method shown is very efficient for batch processing or data migrations where we can blitz a table at a time. There is one note of caution, we need to be certain that no other job or process is writing to the same table using the same method at the same time. If we cannot be certain then we should use an alternative method.

Added efficiency using hashMap key table

This method can be made more efficient by not re-reading the `globalCustomer` table. Provided you have enough memory, it is better to copy the surrogate key (generated) and natural keys (`customerURN` and `source`) into a hashMap. This hashMap can then be used as a lookup, avoiding the need to reload the `customer` table in its entirety from the database, instead of simply reading data already stored in memory.

Ranges

A slight variation in the preceding method is to earmark a range of values prior to writing. This can be achieved by writing a temporary marker record into the table with a key of the current maximum value plus the number of records to be written plus one (or a given range plus one). This means that a second process will start its load at the top of the range, thus avoiding any overlap. Remember, though, to remove the marker record at the end of the writes for the range.

Sequences

Sequences are database objects that will return a unique value every time they are read. To generate surrogate keys, the process simply adds a lookup to the main flow that will select the next sequence value for the table and use the returned lookup.

> Note that the lookup must be made to reload at each row to ensure each row gets a value.

This method is good for both real-time and batch updates, however, not all database versions support sequences.

It is slightly less efficient than the Talend generated sequence method, but this method does have the advantage of being usable by many processes at the same time. It is therefore the best method to use in real-time/web service-based environment.

Auto increment keys

Some databases will allow fields that will automatically generate a new one-up number whenever a record is written to the table. If the key field is set as auto increment then we do not need to generate a key, we simply need to write the record to a table and the database will do the rest.

This method, however, does have a downside in that we need to re-read the table using the natural key to find the database created surrogate.

The LastInsertId component

A slightly more efficient alternative to re-reading using the natural key is to use the `tMysqlLastInsertedId` component in the flow.

This component will automatically add a field to the existing schema and populate it with the most recently written record.

This component will return the last value for a connection, so be very careful to only write one table at a time for a given database session.

Also note that this component is only available for a small subset of databases.

Auto increment procedure

The final option in this list is to use an auto increment key field, but to write the record to the database via a stored procedure. The procedure can then write the record and capture the last value written. This has the advantage of working with most databases, but the disadvantage of having to maintain a stored procedure/function.

Rewritable lookups using an in-process database

The `tHash` components are great for storing intermediate data in memory and are very efficient, but do not allow updates. Database tables allow updates, but aren't as efficient when writing and reading data on a row-by-row basis, especially when there are large numbers of rows to be processed.

This recipe shows how we can get the best of both worlds using a feature of the HSQL database that allows us to define databases that only reside in memory for the given process.

Due to this job being fairly complex, there are a few techniques used that can be found in other chapters of the book, but aren't explained in detail in this chapter. In addition, it will aid understanding if we provide a background for this scenario.

Background

In this recipe we are presented with a list of customers with their countries of residence. We wish to cross-reference their residence country with our list of countries held in our MySQL database and:

- if the country is found, add the country ID to the customer record

- if the country is not found, add a new country to our MySQL table and add the new country ID to the customer record

Getting ready

Open the new job `jo_cook_ch07_0120_inProcessDatabase`.

How to do it...

The first thing we need to do is to create a memory copy of the current MySQL country table, by copying the previous execution position from the persistent table in MySQL:

1. Drag the table schema `countryRef` from the connection **cookbookDB** and select the component `tMysqlInput`.
2. Drag a `tHSQLDBOutput` component onto the canvas and configure it as shown in the following screenshot:

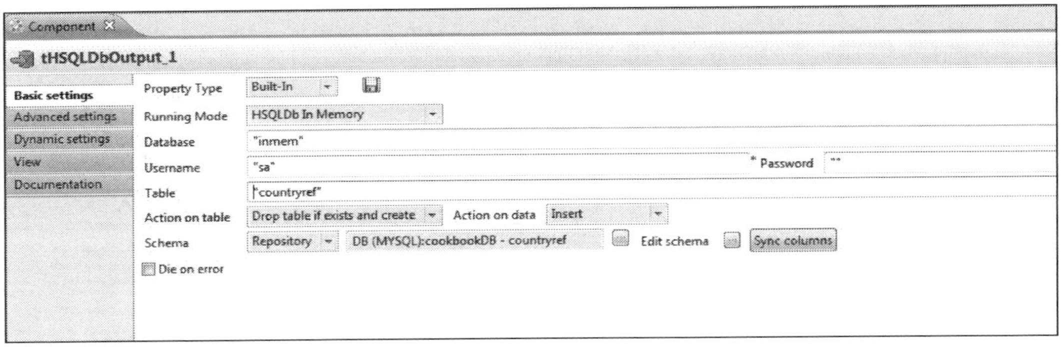

3. Connect `tMySQLInput` to `tHSQLDBOutput` and execute the code.
4. You will see that two rows are copied from the database table into the in-memory table.

   Reading and updating the in memory table

5. Uncomment the final section and join to the previous subjob via an `OnSubjobOk` link as shown in the following screenshot:

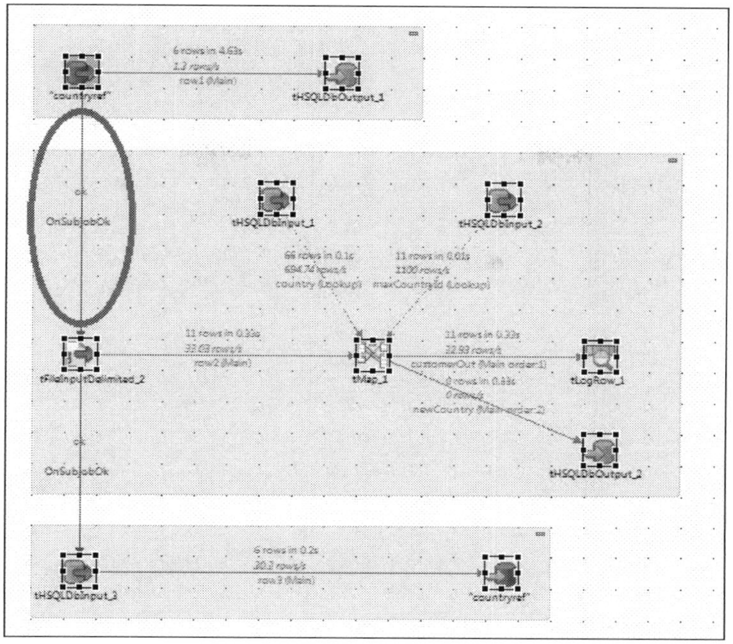

6. Run the job.
7. You will see that four new rows have been added to the `country` table and the customer records all have correct country IDs.

How it works...

The key features of the job are as described in the following section.

In-memory components

All of the HSQLDB components are set up in the same way and use the same database (`inmem`).

Initialize the data

The data is initialized from the persistent copy of the country table.

tMap

There are a few key features to be noted within `tMap`:

- Both the lookups are reloaded at each row. This is to ensure that any in-flight changes are made available immediately after the update.

- We have a lookup for the maximum value of the ID in the country table. This is used when we aren't able to find a country and need a new key, which will be the highest current ID plus one.
- So when writing to the output, we either copy the country key (if the country is found) or we copy the ID for a new country record (maximum ID value plus one). This is achieved using the code: `country.id == null ? maxCountryId.id + 1 : country.id`.
- When a new country is found then we create the new ID using max ID plus one and write it to the `newCountry` flow. This flow is used to insert the new row in the inline table.

Write back

Finally, we need to copy the new version of the table to the persistent country table ready for the next execution.

There's more...

This method is most useful when you need to refer values in a table, but where those values are likely to change during the course of a single execution.

This example is a fairly typical application of this method and while it is possible to achieve the same results using other techniques, this method is by far the simplest to understand and to implement.

It is also incredibly valuable when large numbers of records are to be processed, which would normally mean large numbers of individual reads into the database, which will be very slow.

If the in-memory table is very large then consider using the reload at each row method with a key as detailed in the the recipe *Using reload at each row to process real-time/near real-time data* in *Chapter 4, Mapping Data*.

Memory

As with all memory storage techniques, ensure that you have enough memory to hold all of the reference tables, before and after the execution. Ensuring that you only store the fields that are required in memory will allow you to fit a large number of records in the memory.

See also

- The *Using reload at each row to process real-time/near real-time data* recipe in *Chapter 4, Mapping Data*

8
Managing Files

This chapter contains recipes that show some of the techniques used to read and write data to files. It also contains recipes that show techniques to manage files within a file system. We will cover the following recipes in this chapter:

- Appending records to a file
- Reading rows using a regular expression
- Using temporary files
- Storing data in memory using tHashMap
- Reading headers and trailers using tMap
- Reading headers and trailers with no identifiers
- Using the information in the header and trailer
- Adding a header and trailer to a file
- Moving, copying, renaming, and deleting files and folders
- Capturing file information
- Processing multiple files at once
- Processing control/validation files
- Create and write files depending upon input data

Introduction

It isn't very efficient to process large batches of information via a web service, nor is it particularly desirable to pull data from an application database during peak hours. Thus, many organizations still maintain a file-based overnight batch processes using large extracts in file format.

In addition, many older, legacy applications rely solely on file-based data for communicating with the outside world.

It is therefore very important for the data integration developer to understand many file types and be able to manage them efficiently and effectively.

> This chapter deals with "flat" files, which, for our purposes means files that do not carry their metadata with them, such as XML or JSON, that are described in *Chapter 9, Working with XML, Queues, and Web Services*.

This does not mean that we will only deal with simple files. Some of the recipes in this chapter will deal with complex hierarchical file structures.

Appending records to a file

This simple recipe shows how a file can be built in within different sub jobs by appending data to an existing file. The append method is one way of building complex files, as will be demonstrated in later recipes in this chapter.

Getting ready

Open the `jo_cook_ch08_0010_fileAppend` job.

How to do it...

The steps for appending records to a file are as follows:

1. Copy the complete `subjob1 - copy me` sub job and paste it to create a second sub job.
2. Link the two sub jobs using an `onSubjobOK` link.
3. Open `tFixedFlowInput`, and change `Records from first subjob` to `Records from second subjob`.

4. Open `tFileOutputDelimited` on the new sub job, and tick **Append**, as shown in the following screenshot:

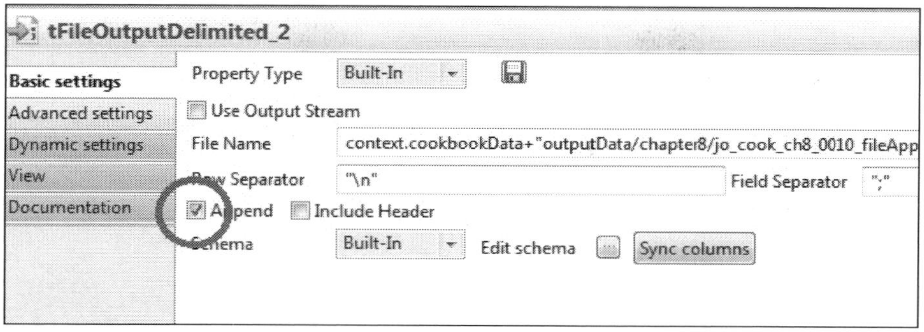

How it works...

The first sub job creates the file, and the second sub job appends to the same file.

There's more...

While relatively trivial, this recipe demonstrates a very powerful method for creating files that do not adhere to the norm, such as files containing a mixture of fixed and delimited data or free format strings.

Concatenating files using the append method

In addition to concatenating records using the append method, it is also possible to use the same method to concatenate many files into one file.

In most cases, the files would be identified using `tFileList`, and then appended to a single output file. One word of caution though; if you forget to set the mode to append, it will result in each file overwriting its predecessor, leaving you with just the output from a single file; the last one to be found.

It also presents an additional problem when the job is run for a second time. In that the file will already exist, and the new data will simply be added to the old data.

> It is thus a good idea when using file append to add a `tFileDelete` component to the beginning of the job. This means that a file is always created anew by the first iteration (but always make sure **Fail on error** is unchecked for the deleted component, otherwise it will fail when you run the job at the first time).
>
> Ensure that the file name is unique for each run, perhaps by adding the process ID to the file name or even the datetime including milliseconds.

Reading rows using a regular expression

Regular expression (**regex**) is a powerful method for pattern matching and replacement within many programming languages, and is outside the scope of this book (a good starting point is the javadocs for regex patterns at `http://docs.oracle.com/javase/1.4.2/docs/api/java/util/regex/Pattern.html`). One interesting use for regular expressions is when dealing with unusual input formats that are difficult to describe using normal delimited or fixed-width file formatting. This recipe shows how regex can be used to identify a set of input columns from an unstructured input row.

Getting ready

The screenshot of the `chapter8_jo_0020_jobLogData.txt` file is as follows:

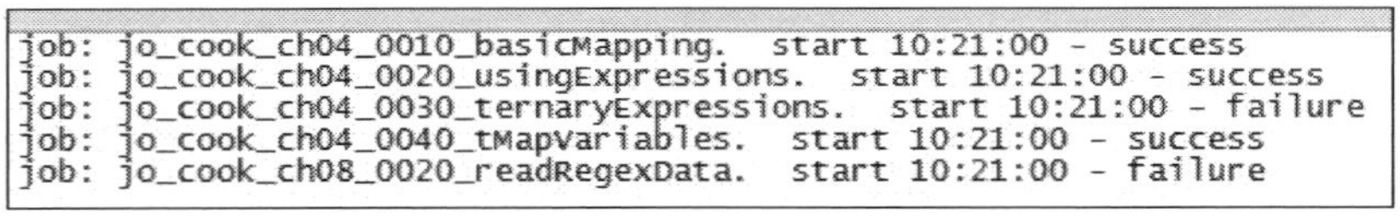

```
job: jo_cook_ch04_0010_basicMapping.  start 10:21:00 - success
job: jo_cook_ch04_0020_usingExpressions.  start 10:21:00 - success
job: jo_cook_ch04_0030_ternaryExpressions.  start 10:21:00 - failure
job: jo_cook_ch04_0040_tMapVariables.  start 10:21:00 - success
job: jo_cook_ch08_0020_readRegexData.  start 10:21:00 - failure
```

You should notice that there is neither an obvious delimiter, nor does each record fit a fixed width format.

Now, open the `jo_cook_ch08_0020_readRegexData` job.

How to do it...

The steps for reading rows using regular expressions are as follows:

1. Open `tFileInputRegex` and enter the following code:

```
"^job:  "+
"([a-zA-Z0-9_]*)"+
"\\. *start *"+
"([0-9][0-9]:[0-9][0-9]:[0-9][0-9])"+
" - "+
"(success|failure)"+
".*"
```

2. Run the job, and you will see that `jobName`, `startTime`, and `status` have been successfully extracted from the string, as shown in the following screenshot:

jobStats		
jobName	startTime	status
jo_cook_ch04_0010_basicMapping	10:21:00	success
jo_cook_ch04_0020_usingExpressions	10:21:00	success
jo_cook_ch04_0030_ternaryExpressions	10:21:00	failure
jo_cook_ch04_0040_tMapVariables	10:21:00	success
jo_cook_ch08_0020_readRegexData	10:21:00	failure

How it works...

Regular expressions require a pattern that will match a whole line of data, with parts of the pattern in brackets being retained and the rest being discarded. A short explanation of the regular expression code for the preceding example is detailed as follows:

- The first line of the regex starts with ^ (the symbol for start of line) followed by the text job and two spaces.
- The second line details that we want a combination of letters, numbers, and underscores. This part of the pattern is in brackets, so is put into the first field; `jobName`.
- The third line details the filler text, which consists of a dot (`\\.` which needs to be escaped), two spaces, the text start, and another space. This text is not in brackets, so is discarded.

- The fourth line details two numbers and a colon repeated three times. This text is in brackets, and is copied to field two in the schema; `startTime`.
- The fifth line consists of a space, then a minus, then a space. This is discarded.
- The sixth line describes a pattern that is either success or failure. This value is retained in the third column in the schema; `status`.
- The final line consists of any number of any characters, and it is discarded.

As mentioned, this is only a brief description of the previous code and of regular expressions. A full explanation of regular expressions is beyond the scope of this book, and it is recommended that you find out more about regular expressions, because they are a powerful means of matching patterns within unstructured strings.

There's more...

You will probably have noticed that the lines in the pattern are organized in terms of patterns to keep and those to discard. The regular expression doesn't need to be specified in this way; however, it does make identifying the fields much easier than if the whole pattern were simply on a single line.

> Java regular expressions will not ignore carriage return or newline characters, unless explicitly told to do so. If you need to create regular expressions that span multiple lines, then simply add `(?s)` to the beginning of a regular expression. This has the same effect as the Java `DOTALL` option.

Using temporary files

Occasionally, it is necessary to create intermediate files within a job that are only used during the lifetime of the job. This recipe shows how to use Talend temporary files.

Getting ready

Open the `jo_cook_ch04_0030_temporaryFile` job.

How to do it...

The steps for using temporary files are as follows:

1. Open the `tCreateFileTemporary` component, and change the name to `customerTemp_XXXX`.
2. Select the options **Remove file when execution is over**, and **Use temporary system directory**.
3. Open the `tempCustomerOut` component, and change **File Name** to `((String) globalMap.get("tCreateTemporaryFile_1_FILEPATH"))`.
4. Repeat the steps for the `tempCustomerIn` component.
5. Run the job, and you will see that data is written to and read from the temporary file.

How it works...

The `tCreateTemporaryFile` component creates an empty file that is then available for writing in the main sub job. The name of the file is stored in the `globalMap` variable `tCreateTemporaryFile_1_FILEPATH`, which is referenced by both the output and input components.

At the end of the job, Talend then deletes the temporary file to free the space.

Temporary files are best used when there are large volumes of data that would or could possibly cause memory issues. For lower volume data, it is recommended that `tHashMap` or an in process table is used instead, because this will create much more performant code. The next section demonstrates the use of `tHashMap` as an alternative for using a temporary file. See *Chapter 7, Working with Databases*, for an example of using the in process table.

There's more...

It is necessary to keep the **XXXX** format in the temporary file name, because Talend uses this to add additional information to the file name to ensure that it is unique for the job instance. This is very important if multiple instances of a job are executed at the same time, because it would be catastrophic if all of the jobs wrote to the same temporary file.

See also

- *Chapter 7, Working with Databases*
- The *Storing intermediate data in memory using tHashMap* recipe

Storing intermediate data in the memory using tHashMap

While not strictly file based, there are alternative methods for storing intermediate data which are more efficient than using temporary files, so long as there is enough memory to hold the temporary data. This recipe shows how to do this using the `tHashMap` component.

Getting ready

Open the `jo_cook_ch08_0040_temporaryDatatHashMap` job. You will notice that this is the same job as in the previous recipe.

How to do it...

The steps for storing intermediate data in memory using `tHashMap` are as follows:

1. Delete the `tCreateTemporaryfile` component.
2. Replace the `tFileOutputDelimited` with a `tHashInput` component, having a generic schema of `sc_cook_ch8_0040_genericCustomerOut`.
3. Replace `tFileInputDelimited` with `tHashInput` component `sc_cook_ch8_0040_genericCustomerOut`.
4. Add the `onSubjobOk` link.
5. Run the job, and the results will be the same as for the previous recipe.

How it works...

`tHashMap` creates an in memory structure that holds all the data in the flow. It can then be used as an input in a downstream sub job.

There's more...

`tHashMap` relies on enough memory being present for *all* the hash mapped data to be stored. If there is not enough memory, then it is best to use a temporary file.

tHashMap is a very useful component for storing data in memory, and can also be used to store lookup data that can be reused across multiple joins. See *Chapter 4, Mapping Data* for more examples of the use of tHashMap.

Reading headers and trailers using tMap

This recipe shows how to parse a file that has header and trailer records, and a record type at the start of a line.

Getting ready

Open the jo_cook_ch08_0060_headTrailtMap job.

How to do it...

The steps for reading headers and trailers using tMap are as follows:

1. Drag a tMap component onto the canvas.
2. Connect the tFileInputFullRow to tMap, and rename the flow to customerIn.
3. Open tMap, and create three new outputs. Name them header, detail, and trailer.
4. Copy the input field line into each of the new outputs.
5. Add the expression filter customerIn.line.startsWith("00") to the header output table.
6. Add the expression filter customerIn.line.startsWith("01") to the detail output table.
7. Add the expression filter customerIn.line.startsWith("99") to the trailer output table.

8. Your `tMap` should now look like the one shown as follows:

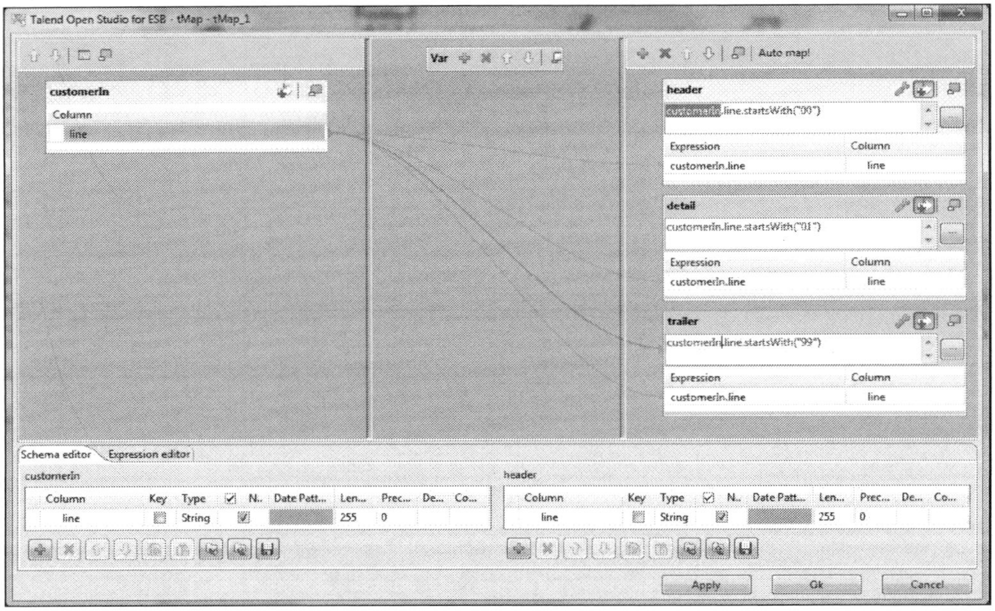

9. Close `tMap`, and drag three `tExtractDelimitedFields` components to the canvas, along with three `tLogRow` components.
10. Join each output from `tMap` to each of the `tExtractDelimitedFields` components.
11. Change the delimiter in each of the `tExtractDelimitedFields` components to comma (`,`).
12. Open the `tLogRow` components, and assign each one a schema from those listed, as follows. This is quickly and easily done by dragging the metadata onto the `tLogRow` component as described in *Chapter 2, Metadata and Schemas*.
    - `sc_cook_ch8_0060_genericCustomerHeader`
    - `sc_cook_ch8_0060_genericCustomerDetail`
    - `sc_cook_ch8_0060_genericCustomerTrailer`
13. Link the `tExtractDelimitedFields` to the `tLogRows`, making sure that you accept the output schema.

14. Your job should now look like this:

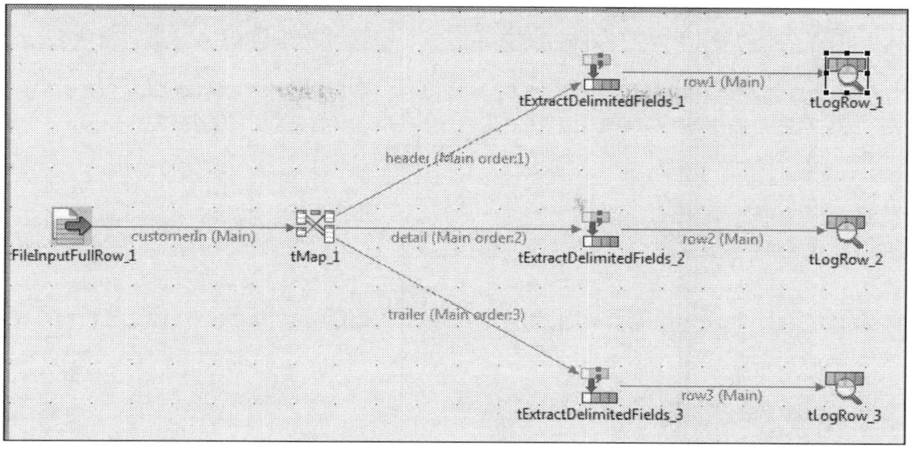

15. Change the `tLogRow` components to the output **Mode** of **Vertical**, and run the job.

How it works...

`tFileInputFullRow` allows us to read a row of any format into `tMap`. This is important, because we do not want records to be rejected due to schema errors at this stage.

The start of each row is then tested for the record type; 00, 01, or 02, the header, detail, or trailer records respectively.

The different rows are then passed to a `tExtractDelimitedFields` component for breaking down into the individual schema columns.

There's more...

This isn't the only method of reading files with headers and trailers, and in fact, the best Talend method would be to use the `tFileInputMSDelimited` component for this example.

This method, however, is much more flexible, in which the conditions for sending in the data as an output to each of the flows does not depend upon a fixed field being present. The next recipe shows this in action.

Reading headers and trailers with no identifiers

This recipe shows how to parse a file that has header and trailer records, but does not have an associated record type. Instead, the header is the first record in the file, and the trailer is the last record in the file.

Getting ready

Open the `jo_cook_ch08_0070_headTrailtMapNoType` job. You will see that it is a slightly changed version of the completed job from the previous recipe; the output schemas have changed.

How to do it...

The steps for reading headers and trailers with no identifiers are as follows:

1. Drag a `tFileRowCount` component onto the canvas.
2. Open the `tFileRowCount`, and change File Name to `context.cookbookData+"/chapter8/chapter08_jo_0070_customerData.txt"`, which is the same as our input file.
3. Connect an `onSubJobOk` trigger from the `tFileRowCount` component to the `tFileInputDelimited`.
4. Open the `tMap`, and add a new variable `rowCount`. Set its expression to `Numeric.sequence("rowNumber",1,1)`.
5. Change the Filter expressions for header, detail, and trailer to those shown as follows:
   - `Var.rowNumber == 1`
   - `Var.rowNumber != ((Integer)globalMap.get("tFileRowCount_1_COUNT"))`
   - `Var.rowNumber ==  ((Integer)globalMap.get("tFileRowCount_1_COUNT"))`
6. Set the detail and trailer output options to **Catch output rejects**.

7. Your `tMap` should now look like this:

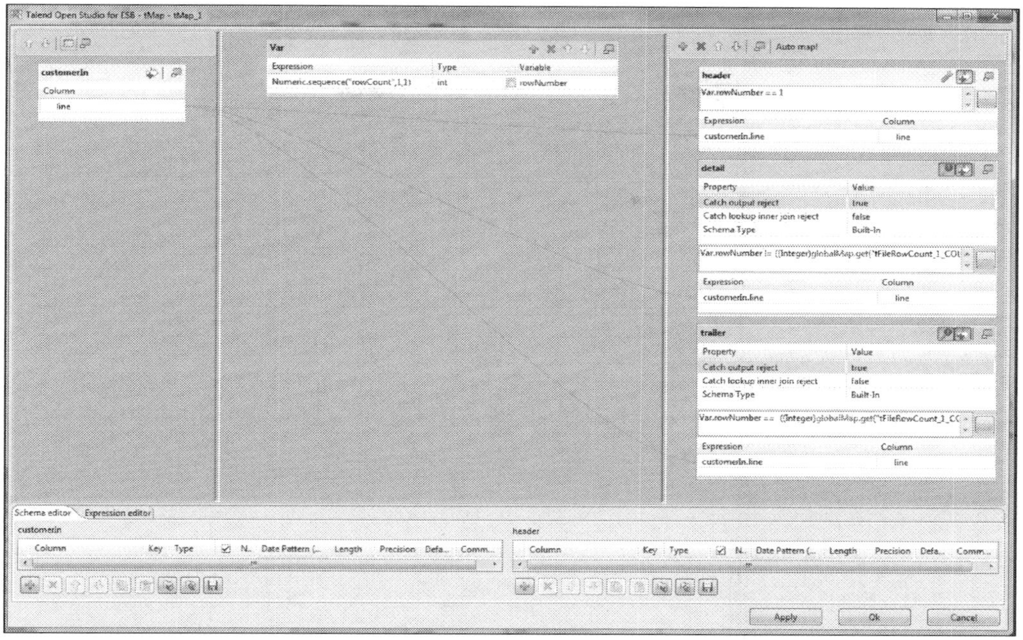

8. Run the job, and you should see the individual row types being printed.

How it works...

The `tFileRowCount` component tells us how many rows there are in the file.

In the `tMap`, we use a sequence to calculate the current line number. If the line number is 1, then we have a header row. If it is equal to the row count (held in `globalMap`), then we have a trailer row, and all other rows are detail rows.

We then use the `tExtractDelimitedFields` to extract the individual delimited fields into a different schema for each of the row types.

Using the information in the header and trailer

This recipe follows on from the previous recipe, but shows how the information in the header can be added to the detail data, and the data in the trailer used for validation, as is typically the case with files of this type.

Getting ready

Open the `jo_cook_ch08_0080_useHeaderAndTrailerInfo` job. This job is the completed job from the previous recipe; however, do note that the `tLogRow` components have now been replaced with `tHashOutput` components. Also, note that three `tHashInput` components have also been added and configured.

How to do it...

We will be performing two main tasks; the first is to use the trailer information to validate the file, and then take a column from the header to use in all the output records.

Validation subjob

1. Drag a `tMap` component onto the canvas, and join the trailer input to it. Rename the flow to `trailerIn`.
2. Open the `tMap` component, and create an output table named `rowCountError`.
3. Drag the input `detailCount` field to the output.
4. Add a new Integer output field named `actualCount`.
5. Add a new Integer variable also named `actualCount`. Set its expression to `((Integer)globalMap.get("tExtractDelimitedFields_2_NB_LINE"))`.
6. Copy this to the output field `actualCount`.
7. Add a filter expression to the output table; `trailerIn.detailCount != Var.actualCount`.
8. Your `tMap` should now look like this:

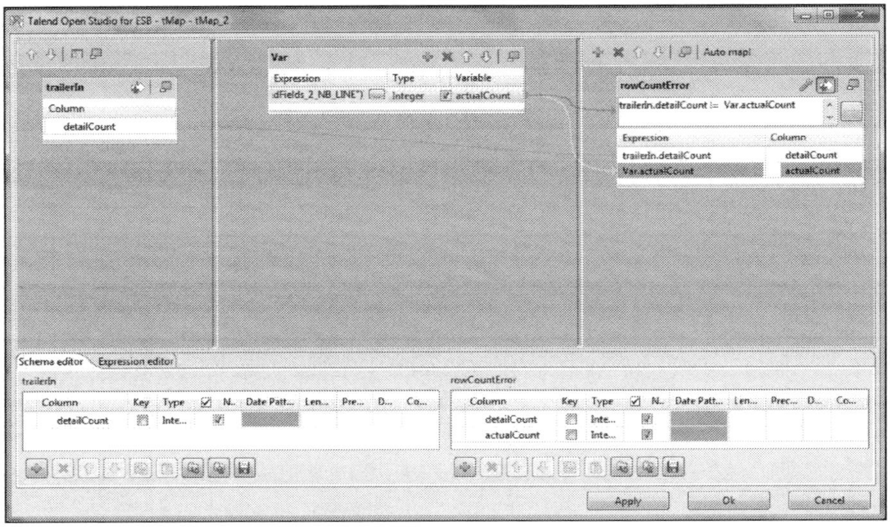

9. Add a `tDie` component, and connect the output of the `tMap` to the `tDie`.
10. Run the job, and you will see that it fails, because the number of rows in the file is 4, yet the trailer says 5.

Use the header information subjob

1. Activate the header and detail `tHashInput` components.
2. Drag a `tMap` component onto the canvas, and join the detail input to it. Rename the flow to `detail1`.
3. Join the header as a lookup to the `tMap`, and rename the flow to `header1`.
4. Create an output named `detailHeader`, and drag all the input detail fields to the output from both the detail and header inputs.
5. Your `tMap` should now look like this:

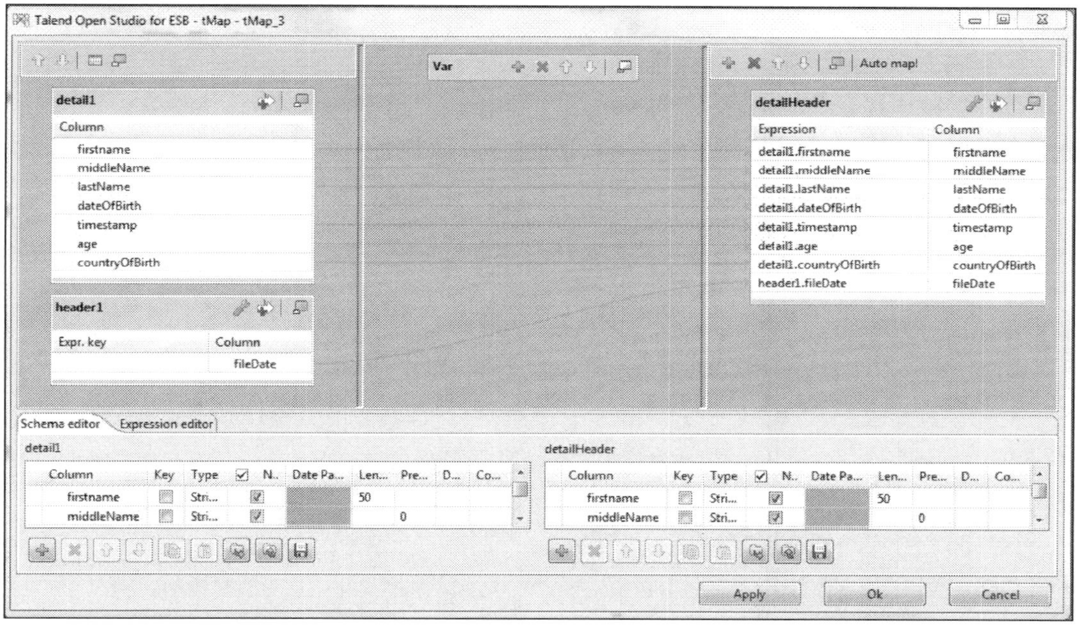

6. Add a `tLogRow`, and join the output of the `tMap` to the `tLogRow` component. Change the `Mode` of the `tLogRow` to `Table`.
7. Manually edit the input file `context.cookbookData+"/chapter8/chapter08_jo_0080_customerData.txt`, and change the final row in the file to `00004`.
8. Run the job, and you will see that the job no longer fails, and that each detail row has the same file data as copied from the header record.

How it works...

The job first separates the header trailer and detail rows, validates the row count in the trailer against the number of physical rows read, and then adds the file date to each detail row.

Validating using the trailer information

The validation sub job compares the row count from the trailer with the actual row count. The only output from `tMap` is controlled by a condition that checks the value of the trailer count with the number of lines (`tExtractDelimitedFields_2_NB_LINE`) passed through the `tExtractDelimitedFields` component, which is stored in `globalMap`.

Using the header information in the detail

The header data is added to the `tMap` as a lookup. You will notice that there are no join links between the detail row and the header, which means that we have an all-all-join. So, every detail record is matched to the header record, thus populating the file date for every detail record.

There's more...

You could choose to copy the header and trailer information into `globalMap` as an alternative to using `tHashMap` components, using a `tFlowToIterate` component in place of the header and trailer components, or a `tJava` component, where the column values are explicitly copied into `globalMap`.

This method does make adding the data to the detail simpler (because no join is needed, just a reference to `globalMap`); however, it also makes the validation slightly more complex, because the compare function does need a row to be created using a `tFixedFlowInput`.

Which method to use is a matter of preference and coding style.

The `tDie` message in this job isn't very useful. If you wish to make it more useful, then change the message to that given as follows:

```
"Error: Counts do not match.  Trailer: "+rowCountError.
trailerCount+".  Actual : "+rowCountError.actualCount
```

An example of copying data to `globalMap` automatically using `tFlowToIterate` can be found in the *Capturing file information* recipe later in this chapter.

To copy data to `globalMap` using `tJava`, see the *Setting context variables and globalMap variables using tJava* recipe in *Chapter 5, Using Java in Talend*.

Adding a header and trailer to a file

This recipe details a method for creating a file with a header and trailer record, which makes use of file append.

Getting ready

Open the `jo_cook_ch08_0090_createHeaderAndTrailer` job.

How to do it...

The steps for adding a header and trailer to a file are as follows:

1. Open the `tFixedFlowInput_1` component.
2. Add the following for the field `fileDate`; `TalendDate.getDate("CCYY-MM-DD")`.
3. Open the `tFixedFlowInput_2` component.
4. Add the following for the field `fileDate`; `((Integer)globalMap.get("tFileInputDelimited_1_NB_LINE"))`.
5. Open `tFileOutputDelimited_1`, and change the type to `Append`.
6. Open `tFileOutputDelimited_4`, and change the type to `Append`.
7. Run the job, and if you examine the output file, you should see that it has created a file with the current date in the header and the correct number of detail lines in the trailer.

How it works...

`tFixedFlowInputs` are used to generate a single row each for the header and the trailer.

The header sub job will create the file and add the header with the field being set to the current date.

The detail sub job adds the detail records using file append.

The trailer sub job adds the trailer record with the count value set to the number of lines read from the customer input file. This ensures that the detail count for the trailer matches the number of lines written.

There's more...

Talend does supply a component for creating complex files; `tFileOutputMSDelimited`; however, this method is not as strict as the `MSDelimited` component, in that records of any schema type can be added in any order at any time during the job.

Thus, this method avoids the need to either structure your job in a way so that the flows merge into a single end component, or to drop the data to intermediate storage prior to merging in a final sub job.

This method usually therefore creates more efficient and readable code.

For these reasons, this is probably the easiest method for creating complex files.

> If you require additional aggregates to be added to the trailer, such as checksums, add a `tAggregate` to the output of the detail sub job, and store the result in a `tHashMap`.

See also

- The *Appending records to a file* recipe in this chapter

Moving, copying, renaming, and deleting files and folders

As well as reading from and writing to files, Talend has a set of components that allow developers to perform file functions without the need to call native operating system commands. This recipe shows the basic file management components.

Getting ready

Open the job `jo_cook_ch08_0100_basicFileCommands`.

How to do it...

In the following recipes, it is worth noting that Talend uses the Linux style forward slash (/) in the file paths, as opposed to the Windows backslash (\).

Copying a file to another directory

1. Drag `tFileCopy` to the job.
2. Set the file name to be `context.cookbookData+"/chapter8/chapter08_jo_0100_copyFile.txt"`.
3. Set the output directory to be `context.cookbookData+"/outputData/chapter8"`.
4. Run the job, and you will see that the new file has been created: This is a simple copy.

Copying file to a different name

1. Open `tFileCopy`, tick the **Rename** box, and then add a **Destination filename** of `chapter08_jo_0100_copyFileRenamed.txt`.
2. Run the job, and you will see that there is now a renamed copy of the file.

Renaming a file

1. Open `tFileCopy`, and change the **Input filename** to be `context.cookbookData+"/outputData/chapter8/ chapter08_jo_0100_copyFileRenamed.txt"`.
2. You will see that the input file is in the same directory as the **Destination directory**.
3. Change the **Destination filename** to `chapter08_jo_0100_renamed.txt`.
4. Click the box **Remove source file**.
5. Run the job, and you will see that the original file has been renamed.

Moving a file

This is the same as the previous (see The *Copying file to a different name* recipe), but click the box **Remove source file**.

Deleting a file

To delete a file, simply add the file path to the `tFileDelete` component.

How it works...

As you will see, the `tFileCopy` is used to copy, move, and rename files, depending upon the options selected.

The `tFileDelete` component is simply used to delete files.

There's more...

You should have noticed that the `tFileDelete` and `tFileCopy` components allow us to tick boxes to copy and delete directories as required. It does go without saying that the utmost care should be taken when deleting files, and even more especially when deleting directories using Talend.

Capturing file information

Another useful Talend feature is the ability to capture information about a file for use within downstream processing, most probably to perform validation prior to processing.

Getting ready

Open the `jo_cook_ch08_0110_fileInformation` job.

How to do it...

The steps for capturing file information are as follows:

1. Drag a `tFileProperties` component from the right-hand panel. Open `tFileProperties`, and set the file name to `context.cookbookData+"/chapter8/chapter08_jo_0110_customerData.txt"`.
2. Drag `tFlowToIterate` to the canvas, and link the row from `tFileProperties` to it. Name the flow `properties`.
3. Drag `tFileRowCount` to the canvas and set the filename to match the `tFileProperties` component.
4. Add `onSubjobOk` from `tFileProperties` to `tFileRowCount`, and then to `tFixedFlowInput`, so that your job looks like the one shown as follows:

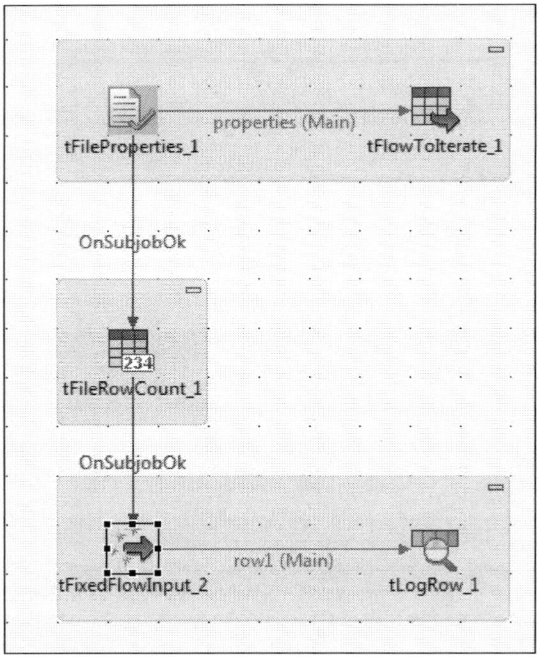

5. Open `tFixedFlowInput`.
6. Add `((Long)globalMap.get("properties.size"))` to the field **fileSize**.

7. Add `((Integer)globalMap.get("tFileRowCount_1_COUNT"))` to the field **numberOfRows**.
8. Your `tFixedFlowInput` should look like the one as follows:

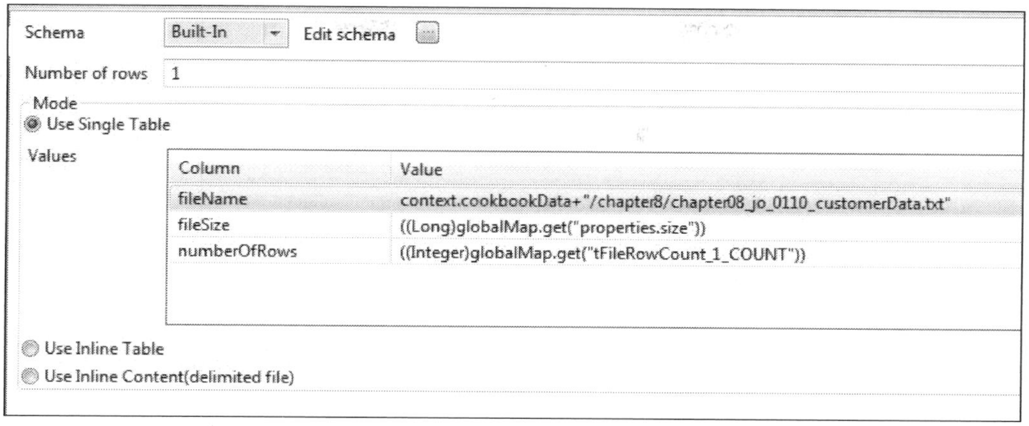

9. Run the job, and you will see the file information in the console.

How it works...

The `tFileProperties` component captures file information and passes the data in a row to the next component. The `tFlowToIterate` component is used as a shorthand method for adding the file information to `globalMap`.

The `tFileRowCount` component counts the number of rows in a file, and presents the count as a `globalMap` variable.

The final sub job shows the data held in `globalMap` being used in a process flow.

There's more...

The final sub job simply prints out some of the information; however, a good, real-life example is to use the file size from the properties to check against the file size written in a file trailer record or a validation file. This would ensure that a file transmitted from, a third party application, for example, is received in its entirety before it is processed by the receiving application.

One field in `tFileProperties` can be difficult to use; the file creation datetime, which is a complex string format of a date. If you need to read this into a date column, then use the following date pattern:

```
TalendDate.parseDateLocale("EEE MMM dd HH:mm:ss z
yyyy",input_row.mtime_string,"EN")
```

where `EN` is the locale that you may need to change.

Processing multiple files at once

Often, with batch processes, it is required that multiple files are processed by the same job in a single tranche. This example shows how this can be achieved by merging a group of input files into a single output.

Getting ready

Open the `jo_cook_ch08_0120_multipleFiles` job. You will notice that it is currently reading a single file to a temporary file, and then copying the temporary file to a permanent output.

How to do it...

The steps for processing multiple files at once are as follows:

1. Add a `tFileList` component, open it, and set the directory to `context.cookbookData+"/chapter8"`.
2. Click on the **+** button under the **Filemask** box, and add the filemask `"chapter08_jo_0120_customerData_*.txt"`.

3. Your `tFileList` should look like the one shown, as follows:

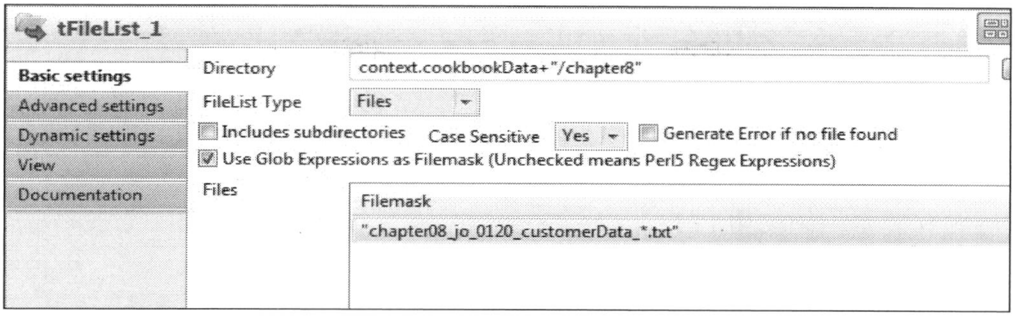

4. Move the `OnSubjobOk` from the `tFileInputDelimited` to the `tFileList`.
5. Add a `tJava` component.
6. Right-click on `tFileList` and select **Row**, then **Iterate**, and link to the `tJava`.
7. Right-click on the `tJava` and select **Trigger**, then `OnComponentOk`.
8. Link it to the `tFileInputDelimited (customer)` component.
9. Open the `tFileInputDelimited` component, and change the file name to `((String)globalMap.get("tFileList_1_CURRENT_FILEPATH"))`.
10. Move the `OnSubjobOk` link from `tFileInputDelimited (customer)` to the `tFileList` component.
11. Your job should look like the one shown as follows:

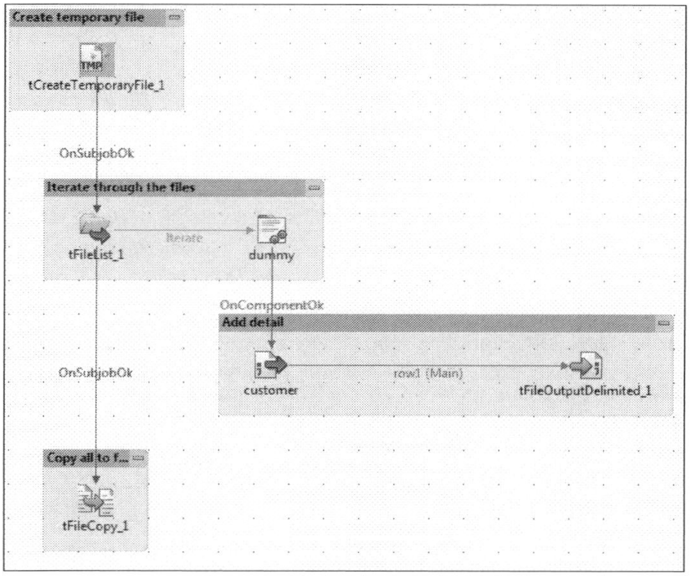

12. Run the job, and you will see that the output file contains information from the three input files.
13. To make the job output more useful, open `tJava` and insert the following code `System.out.println("Processing file: "+((String)globalMap.get("tFileList_1_CURRENT_FILE")))`.
14. Run the job again, and you will see that the console now logs the individual files as they are found.

How it works...

This job merges all files in a directory into a temporary file ready for processing as a single entity; in this case, renaming the temporary file to a permanent output file name.

The `tFileList` component is an iterator that is triggered by each file found that fits the specified mask.

So as each file is found, the file details are stored in `globalMap`, and then all linked components and sub jobs will be processed until no more files are found.

As you can see from the job, the `tFileInputDelimited` component reads from the file specified in `globalMap` by `tFileList`, and `tFileOutputDelimited` writes to the `globalMap` variable specified by `tCreateTemporaryFile`.

Once all files have been read and processed, `tFileList` is then complete, and the `onSubjobOk` link will be triggered, thus copying the temporary file into a final permanent merged file.

There's more...

In this job, we have only one sub job that is executed as part of the Iterate, but it is probably more common to have many. In a traditional programming language, this would mean that all the processing linked to the Iterate would be in a programming loop.

It is also possible to have further iterations below the first one, for instance, if you are navigating your way down a set of directories to find input files for processing.

> The `tJava` component named `dummy` is just that. It performs no logic (though I will often add in logging line detailing the file name) and is present in the code just to make it more readable. This is because it allows the processing for each iteration to sit in individual sub jobs as if they are within a normal, atomic job that processes just one file.

Processing control/validation files

Some organizations prefer to use a companion (control/validation) file containing file information instead of storing the information in the file header or trailer. This means that the detail file is much simpler to process, because it is a normal flat file.

In this recipe, the control file has the same name as the detail file; however, it is suffixed with `.ctrl` rather than `.txt`. This recipe shows how the control file is processed.

Getting ready

Open the `jo_cook_ch08_0130_controlFile` job. You will see that `tFileList_1` is looking for files with the mask of `chapter08_jo_0130_customerData*.txt`. There are two of these in the directory.

How to do it...

The steps for processing control/validation files

1. Copy the first sub job.
2. Change the new `tFileList` mask to `StringHandling.EREPLACE(((String) globalMap.get("tFileList_1_CURRENT_FILE")),"txt","ctrl")`.
3. Open `tJava_2` and change the command to `System.out.println("Found control file: "+((String)globalMap.get("tFileList_2_CURRENT_FILE")));`.
4. Connect the first and second sub job using `OnComponentOk`.
5. Repeat the same for the second and third sub jobs.

6. Your job should now look like this:

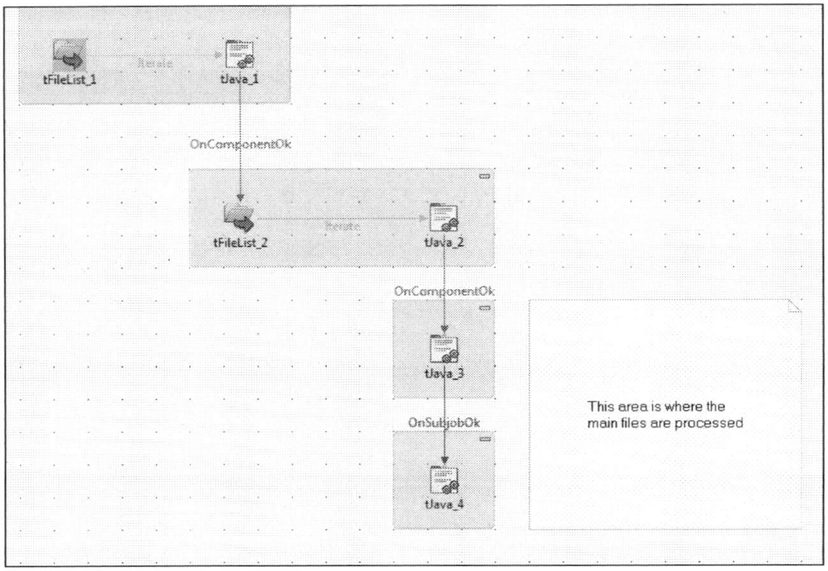

7. Run the job and you will see that the main process is called once per file/control combination.

How it works...

The first `tFileList` looks for files that fit the mask `"chapter08_jo_0130_customerData*.txt"`, of which there are three.

For each `.txt` file, it finds the file that fits the mask, and then performs another `tFileList`. This time, however, the mask is the actual file name, but with `.txt` replaced with `.ctrl`. This has the effect of searching for a control file that has exactly the same name as the text file.

Once a match is found then we have both file names in `globalMap` together, and the file details can be validated and processed by whatever means within the main processing section (represented here by `tJava_3` and `tJava_4`).

There's more...

In the version of the job that we have just coded, if a `.txt` file arrives without a control file then it is simply ignored.

In a production version of this job, we would also add a validation step to check that the control file is found for a job. This can be achieved with an `if` link that checks `((Integer) globalMap.get("tFileList_2_NB_FILE")) !=1`, shown as follows:

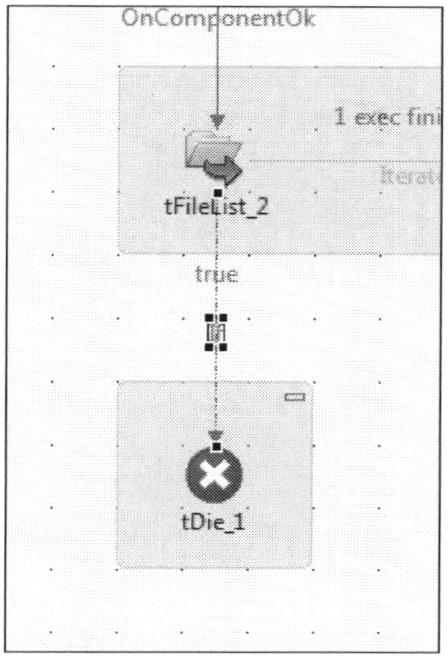

Creating and writing files depending on the input data

Sometimes it is required that multiple files are written from a single data source where the file name is dependent upon the data held within the row. This recipe shows how this can be achieved.

Getting ready

Open the `jo_cook_ch08_0140_filesFromInputData` job.

How to do it...

The steps for creating and writing files depending on the input data are as follows:

1. Run the job, and you will see that the file `dummy.txt` has been created and populated with six rows.
2. Open the `tJavaRow` component, and you will see that the move of data from input to output has already been performed.

3. Add in the following code after the generated code:

```
// test for change of input_row.key
if (Numeric.sequence(input_row.key, 1, 1) == 1 ) {
  outtFileOutputDelimited_1.flush();

  // if this is the first record then do not flush and close - do
not want to create dummy.txt
  // otherwish if sequence > 1 then we will close the previous
file
  if(Numeric.sequence("all", 1, 1) !=1 ) {

    outtFileOutputDelimited_1.close();
  }

  // build the new file name
  fileName_tFileOutputDelimited_1 = context.cookbookData+"/
outputData/chapter8/"+input_row.key+".txt";

  // create new writer for the new filename.  Talend uses this for
writing the record
  outtFileOutputDelimited_1 = new java.io.BufferedWriter(
              new java.io.OutputStreamWriter(
                  new java.io.FileOutputStream(
                      fileName_tFileOutputDelimited_1,
                      false), "ISO-8859-15"));
}
```

4. Run the job. You will see that besides the dummy file, there are three additional files: `a.txt` containing the records with key `a`, `b.txt` containing records with key `b`, and `c.txt` containing rows with key `c`.

How it works...

The code in `tJavaRow` makes use of the fact that Talend code is a series of loops within loops. Because the `tJavaRow` loop is within the `tFileOutputDelimited` loop in the generated Java code, we can change variables within the inner loop, which will affect the processing within the outer loop.

The variable that we will change is the writer that Talend uses for the `tFileOutputDelimited` component.

tJavaRow code explained

The `Numeric.sequence` command uses `input_row.key` as the name, thus, causing a new sequence to be created whenever the key changes. Thus by testing the sequence as 1, we know that the key has changed.

Once we know that the key changed, we can then close the previous file.

Then we create a new file name consisting of the output directory plus the `input_row.key` suffixed with `.txt`. Thus if the key is changed we create a file named `a.txt`.

The next statement then creates a new writer for the `tFileOutputDelimited` component and Talend will use this writer when writing to the output.

There's more...

This method will only work with sorted input data. It is possible to create much more sophisticated file management routines using similar principles that would not need to have the data pre-sorted, however, this isn't covered in this book.

In addition, this method does not remove the `dummy.txt` file. For production versions of this code it would be worthwhile adding `tFileDelete` to the job to remove the dummy file.

9

Working with XML, Queues, and Web Services

This chapter describes some of the features of the Talend data integration suite that interfaces with technologies used in the Talend ESB (Enterprise Service Bus) Studio. We will cover the following recipes in this chapter:

- Using tXMLMap to read XML
- Using tXMLMap to create an XML document
- Reading complex hierarchical XML
- Writing complex XML
- Calling a SOAP web service
- Calling a RESTful web service
- Reading and writing to a queue
- Ensuring lossless queue using sessions

Introduction

It is for this chapter that we are using Talend Studio for ESB. This chapter is an amalgam of tools and techniques associated with low latency or real-time processing. It also covers the areas where the Talend DI tool set overlaps with the Talend ESB tool set.

But first, let's look at some of the key principles required for this chapter:

- **tXMLMap**: `tXMLMap` is the XML equivalent of `tMap`, providing most of the same functionality as `tMap`, but with the added ability to process XML data as well.
- **XPATH**: `tXMLMap` is good for moderately complex XML; however, processing complex multi-level XML is more complex. This is where XPATH is used: to decompose the input XML into more manageable chunks.
- **tXMLOutput, tWriteXMLField:** These components are used to create complex multi-level XML structures from flat structures.
- **Web services:** The Talend studio for ESB provides simple to use capabilities for creating and consuming both SOAP and RESTful web services.
- **Message Queues**: Talend ESB contains a copy of **ActiveMQ**, which will be used for the queue based recipes in this section.

Using tXMLMap to read XML

This recipe shows how we can convert an XML record stored in a file into a format that is readable by `tXMLMap`, and how we can then read and process the data in the XML record.

Getting ready

Open the job `jo_cook_ch09_0010_readXMLFile`.

How to do it...

The first stage of this process is to convert the XML file into **Java Document** format for use by the downstream component.

1. Drag a `tFileInputXML` component onto the canvas.
2. Edit the schema and add a column named **payload**. Make it a type of **Document**, as shown in the screenshot:

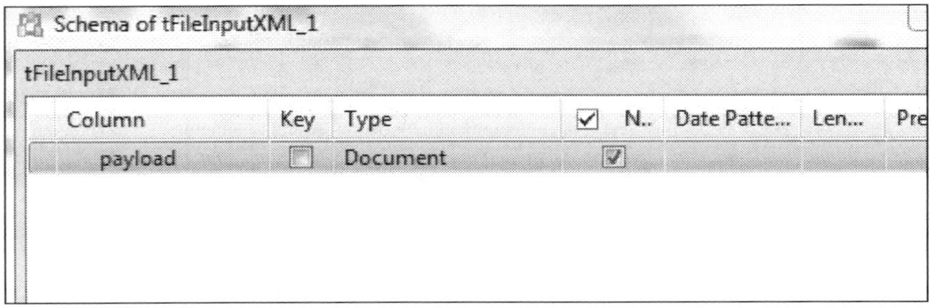

3. Open the `tFileInputXML` component and change the **File name/Stream** field to `context.cookbookData+"/chapter9/chapter09_jo_0010_customerData.xml"`.
4. Change the **Loop Xpath query** field to `"/"`.
5. Add an **Xpath query** of `"."`, and tick the box **Get Nodes**.
6. Your `tFileInputXML` should look like the one shown in the next screenshot:

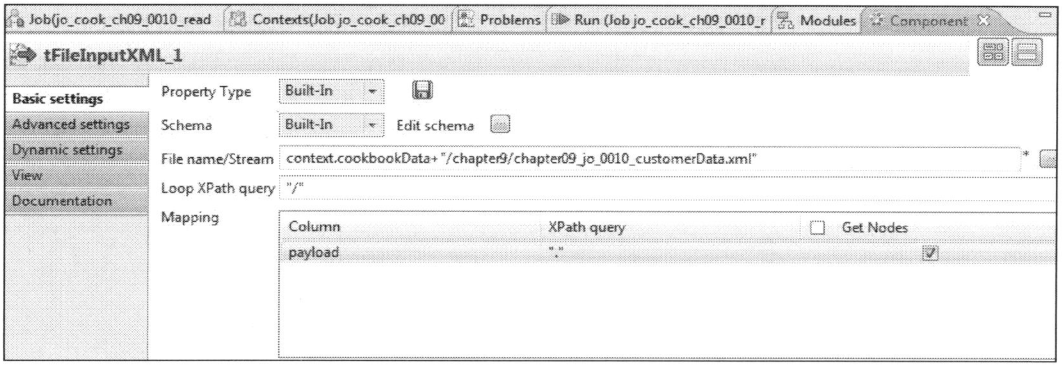

Reading using tXMLMap

7. Add a `tXMLMap` component to the canvas and link to the `tFileInputXML` component.
8. Open the `tXMLMap` component and right-click on **payload**.
9. Select **Import from file**.

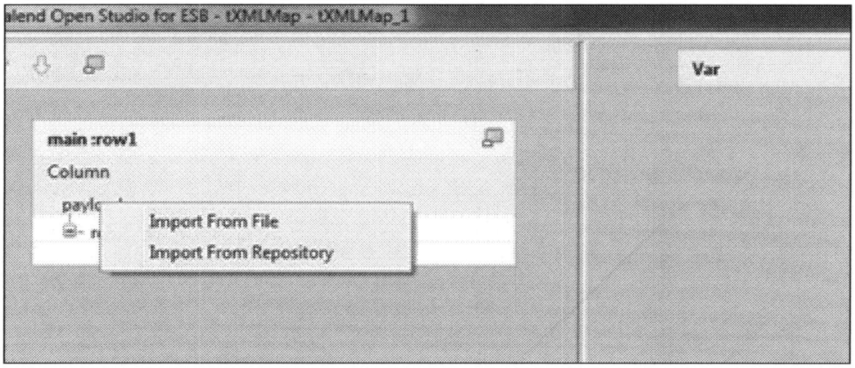

10. Navigate to the input xml file in the folder for this chapter, and when you select the file you will see that the XML structure has now been added to the `tXMLMap` component's input table.

11. Add an output table named `customerOut`, and drag the fields from the input to the output. Your `tXMLMap` should now look like the one in the next screenshot:

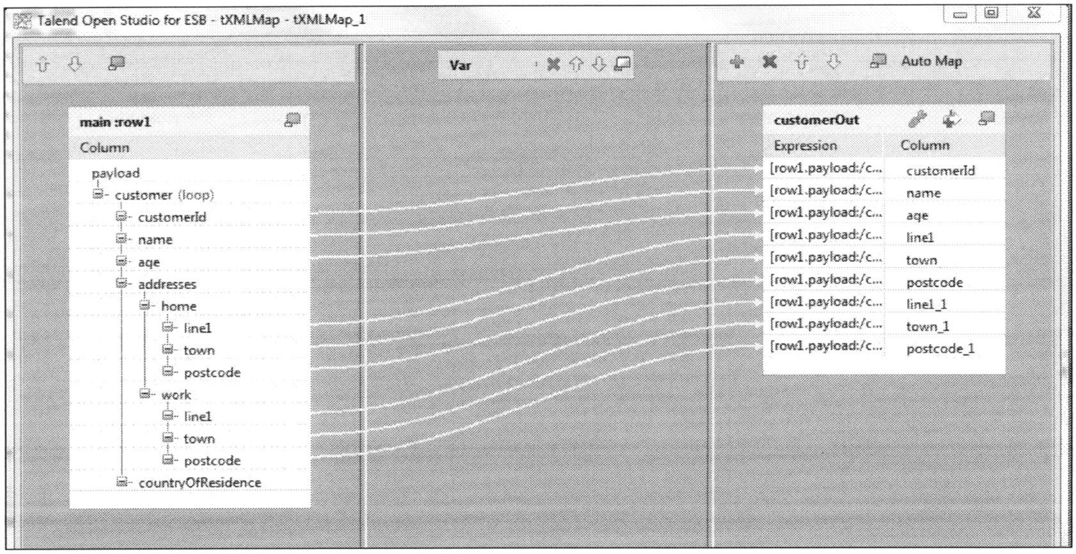

12. Add a `tLogRow` to the job, connect it to the output of `tXMLMap` and then run the job. You will see that the XML data has now been flattened into a normal Talend row.

How it works...

The `tXMLInput` component uses XPATH to convert the input XML into a Java Document object, so that an XML tree can be created by the `tXMLMap` component.

Note that the XPATH settings are not covered in this book. For more information on XPATH, you may wish to visit `http://www.w3schools.com/xpath/`.

By pointing `tXMLMap` at our XML file, we were able to import the XML structure from the file, so that we could manipulate the fields individually.

Once the document tree has been defined, elements can then be copied from the output to the input, as with a normal `tMap`.

There's more...

Note that the `tXMLMap` component does have its limitations though and isn't the best component to use in in all scenarios.

Document objects

The Java Document object is the key to being able to define input and output trees in tXMLMap. If we do not define a document either as input or output, then the tXMLMap component performs in the same way as a tMap component, so if you aren't processing input and/or output XML, then use tMap, because it has more functionality.

XML Structure

In this recipe we used a populated XML file to define our XML structure. While this is fine for an example, it would be unusual in the real world.

It is more likely that we would use an **XML Schema Definition** (**XSD**) to define the format of the XML structure, because we cannot always guarantee that our file does not have some optional elements missing.

Using tXMLMap to create an XML document

This recipe is the reverse of the previous recipe, in that we'll be reading in a flat format and converting it to an XML document for output. It is recommended that you have understood the previous recipe prior to attempting this one.

Getting ready

Open the job jo_cook_ch09_0020_createXMLDocument file.

How to do it...

The first stage of the process is to convert the input data into a Java Document that can store the XML.

1. Drag a tXMLMap component onto the canvas, and link the tFileInputDelimited component to it.
2. Create an output table named customerDocumentOut, and add a field named payload. Make the field a type of **Document**.
3. You will see that the field in the output table has changed to become a simple XML structure.
4. As we did in the previous recipe, retrieve the XML format from the file containing our target XML structure.
5. Drag the fields from input to output, and set the countryOfResidence component to UK.

6. Your tXMLMap component should look like the one in the next screenshot:

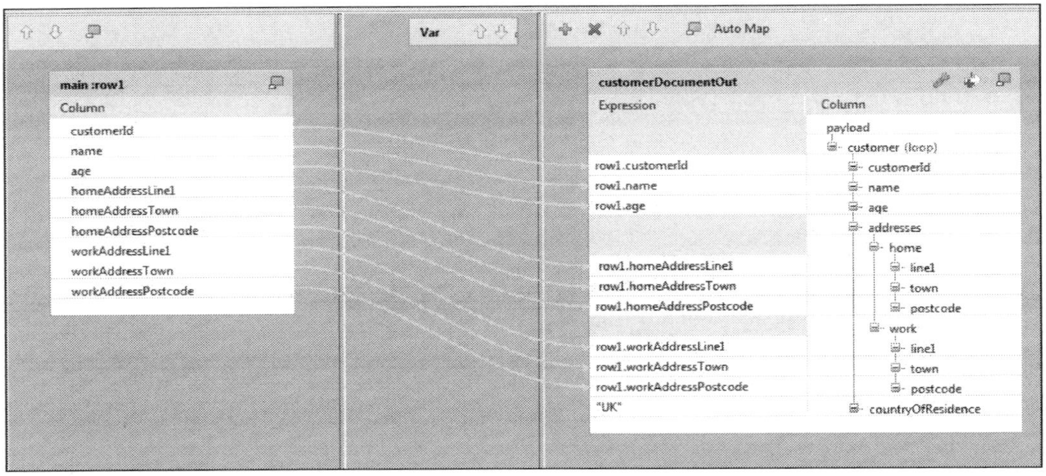

Output the Document to a file

7. Add a tFileOutputXML component and link it to the tXMLMap component.
8. Open tFileOutputXML, tick the box **Incoming record is a document** and set the File Name to context.cookbookData+"/outputData/chapter9/jo_cook_ch9_0020_customer.xml".
9. Run the job file to create the XML file.

How it works...

As discussed in the first recipe, defining the output type of Document allows us to define an XML format within the tXMLMap component into which we can then map our input data.

The tFileOutputXML component by default will create an XML structure from a normal schema; however, it is possible to force it to handle a document as we did in this recipe.

There's more...

We have seen in this recipe how we can map from XML to a Talend schema and the reverse, but tXMLMap does allow us map combinations of inputs (flat or XML) with combinations of outputs, so we can reformat one XML format into another, or join an XML file with a second XML file to produce a normal Talend record.

Reading complex hierarchical XML

The first two recipes show how `tXMLMap` can be used to map between XML formats visually, much like the `tMap` component; however, it can become overly complex and difficult to manage when there are multiple levels of hierarchy and multiple loops within the XML. This recipe shows how we can deconstruct a more complex XML record into individual sets of data while ensuring that the hierarchical relationships between the data are not lost.

Getting ready

Open the job `jo_cook_ch09_0040_readComplexXML` file. `If you` view the input file `chapter09_jo_0040_orderDate.xml`, you will see that we have a hierarchy of customer that has many orders, and orders have many items.

How to do it...

First, we will create a customer schema using the XML schema wizard.

1. In the metadata panel under **File XML** | **Chapter 09** right-click and select the option **Create file xml**.
2. Name the XML file `sc_cook_ch9_0040_XMLorderDataCustomer`.
3. Select **Input XML**, then click on **Next**.
4. Click on Browser to select the XML file `C:/cookbookData/chapter9/chapter09_jo_0040_customerData.xml`.
5. In the **Schema Viewer**, you can check that this is the correct file then click on **Next**.
6. Drag the field `customer` from the **Source Schema** panel to the **Target Schema** panel **Xpath loop expression**.
7. Drag `name` and `age` to the **Target Schema** panel **Fields to extract**.
8. Drag the field `customer` from the **Refresh Preview** panel, and you will see the values as they will appear in the schema.

9. Your screen should now look like the next screenshot:

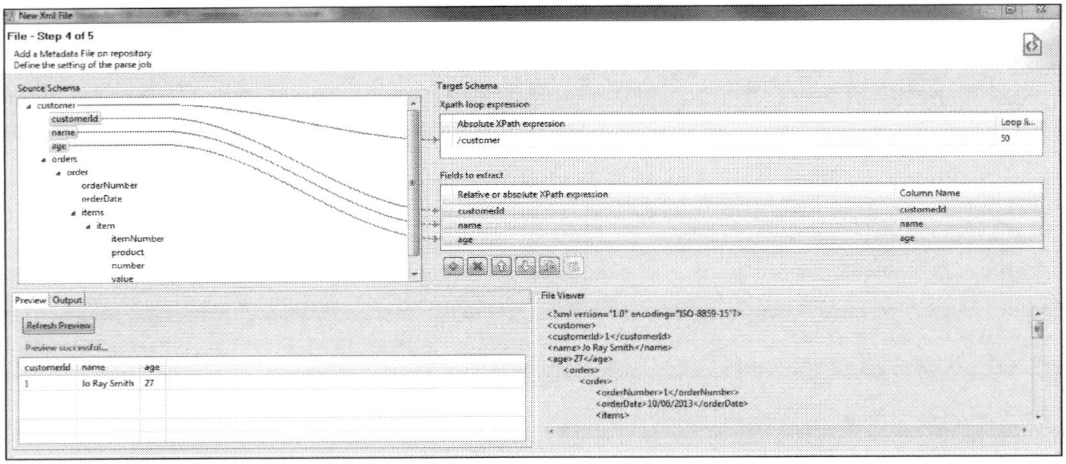

10. Click on **Next**.
11. The next step allows you to validate and change the extracted field names and lengths if you need to. For this recipe, we will not worry about this.
12. Click on **Finish** to complete the schema.

    Creating order schema

13. Repeat the steps above for a schema named `sc_cook_ch9_0040_XMLorderDataOrder`.
14. Map the `customerId` and the order fields so that your mapping looks like the one in the next screenshot:

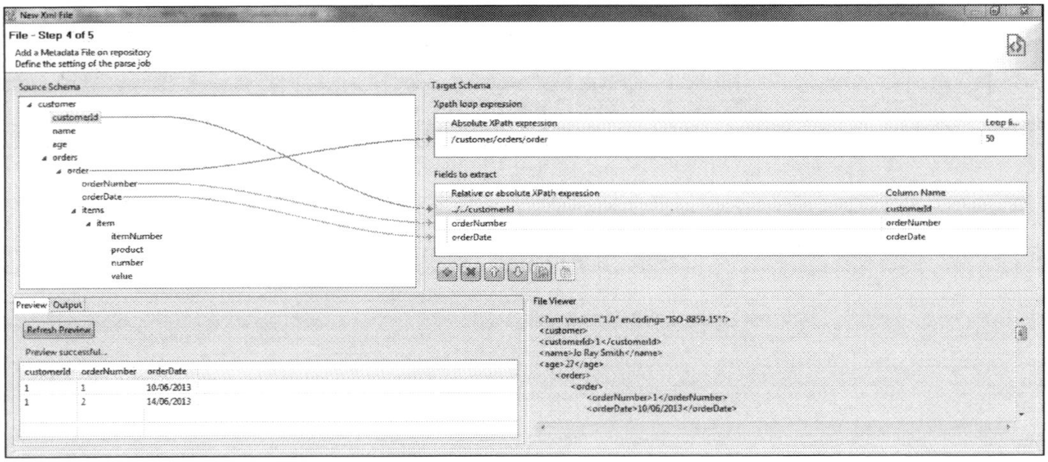

Creating order item schema

15. Repeat the steps above for a schema named `sc_cook_ch9_0040_XMLorderDataOrderItem`.
16. Map the `customerId`, `orderNumber`, and the `order item` fields so that your mapping looks like the one in the next screenshot:

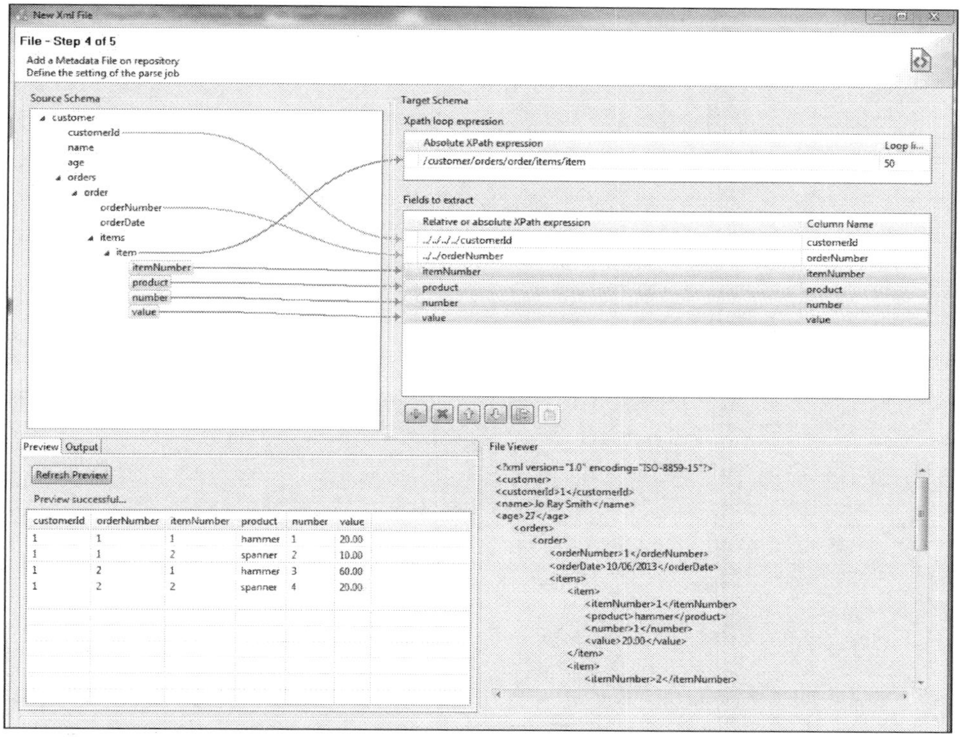

Adding to the job

17. Finally, drag all three schemas to the canvas, selecting the component type of `tFileInputXML`, join them up as shown in the next screenshot and run the `job`.

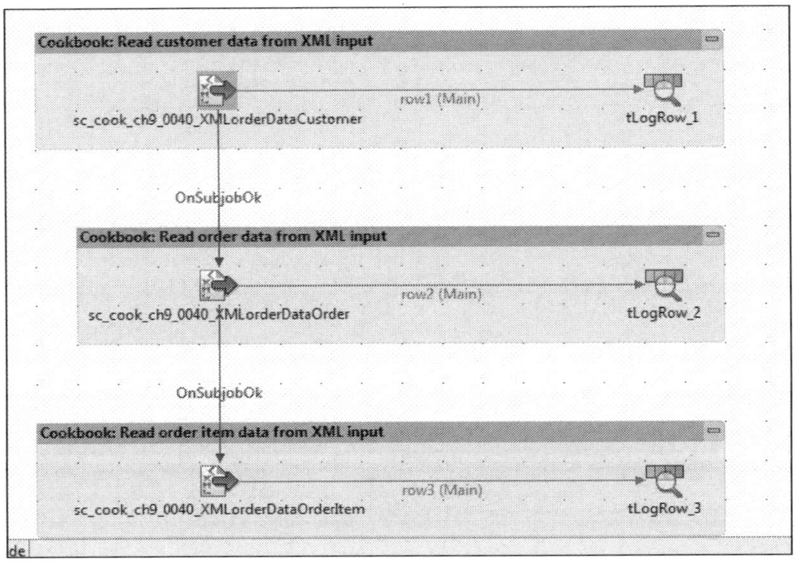

How it works...

The XML schema component allows us to map data from the XML structure into a flattened Talend schema easily, ready for use in the downstream components.

First, we defined an XML schema to extract just the `customer` fields.

Then we did the same for the `order` fields, but remembered to also extract the key for the `customer`, which is `customerId`. This will ensure that for each set of order data, of which there are two, the `customerId` is present.

We repeated this process again for the `orderItem` fields, remembering to extract the `customer` and `order` fields.

Finally, we dragged the schemas to the canvas, linked them and added the `tLogRow` outputs.

There's more...

This method is the basis for a very useful Talend design pattern, and the key principles and how it can be used are described ahead.

Managing the relationships

The thing to remember about this method is that for each branch we process from the XML tree, we need to capture the keys for the parent branches, so that we do not lose the relationships that are implicit in the structure of the input XML.

File information

In this recipe, we changed the file path to built in for this example, and added in the name relative to our cookbook context variable. There is also the option to store the file and XPATH information to a context if you so desire.

XML to database mapping

This design pattern is perfect for mapping an XML structure to a relational (third normal form) database. When viewing the log output, we can see that the XML loops have been normalized into individual entities (`customer`, `order`, and `order item`), and that we have captured the primary and foreign keys for each of the table entities.

See *Chapter 7, Working with Databases* for an example of writing hierarchies to a database.

XPATH

You may have noticed that the XML file wizard produces XPATH expressions when creating the schema, and it is also noteworthy that this isn't the only component to use XPATH to extract information from an XML structure.

Web service XML

When reading XML data from say a web service, it would not be efficient to write it to a disk file prior to reading the data, so the same method can be applied to extract the data, but we would use `tExtractXMLField` rather than `tFileInputXML`. This method is slightly harder, in that there isn't a drag-and-drop editor, so the XPATH expressions must be done by hand.

Writing complex XML

This is a very useful recipe for building complex XML structures containing many looping elements and deep hierarchies, and once the principles are understood, it is simple and quick to implement. If you use XML frequently, then we hope that this will become one of your staple recipes.

To make this exercise more understandable, it is necessary to understand a little about the method prior to using it.

Understanding the XML structure

The XML structure we are aiming to create is shown in the following screenshot:

```xml
<customer>
    <customerId>1</customerId>
    <name>Jo Ray Smith</name>
    <countryOfResidence>Germany</countryOfResidence>
    <orders>
        <order>
            <orderId>1</orderId>
            <orderType>Card</orderType>
            <orderDate>01/01/2013</orderDate>
            <orderTotal>21.01</orderTotal>
            <items>
                <item>
                    <orderItemId>1</orderItemId>
                    <itemDescription>Hammer</itemDescription>
                    <itemQuantity>1</itemQuantity>
                </item>
                <item>
                    <orderItemId>2</orderItemId>
                    <itemDescription>Spanner</itemDescription>
                    <itemQuantity>2</itemQuantity>
                </item>
                <item>
                    <orderItemId>3</orderItemId>
                    <itemDescription>1 inch nails</itemDescription>
                    <itemQuantity>100</itemQuantity>
                </item>
            </items>
        </order>
        <order>
            <orderId>2</orderId>
            <orderType>Cash</orderType>
            <orderDate>02/07/2013</orderDate>
            <orderTotal>200.76</orderTotal>
            <items>
                <item>
                    <orderItemId>4</orderItemId>
                    <itemDescription>Hammer</itemDescription>
                    <itemQuantity>1</itemQuantity>
                </item>
                <item>
                    <orderItemId>5</orderItemId>
```

As you can see, a customer can have many orders, and an order can have many order items.

Node

> I am using the term **node** to describe an XML tag that contains one or more other tags or nodes. For example a customer node may contain many order nodes.

Method

We will build a three-tier XML structure building the hierarchy one level at a time:

1. First, we build the customer node.
2. Then, we build an orders node that contains many individual order nodes and add them as a child of the customer node.
3. Finally, we will build the order items node that contains one or more items and add them to the individual order nodes.

Java DOM

This recipe depends upon the **Java DOM** (XML document) format and three code routines that have been built to manipulate it; however, beyond knowing how to use the routines, this method does not require an in-depth knowledge of Java XML Documents.

Getting ready

Open the job `jo_cook_ch09_0050_writeComplexXML`. If you look at the whole job, you will notice that it seems to have a hierarchy, a little like the XML structure itself.

How to do it...

The first action is to create the top-level node, `customer`:

1. Add a `tWriteXMLField` component to the canvas, and add a row from `tFixedFlowInput_2`.
2. Open `tWriteXMLField_1` and change `rootTag` in the right-hand panel to `customer`.
3. Drag the columns `customerId`, `name`, and `countryOfResidence` from the left-hand panel to the right-hand panel onto the field `customer`.
4. You will be prompted as to how you wish to treat the fields. Select the default, **Create as sub element of the target node**.

5. Right-click on the field `customerId` in the right-hand panel and select the option to **Set As Loop Element**. You will notice that the error condition in the top left hand corner disappears.
6. Your `tWriteXMLField` should now look like the one in the next screenshot:

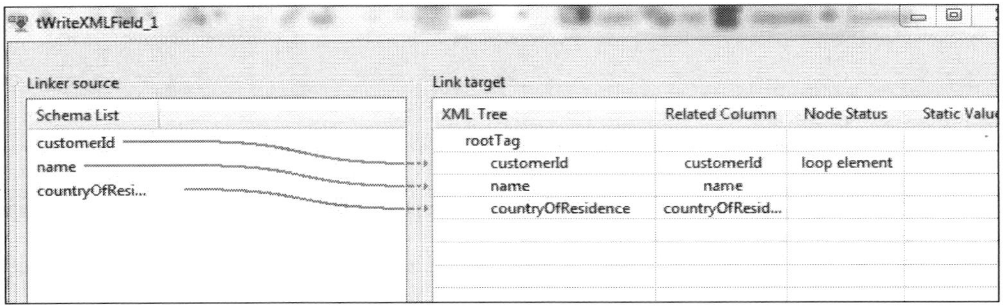

7. Finally, in the component panel for your `tWriteXMLField`, open the schema and add a String field to the right-hand side called `customerXML`, as shown in the next screenshot:

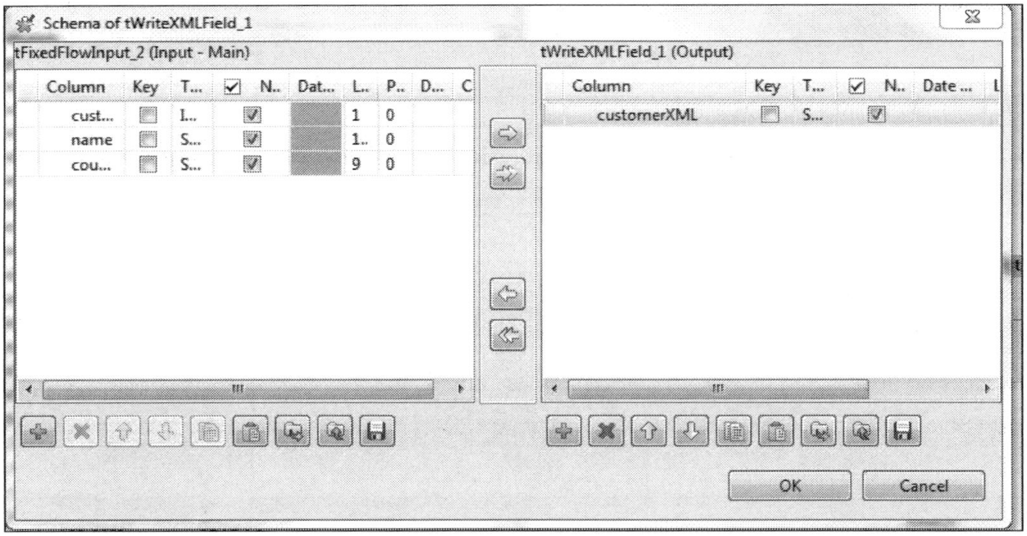

Creating the customer document

8. Add a `tJavaRow` component, link it to the `tWriteXMLField` component, and open it.

9. Add the following code:

```
// Initialize the document using the customer details
  and then write it to globalMap
globalMap.put("customerXML",XMLUtils.createDomFromString
  (input_row.customerXML));

System.out.println("*********************
  Customer xml *******************************");
System.out.println(XMLUtils.DOMToString(
(org.w3c.dom.Document) globalMap.get("customerXML")));
```

10. Run the job, and you will see the customer Strings and customer documents.

    Creating the orders XML String

11. Activate the next subjob and `tJava_2`.
12. Open `tMap_3`, and you will see that we are finding the orders for the given `customerId`, which are then stored in the orders hash map.
13. Open `tWriteXMLField_2`, and you will see that this time we have created two levels; `orders` and within that, `order`, and that we have set the **loop element** to be the `order` node. This allows us to store the individual order nodes in the top-level `orders` node.
14. Open the component panel for the `tWriteXMLField_2` component, click on the **+** button for the **Group By** section, and select the field `customerId` as shown in the next screenshot. This ensures that only one string will be written with all the orders for the customer in it.

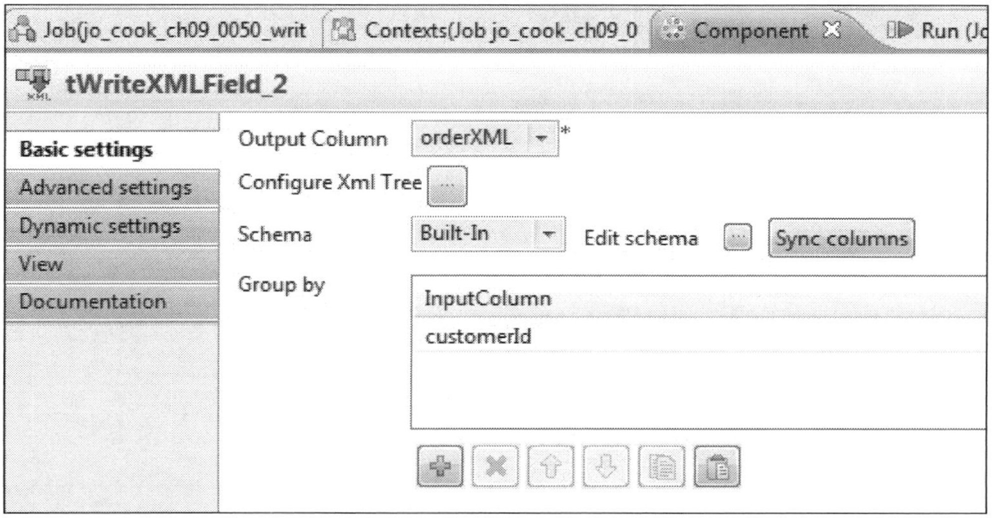

15. Open `tJavaRow_3` and add the following code:

```
System.out.println("********************** Order XML *************
******************");
System.out.println(input_row.orderXML);

// read the document
org.w3c.dom.Document customerXML =
  (org.w3c.dom.Document) globalMap.get("customerXML");

XMLUtils.addChildAtPath
  (customerXML, "/customer", input_row.orderXML);

//Put the document back into globalMap
globalMap.put("customerXML",customerXML);
```

16. Run the job, and you will see the `orders` XML structure that is generated and how it has been added to the `customer` XML. Note how for `customerId = 1` there are multiple order records within the `orders` node.

Adding the order items

17. Reactivate the remaining components. If you examine the components you will see that they are set up in the same way as the `order` XML creation, except the parent is now `order`, and thus the group is now by `orderId`.
18. Open `tJavaRow_4` and insert the following code:

```
System.out.println("********************** Order item XML ********
***********************");
System.out.println(input_row.itemXML);


// read the document
org.w3c.dom.Document customerXML =
  (org.w3c.dom.Document) globalMap.get("customerXML");

// write the order items XML into the main structure
  where the order node has an id = the current id
XMLUtils.addChildAtPath(customerXML, "/customer
  /orders/order[orderId = "+((Integer)globalMap.get
  ("order.orderId"))+"]", input_row.itemXML);

// put the main XML back into globalMap
globalMap.put("customerXML",customerXML);
```

```
System.out.println("********************** Document
  with item added *******************************");
System.out.println(XMLUtils.DOMToString(
  (org.w3c.dom.Document) globalMap.get("customerXML")));
```

19. Note the highlighted section. This will be explained later.
20. Run the job, and you will see that individual `item` nodes are grouped within the `items` node and that the correct `items` nodes have been added to the correct `order` nodes.

How it works...

This is probably the most complex exercise in the book to explain, so while you are reading this, we would recommend that you also reference the output of the job. The job log has been designed to illustrate the concepts in the section *Putting It All Together*.

So here we go...

This method revolves around five main principles:

- `tWriteXMLField` allows us to build XML strings from the input data.
- Code utilities allow us to create a document, add nodes to it, and then convert it back to a String.
- `tFlowToIterate` allows us to create Talend looping sections for managing repeating groups of child nodes.
- `tHash` components allow us to store the keys for the parent elements that we then use to find the data for the child elements. These keys also allow us to locate the correct node to which the children need to be added.
- XPATH condition logic that allows us to add order items into the relevant node using the `orderId` field as the key.

And here, they are explained in more detail.

tWriteXMLField

`tWriteXMLField` allows us to build XML Strings from flat data. When building the top-level node, its use is simple and obvious, but when we come to building the repeating nodes, you must remember to add a `Group By` field.

Code utilities

You will notice that we used three methods in the code routine `XMLUtils`:

- `createDomFromString`: We took the customer XML String and created a new Document from the String.
- `addChildAtPath`: This will take an XML String, and add it into an existing node in the Document. It uses an XPATH expression to locate the correct node.
- `DOMToString`: This converts a Document into a String.

tFlowToIterate

`tFlowToIterate` is used whenever we have a node that contains repeated children. In our case, this is `customer` and `order`.

tHash components

The `tHashOutput` components are used to store the keys for the repeating parent elements. These keys are then used to drive a lookup process to join to the child data, so that it can be added to the parent node.

XPATH Condition

You will have noticed that when adding the `items` node, the `addChildAtPath` expression was more complex than for the orders node. This is because it uses an XPATH condition. If we take `orderId` of `1` for this example, the condition would be expressed as the following:

```
/customer/orders/order[orderId = 1]
```

which is translated as the order node where the orderId = 1.

Putting it all together

So, putting all of this together, here is what we did in this recipe:

1. We first created an XML string version of the customer data using `tWriteXMLField`.
2. Using `createDomFromString`, we then created a Document object for the customer.
3. Using the `customerId` as the key, we then found all the orders for that customer using `tMap`.
4. We used the order data to create a node (`orders`) that consisted of all the individual order nodes using `tWriteXMLField`. We also stored the key values for the `orders` in a `tHashOutput` component for later use with the `order items`.
5. Next, we used `addChildAtPath` to add the node containing all the `orders` into the `customer` node.

6. Then, for each order, we performed the following steps:

    1. Get the order item data for all items within the order.
    2. Create an XML string (items) containing all the individual order item nodes for the current order iteration.
    3. Add the items XML string to the Document under the relevant order using an XPATH expression that uses the `orderId` as a condition, to ensure that the items node was inserted into the correct order node.

There's more...

But that's not all that we think you need to know about this recipe.

Job "shape"

In the *Getting ready* section, I mentioned that the job itself has a hierarchy. It is visible to one level in this job; however, when you are using much deeper hierarchies, it becomes totally obvious and gives a rough indication as to the shape of the XML hierarchy being built.

We have changed the color of the subjobs for the order level in this job to make this more obvious, and this is something you may wish to adopt. Subjob colors can be changed in the subjob component tab.

We would recommend that you try this with a deeper hierarchy; for example, country has regions as branch has employees, to get accustomed to working with multiple nested levels. Then, try with additional nodes at the same level, for example customer has many addresses, many telephone numbers and many e-mail addresses, to get you accustomed to building lots of additional nodes under the same parent node. With practice, this technique can help you produce extremely complex XML structures quickly and efficiently.

Calling a SOAP web service

This recipe shows how a SOAP-based web service can be called from Talend. We will be using a very simple Talend web service that will return the weather conditions in a given city.

Getting ready...

1. Open the job `jo_cook_ch09_weatherService` and run it. You will see the output in the console, the last line of which will be `web service [endpoint: http://localhost:8090/services/cookbookWeatherService] published`.
2. This means that the web service is now available to be called by our consumer job.
3. Now open the job `jo_cook_ch09_0060_consumeSOAP`.

How to do it...

1. Drag a `tESBConsumer` component to the canvas and open it.
2. Change the **WSDL** to `http://localhost:8090/services/cookbookWeatherService?wsdl`.
3. Tick the box for **Populate schema to repository on finish**. This will ensure the XML metadata schemas we need for the SOAP request and response are created in the repository for us to use later.
4. Click on the button to refresh the details, as highlighted in the following screenshot, and you will see that the details for the web service we are calling have been populated.

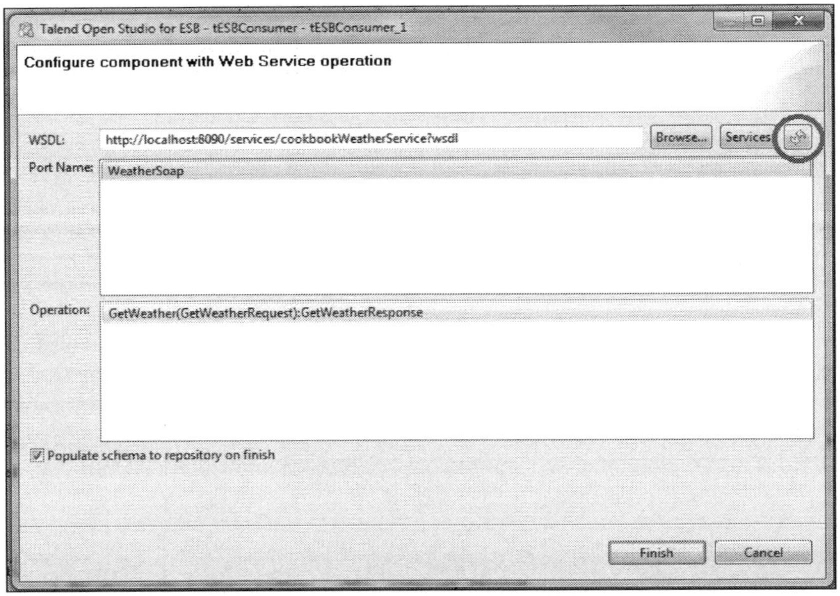

5. Click on **Finish**.
6. Add `tXMLMap` before the `tESBConsumer` component and `tLogRow` after and join as shown in the next screenshot:

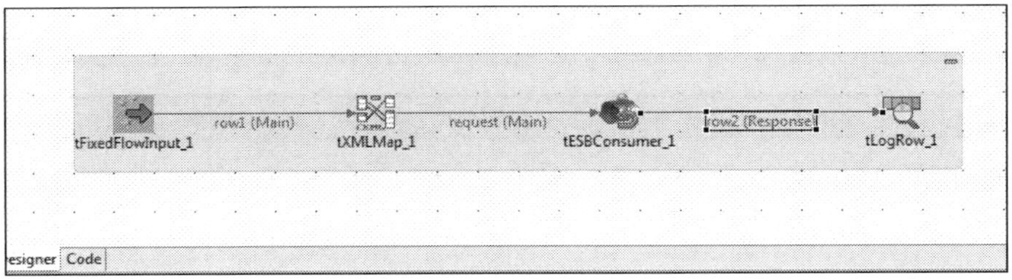

7. Open the `tXMLMap` component and import the request from the repository for the output table from the repository location shown in the next screenshot:

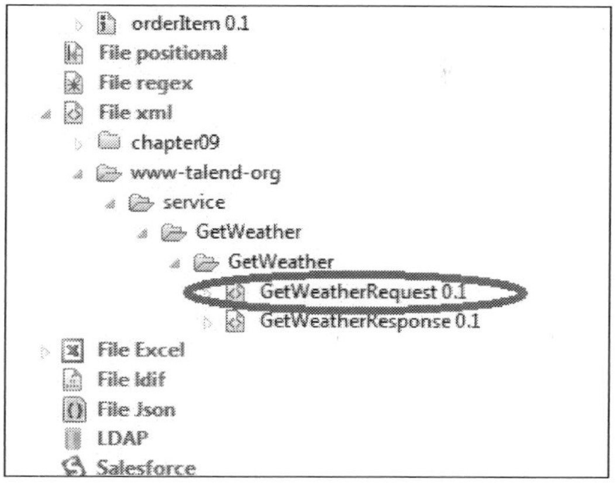

8. Now you can copy the input `city` field to the output request `city` field as shown in the following screenshot:

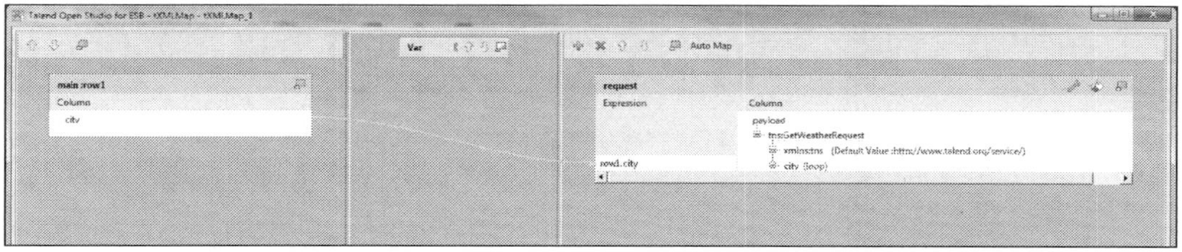

9. Run the job. The response XML will appear in the console.
10. You can now stop the job `jo_cook_ch09_weatherService`.

How it works...

The `tESBConsumer` component will connect to the service and use the WSDL definition to create the XML schemas required for the SOAP request and response.

The XML schema for the request is then defined in the `tXMLMap` component and the input columns are mapped to the XML request.

There's more...

This job calls a very simple web service with a flat XML structure, so the same result could be achieved much more simply using `tWebServiceInput`. However, it should be noted that the `tWebServiceInput` component is very limited in terms of complexity of request and response. The method used in this recipe provides a pattern for use with SOAP services where the request and the response can be very complex.

Decoding the response

When the `tESBConsumer` component creates the request XML it also creates the response XML that can be used in `tXMLMap` to decode the response into a Talend schema.

Using web service calls in-flow

This service does not return the input information when the output is returned, so the job as set up currently requires additional work to output the city and the weather in the same row.

If there is a requirement to do this then the flow as shown here can be added to a `tMap` component as a lookup with reload at each row active. The input data can then be configured via `globalMap` variables set from the input fields.

Calling a RESTful web service

This recipe shows how a RESTful web service can be called from Talend. The REST service we will be using is a Google maps service, so you will need to be connected to the Internet to perform this recipe.

Getting ready

Open the job `jo_cook_ch09_0070_consumeRestService`.

How to do it...

1. Drag a `tRESTClient` component onto the canvas.
2. Set the **URL** to `http://maps.googleapis.com` the **Relative Path** to `"maps/api/geocode/xml"`.
3. Add two **Query Parameters** `"address"` with a value of `"Trafalgar Square"` and `"sensor"` with a value of `"false"`.

4. Your `tRestClient` should look like the one below:

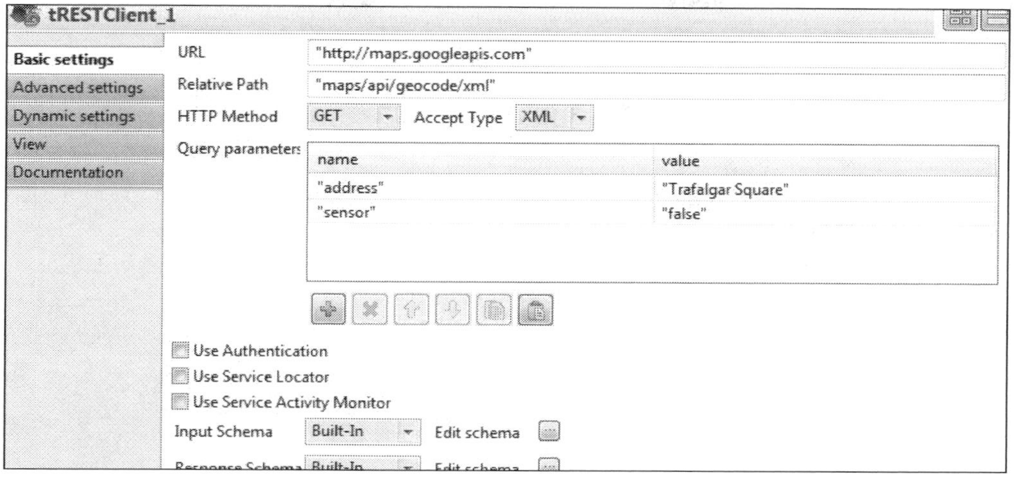

5. Link a `tLogRow` component to the response and error flows out of the `tRestClient` component.
6. Run the job.

How it works...

The `tRestClient` is a component that enables us to define all of the features of a REST request. In this case, we define the URL of the Google APIs, and then the Geocoder API within the maps functions.

Finally, we define the address for which we wish to provide the information.

There's more...

This recipe is similar to the previous SOAP recipe; however, the request does not require as much setup as the SOAP recipe.

The downside of this method as it stands, is that the data is held in parameters, so we can only do one request at a time.

Similarly to the SOAP request, if we wish to use this component in-flow, we'll need to add a `tMap` component in reload at each row made, and use the `tRESTClient` component as a lookup, where the **Query Parameter** for `address` in the `tRestClient` component would be specified via `globalMap` variables.

Reading and writing to a queue

Talend ESB is supplied with the Apache ActiveMQ software for creating message queues and topics. This recipe shows how we can write to and read from an ActiveMQ queue.

Getting ready

First, we'll need to start ActiveMQ.

1. Navigate to the folder <talend installation folder>\Runtime_ESBSE\activemq\bin and double-click on the file activemq.bat.
2. This will open a command window. Do not close this command window while you are doing this recipe.
3. You can access the ActiveMQ administration console by opening the URL localhost:8161/admin. This will allow you to view your queues and topics.
4. Open the job jo_cook_ch09_0080_readWriteQueue.

How to do it...

The first thing to do is to write a message to a queue.

Writing to the queue

1. Drag a tMomOutput component to the canvas.
2. Create a flow between the tFileInputXML and the tMomOutput components.
3. Open the component and set the **MQ Server** to **ActiveMQ,** the **To** field to **customerData,** and the **MessageType** to **Queue**. Your tMomOuptut should look like the one in the next screenshot:

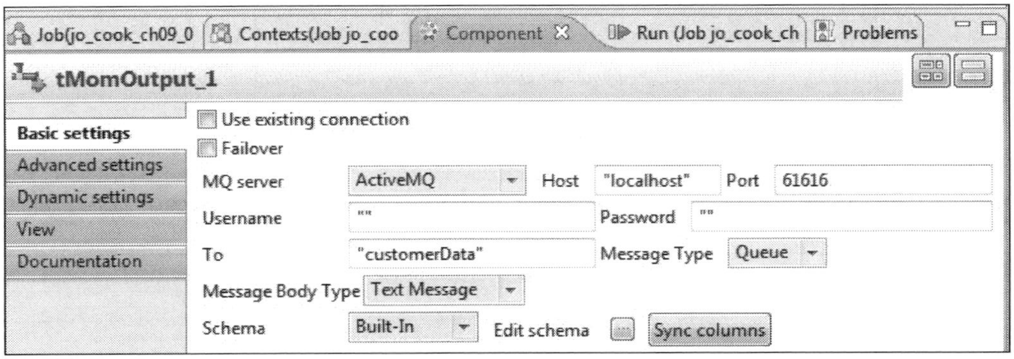

4. Run the job.

5. Open a browser and navigate to the URL `http://localhost:8161/admin`
6. Click **Queues** on the navigation bar. You will see the queue you just created with one message enqueued.
7. Double-click on the link `customerData`, and then click on the message.
8. You should now see the customer XML data in the message.

Reading the message from the queue

9. Now deactivate the subjob that writes to the queue.
10. Copy a `tMomInput` component to the canvas and change the settings to match those for the `tMomOutput` component, as shown below:

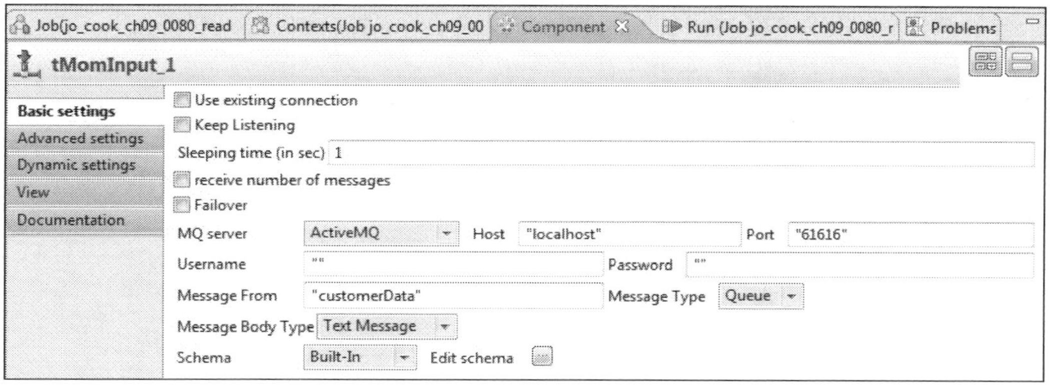

11. Add a `tLogRow` component and run the job.
12. The message will now be displayed in the log.
13. Return to the browser and click on the **Queues** option on the navigation bar
14. You will see that the number of pending messages is now **0**.

How it works...

The first subjob wrote an XML message to the queue named `customerData`. We then viewed the customer data in the queue.

The second subjob then read the XML message from the queue, and we were able to see that the message had been removed (dequeued).

There's more...

The `tMomOutput` and `tMomInput` components in this recipe were configured manually and will commit records as soon as they are read and/or written.

The next recipe shows how we can treat data being read or written from a queue as a transaction in a similar fashion to the session based transaction in the database chapter.

Ensuring lossless queues using sessions

In any production system, it is imperative that the data isn't lost when being read/written to or from a data source/target. This recipe shows how this is achieved when reading and writing to queues using the `tMom` component.

Getting ready

Open the job `jo_cook_ch09_0090_loss1esQueues`.

How to do it...

In a similar fashion to creating sessions with a database, we will first add ActiveMQ connection that will create the session.

1. Open the `tMomConnection` component to the canvas and tick the box **Use Transacted**.
2. Open the `tMomOutput` component and tick the **Use existing connection** box.
3. Set the **To** field to **losslessQueue**, and the **Message Type** to **Queue**.

   Add the rollback and commit components

4. Drag a `tMomCommit` component to the canvas and link this to the `tFixedFlowInput` using an `OnSubjobOk` trigger.
5. Open the component and set the **MQ Server** to **ActivMQ**.

   Successful run

6. Run the job and then check the queue in the web browser.
7. You will see that the queue `losslessQueue` has been created with 10 messages enqueued.
8. Delete the queue.

Failed run

9. Open the `tMap` component and change the **Expression** field in the table `killjob` to `Numeric.sequence("s2",1,1) > 8`.
10. Run the job and then check the queue in the web browser.
11. You will see that the queue `losslessQueue` has been created, however there are 0 records enqueued.

How it works...

We first created a session that allows transaction style processing by defining a `tMomConnection` component as **transacted**.

We then ensured that our `tMomOutput` component is linked to the session by setting the **Use existing connection** option to **true**.

When we ran the first time, rows were sent down the flow `killjob`, so all 10 records are written to the queue when the commit is processed.

Then, the condition in the `tMap` component is set to mimic a job failure on the eigth record. When we ran the job after the condition was changed, the commit was never processed, so none of the records written to the queue were persisted.

There's more...

Like the database sessions, the rollback on a queue is automatic if a job fails, so the job only needs to have a `tMomCommit` component.

The `tMomInput` component works in the same way as the `tMomOutput` when using a connection, in that messages written to the queue will be removed if no commit takes place.

10
Debugging, Logging, and Testing

This chapter contains exercises that illustrate the methods provided by Talend to locate and correct code, display logging information, and create test data. They are as follows:

- Finding the location of compilation errors using the Problems tab
- Locating execution errors from the console output
- Using the Talend debug mode – row-by-row execution
- Using the Java debugger to debug Talend jobs
- Using tLogRow to show data in a row
- Using tJavaRow to display row information
- Using tJava to display status messages and variables
- Printing out the context
- Dumping console output to a file from within a job
- Creating simple test data using tRowGenerator
- Creating complex test data using tRowGenerator, tFlowToIterate, tMap, and sequences
- Creating random test data using lookups
- Creating test data using Excel
- Testing logic – most used pattern
- Killing a job from within tJavaRow

Introduction

When our code eventually runs as a production job, it is expected that it will be robust, reliable, and bug free. For this to happen, it will usually pass through various stages of testing, including the unit test stage performed by the developer.

This section shows some of the methods that can be used to ensure that developers can find and fix problems quickly during this testing phase.

Debugging

The ability to find and locate issues within code quickly and efficiently is the key to successful delivery of projects. Talend provides methods for debugging, and so does Eclipse.

Logging

Talend provides useful components for logging and capturing errors in `tWarn`, `tDie`, and `tFlowMeter`. It also provides mechanisms for logging information to the console, which can be a quick and valuable debugging tool, and is a vital part of the developers' armory. It is often quicker to send and view messages and information to the log output during development than it is to do the same to say a database or files.

Testing

It is obvious that code needs to be tested, and creation of unit testing data is usually part of the developer's responsibilities. In many cases, Talend can be utilized as part of the test data creation process to enable jobs to be properly tested.

Find the location of compilation errors using the Problems tab

When you begin working with Talend, you will inevitably hit compilation errors when you run a job. This recipe will show you how to easily identify the errors using Talend.

Getting ready

Open the `jo_cook_ch10_0010_findCompilationErrors` job.

How to do it...

The steps for finding the location of compilation errors using the Problems tab is as follows:

1. Run the job, and Talend will notify you that the job has compilation errors. Click on **Cancel** to stop the job executing.

2. Now click on the **Problems** tab, and you will see the errors, as shown in the following screenshot:

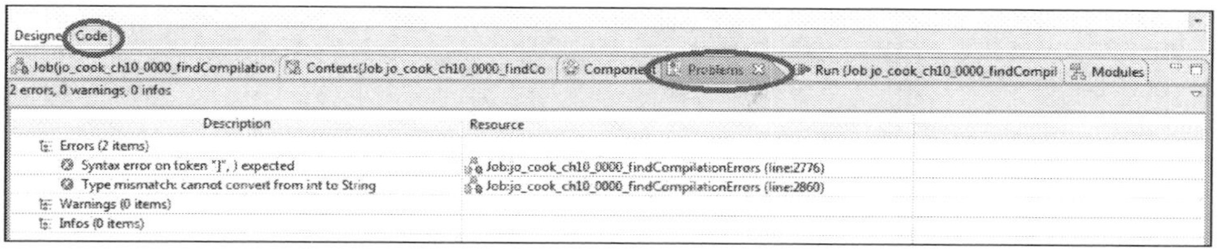

3. If you click **one each on** you will see that the focus moves between the two `tMap` components. This means that there is an error in each of the `tMap` components.
4. To locate the error exactly, click on the **Code** tab, highlighted in the previous diagram.
5. You should now see the generated Java code and that there are two red markers on the right-hand side of the code.

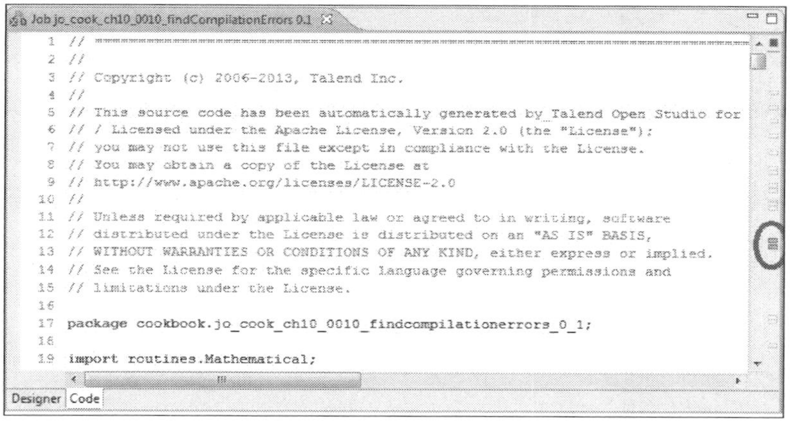

Job jo_cook_ch10_0010_findCompilationErrors 0.1
// Copyright (c) 2006-2013, Talend Inc.
// This source code has been automatically generated by_Talend Open Studio for
// / Licensed under the Apache License, Version 2.0 (the "License");
// you may not use this file except in compliance with the License.
// You may obtain a copy of the License at
// http://www.apache.org/licenses/LICENSE-2.0
// Unless required by applicable law or agreed to in writing, software
// distributed under the License is distributed on an "AS IS" BASIS,
// WITHOUT WARRANTIES OR CONDITIONS OF ANY KIND, either express or implied.
// See the License for the specific language governing permissions and
// limitations under the License.
package cookbook.jo_cook_ch10_0010_findcompilationerrors_0_1;
import routines.Mathematical;
Designer
Code

6. Click on the top marker, and it will automatically take you to the line shown as follows:

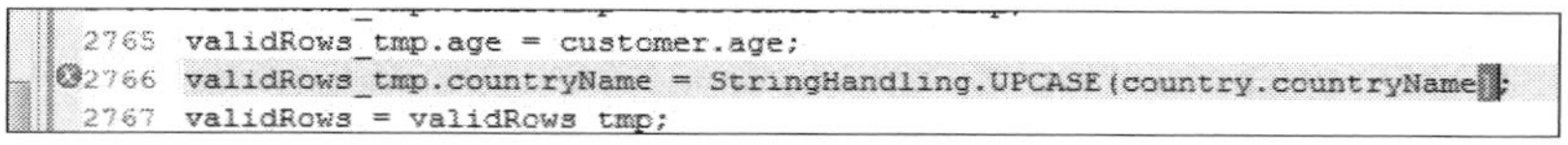

2765 validRows_tmp.age = customer.age;
2766 validRows_tmp.countryName = StringHandling.UPCASE(country.countryName];
2767 validRows = validRows_tmp;

7. This matches the line in the **Problems** tab with the error **Syntax error on token "]",) expected**.
8. Click on the second marker, and it shows the line:

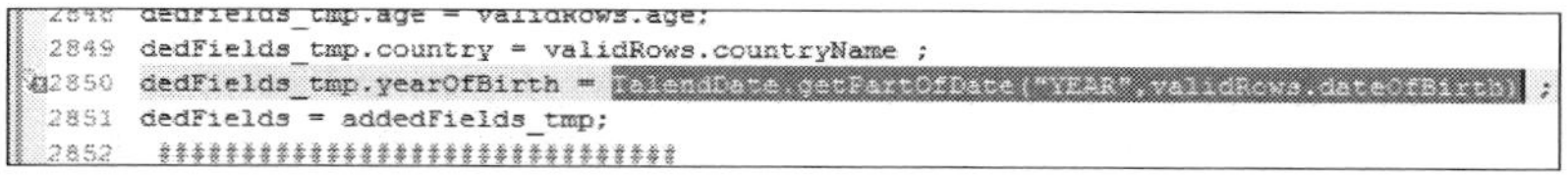

2849 dedFields_tmp.country = validRows.countryName ;
2850 dedFields_tmp.yearOfBirth = TalendDate.getPartOfDate("YEAR",validRows.dateOfBirth) ;
2851 dedFields = addedFields_tmp;
2852 ################################

9. This matches the second error in the **Problems** tab.

How it works...

When Talend recognizes that there are one or more compilation errors during execution, it will populate the **Problems** tab with the errors. Crossing over to the Java code enables the exact lines to be located and fixed.

To fix the problems mentioned previously, replace the `]` with `)` in the first `tMap`, and change the type of `yearOfBirth` to `Integer` in the output schema of the second `tMap`.

There's more...

If you follow the best practice regarding keeping changes small and executing often, then you won't have to use this method often, because you should be aware of what changes you have made since the last successful execution.

That said, it is a very quick and easy way to find lines that have errors and very useful when you have lots of fields within a `tMap` or other component.

Locating execution errors from the console output

This recipe shows that the often complex errors returned by Java can, in the main, be located fairly easily if you know how.

If you are already familiar with Java, this exercise is trivial; however, if you are not then Java errors can often seem very intimidating.

Getting ready

Open the `jo_cook_ch10_0020_findExecutionError` job.

How to do it...

The steps for locating execution errors from the console output are as follows:

1. Run the job. It will fail with a **null pointer** error. Note the line number from the first line of the list of lines; 2636.

```
Exception in component tMap_1
java.lang.NullPointerException
    at cookbook.jo_cook_ch10_0020_findexecutionerror_0_1.jo_cook_ch10_0020_findExecutionError.tFileInputDelimited_1Process(jo_cook_ch10_0020_findExecutionError.java:2636)
    at cookbook.jo_cook_ch10_0020_findexecutionerror_0_1.jo_cook_ch10_0020_findExecutionError.runJobInTOS(jo_cook_ch10_0020_findExecutionError.java:3898)
    at cookbook.jo_cook_ch10_0020_findexecutionerror_0_1.jo_cook_ch10_0020_findExecutionError.main(jo_cook_ch10_0020_findExecutionError.java:3761)
```

2. Open the **Code** tab and press *CTRL + L*.

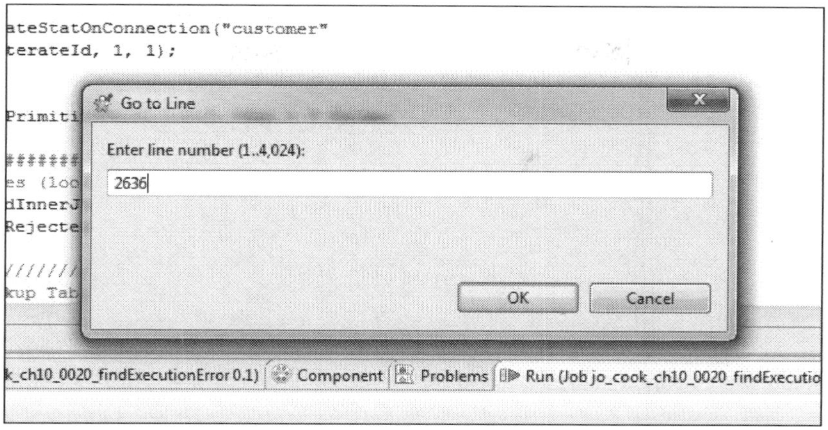

3. Type `2636` as the line number, and you will be taken to the following line:

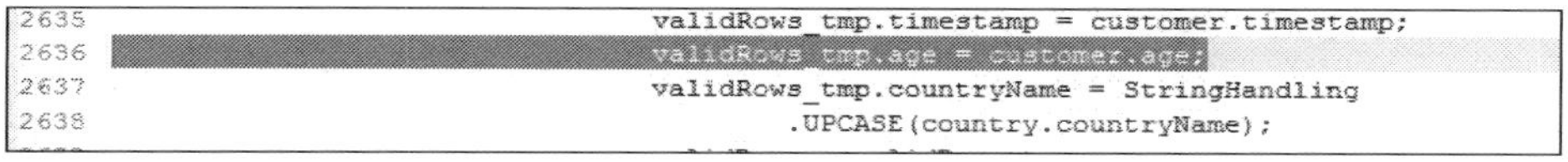

2635 validRows_tmp.timestamp = customer.timestamp;
2636 validRows_tmp.age = customer.age;
2637 validRows_tmp.countryName = StringHandling
2638 .UPCASE(country.countryName);

4. This is the line that caused the job to fail. There is null data in the `customer.age` field.

How it works...

It is fairly obvious from the message that the error occurred in `tMap_1`, but it's not so obvious unless you know Java error messages. Unlike compilation errors, Talend does not list the error in the problems log, so a bit of combined Talend and Java understanding is required here.

In most cases, the first line of the main body of the error message will show the job and line number for the error. In our case, you will see that the first line ends with:

```
jo_cook_ch10_0020_findExecutionError.java:2636
```

This is the line number of the error within the job.

When working in the **Code** tab, *CTRL + L* will take you to a line number, in our case, `2636`. This is the line that failed, and we can see that the field is the customer age field.

From the job, we can also see that three rows had been read from the input, but only two have been processed. This means that we have an error with the third row in the file.

When you look at the `chapter10_jo_0020_customerData.csv` file, you will see that the **age** field for the third row is blank.

If you also look at `tMap_1`, you will see that the **age** field is non-nullable.

Thus, it is the blank age value that is causing this job to fail with a null pointer exception.

If you change the blank age to an integer value in the file, then the job should run ok.

There's more...

This method is a general rule of thumb and works for many Talend errors. Sometimes, the error message occurs within a Java method for which there is no source code. In these cases, it may help to use the Java debugging method as described later in this chapter.

> Sometimes for deployed jobs in different environments the line numbers in the errors do not match the line numbers in the Studio version of the code. It is thus a good idea when deploying the code to ensure that the source code is also deployed. The line number in the error will always match the line number in the deployed code.

See also

- *Using the Java debugger to debug Talend jobs recipe* later in this chapter

Using the Talend debug mode – row-by-row execution

This recipe will show how we can find Talend data issues by watching the data as it flows between components using the Talend debug mode.

Getting ready

Open the `jo_cook_ch10_0030_useDebugMode` job.

How to do it...

The steps for using the Talend debug mode are as follows:

1. Open the run tab, and select the **Debug Run** option on the left-hand side as shown in the following screenshot:

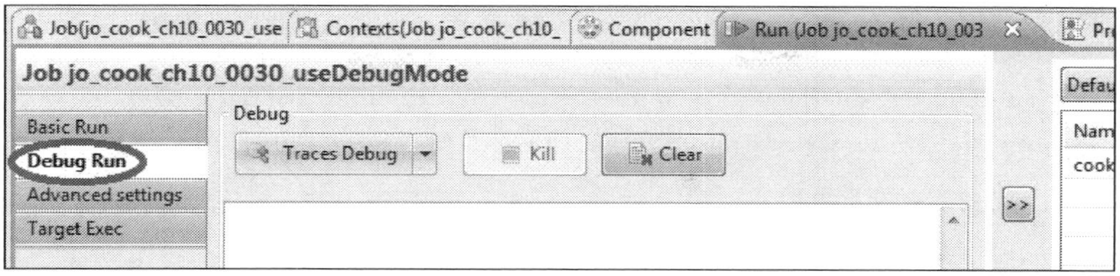

2. Click on **Traces Debug** and the job will execute, and you can watch the data in the rows as they progress along the main flow of the sub-job until the error is hit, and the job fails.

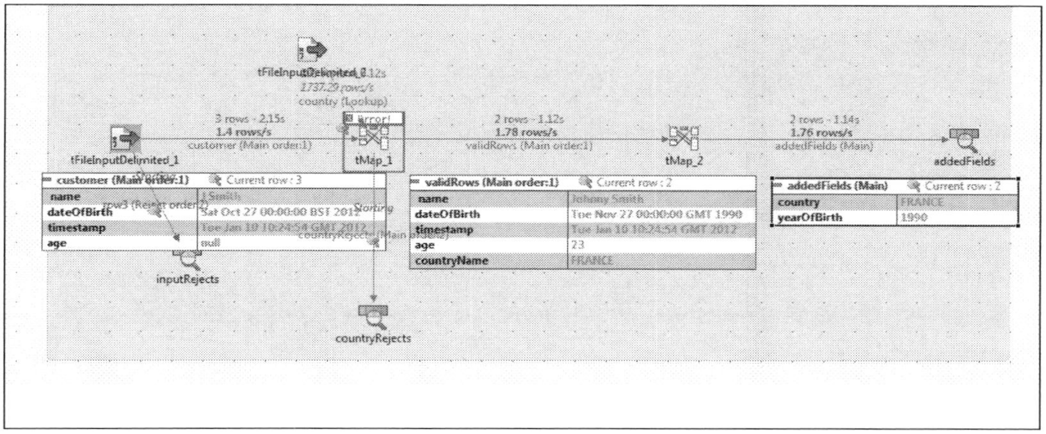

How it works...

Being able to view the data progressing through the job in real time allows us to see that the third row failed. Because the reported error is a null pointer exception and the only field in the row that has a null pointer is the age, we can confirm if the input age value is incorrect.

There's more...

You will notice that the execution of a job is slowed down considerably by using this method for debugging because of the amount of data that is refreshed on the screen. This means that this method isn't the most practical method for large volumes of data, unless you are happy to wait for a while for the job to fail.

In case of larger datasets, it is better to use either logging or Java methods to debug the code.

See also

- The *Locating execution errors from the console output* recipe in this chapter
- *The Using the Java debugger to debug Talend jobs* recipe in this chapter

Using the Java debugger to debug Talend jobs

Occasionally, it is necessary to delve deeper into the Java code generated by Talend in order to locate and understand the cause of a bug. This recipe is a very light introduction for debugging Talend code using the Java debugging mode in Talend.

Getting ready

Open the `jo_cook_ch10_0040_useJavaDebugger` job.

How to do it...

The steps for using the Java debugger to debug Talend jobs are as follows:

1. Select the **Debug Run** option from the **Run** dialogue and click on the down arrow for the run type. Select **Java Debug** to run using the Java option.

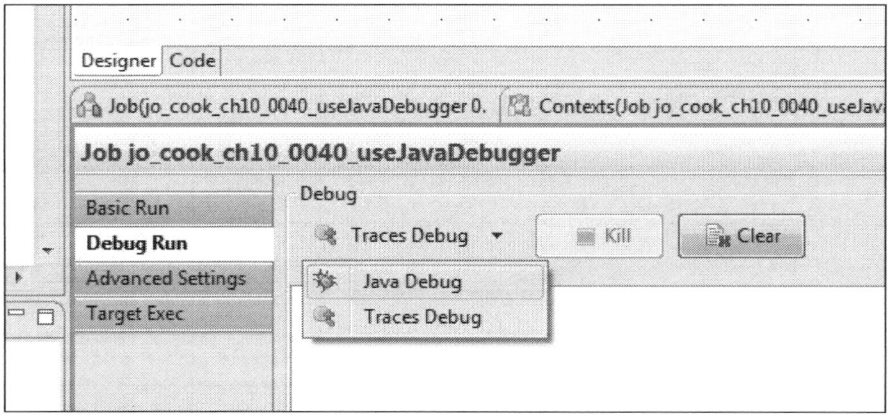

2. Confirm the perspective switch by clicking **Yes**.

3. Click the resume icon to start the job running.

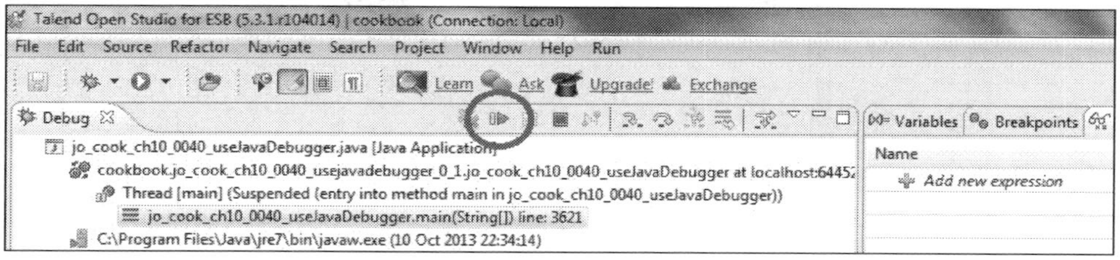

4. The job will execute and return an error. Scroll through the console output (bottom panel), and you will see the error, as shown in the following screenshot:

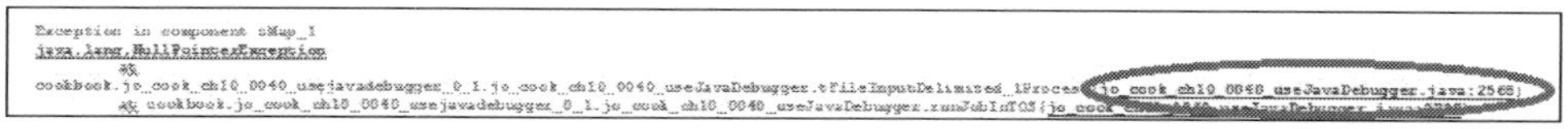

5. Click the hyperlink for line 2574. This will take you to the line that is causing an error.

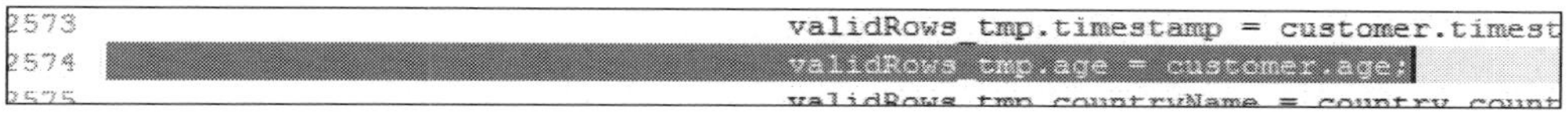

Adding a breakpoint to allow inspection of data:

6. Right-click on the line number, and select **Toggle Breakpoint**. The line now has a blue button next to it.

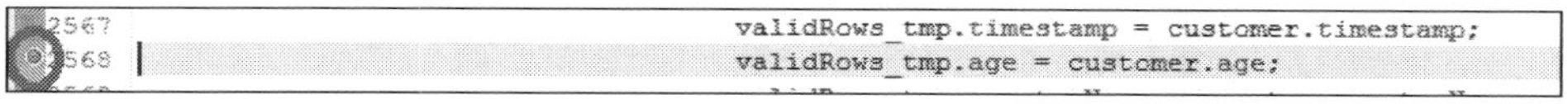

7. Run the job again using the **Debug** button, then the resume button, and it will stop before the line is executed.

8. Highlight the code `customer.age` using the mouse, then right-click and select **Inspect**. You will see that the value is 23.

9. Right-click again and select the option **Watch**. Repeat this for the customer name. You will see that these fields have been added to the watch list in the top right hand corner, as shown in the following screenshot:

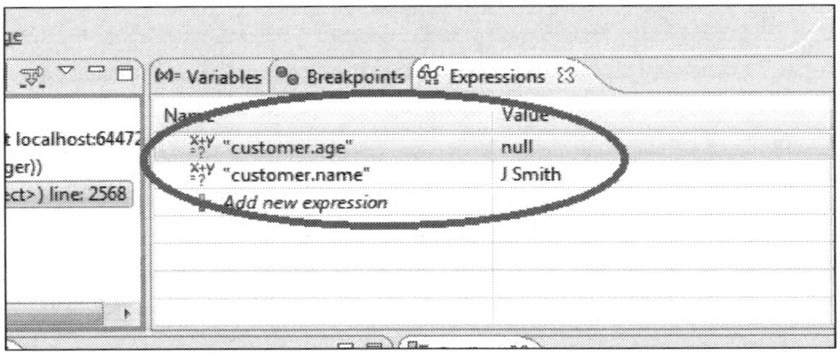

10. Click the resume button twice more, and you will eventually hit the row where the value is null. This will give you the name of the customer (**J Smith**) for the erroneous age.
11. End the job by clicking on the resume button.

    Adding a conditional breakpoint to find the row quickly:

12. Right-click on the line where we previously added the breakpoint (2574). Select the option **Breakpoint properties**. This will open the following condition dialog, as shown in the next screenshot.
13. Select **Conditional** breakpoint, and type `customer.age == null` into the text field as shown in the following screenshot:

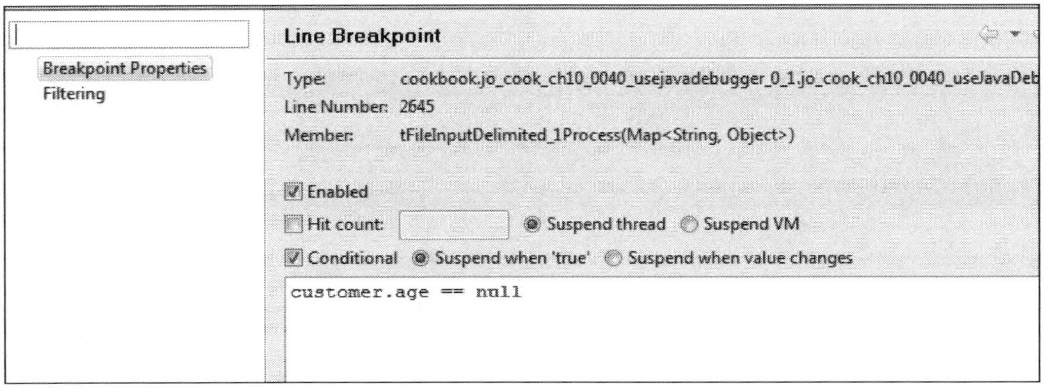

14. Run the job using the bug button and the resume button, and you will now see that the debugger stops on the record with the null value for age.

How it works...

Adding a breakpoint tells the debugger to stop before the line is executed, which allows us to then view values of fields, and add them to the watch list if required.

When the resume button is then pressed, it will continue execution of the job until the next breakpoint is reached, or the job finishes. In our case, because the error is on the fourth row, the breakpoint will be hit two more times before we find the record with a null age.

Adding conditional breakpoints enables us to skip records, in which we aren't interested, and only break the process for inspection when the condition is met. This is why when we start the job and click resume, the first value for age in the watch list is null.

There's more...

The Java debug perspective allows for much more in-depth debugging; however, some Java knowledge is essential for use, as is the knowledge of how Talend builds the Java code. Both are outside the scope of this book.

This is only a very brief introduction to the Java debugger in Talend, which is actually based upon the Eclipse debugger. More information and useful techniques for using the Eclipse debugger can be found at the following link:

`http://www.vogella.com/articles/EclipseDebugging/article.html`

Using tLogRow to show data in a row

This recipe demonstrates some simple but interesting features of tLogRow, one of the simplest components in Talend.

Getting ready

Open the `jo_cook_ch10_0050_tLogRow` job and run it. This is the default format for tLogRow.

How to do it...

The steps for using tLogRow display data in a row are as follows:

1. Open the `tLogRow` component and change the **Field Seperator** to `,` and execute. This will give you a CSV output.

2. Click on the option **Use fixed lengths for values**, and set all the **Length** columns to `30`. You will see a formatted output. If not ,then you will need to copy the console output to a text editor. Note that you will need to use *CTRL + A* followed by *CTRL + C* to copy, because right-click does not work in the console.
3. Now, change the **Length** columns to `-30`. Notice that, the information is now left-justified rather than right-justified.
4. Close `tLogRow` and change the component name from `tLogRow_1` to `customers`.
5. Open the `tLogRow` component and change the type to `Vertical`.
6. You will see that the output is now a set of name/value pairs, and the name is still being shown as `tLogRow_1`. This is the **Unique name**.
7. Open the tLogRow component and select the option **Print label**. Run the job.
8. You will see that the heading is now `customers`.

How it works...

As you can see, the tLogRow component is a very flexible method for adding runtime logging information, and for aiding in the debugging process.

`tLogRow` uses Java print formatters under the covers to enable a variety of different methods of logging row data.

> If you do use `tLogRow` for debugging, then remember to either remove it or deactivate the component prior to releasing the code to test.

There's more...

The **Vertical** feature with **Print label** is very useful when you have multiple `tLogRow` components in a job. It allows them to be distinguished more easily.

`tLogRow` is a valuable tool for logging and debugging; however, it can really slow down execution when run in the Studio. For larger volumes of log data, consider either:

- Exporting the job and running as a batch process. You can then redirect the log output to a file.
- Use the *Dumping console output to a file from within a job* recipe in this chapter to dump the log information to a file.
- Write the data to a temporary file rather than `tLogRow`.

Using tJavaRow to display row information

Although `tLogRow` is flexible and very useful, it does have some limitations, in that it only prints what is defined in a schema. `tJavaRow` doesn't have the same limitations. This recipe will show you how it can be utilized.

Getting ready

Open the `jo_cook_ch10_0060_tJavaRow` job.

How to do it...

The steps for using tJavaRow to display row information are as follows:

1. Run the job. You will see data in the console output sorted by customer key.
2. Remove the `tLogRow` component, and add a `tJavaRow` component in its place.
3. Open the `tJavaRow` component and add the following code:

```
//Test for change of key and print heading lines if key has
changed
if (Numeric.sequence(input_row.name, 1, 1) == 1){
    System.out.println("\n\n******************* Records for
customer name: "+input_row.name+" **********************");
    System.out.printf("%-20s %-20s %-30s %-3s \n","name","DOB","ti
mestamp","age");
}

// print formatted output fields
System.out.printf("%-20s %-20s %-30s %-3s \n",input_
row.name,TalendDate.formatDate("dd/MM/yyyy",input_row.
dateOfBirth),TalendDate.formatDate("dd/MM/yyyy  HH:mm:ss",input_
row.timestamp),input_row.age+"");
```

4. Run the job, and you will see that the simple list of records is now grouped within headings, as shown in the following screenshot:

```
******************** Records for customer name: Jo Smith **********************
name                 DOB                 timestamp                    age
Jo Smith             27/11/1990          10/01/2012  10:24:54         23
Jo Smith             27/11/1990          10/01/2012  10:24:54         23

******************** Records for customer name: Johnny Smith ******************
name                 DOB                 timestamp                    age
Johnny Smith         27/11/1990          10/01/2012  10:24:54         23
Johnny Smith         27/11/1990          10/01/2012  10:24:54         23

******************** Records for customer name: J Smith ***********************
name                 DOB                 timestamp                    age
J Smith              27/10/2012          10/01/2012  10:24:54         11
J Smith              27/10/2012          10/01/2012  10:24:54         11
J Smith              27/10/2012          10/01/2012  10:24:54         11

******************** Records for customer name: J Jones ***********************
name                 DOB                 timestamp                    age
J Jones              27/11/1980          10/01/2012  10:24:54         33
J Jones              27/11/1980          10/01/2012  10:24:54         33
```

How it works...

`System.out.println()` is the Java function to print a line of text to the console, and is what you will most commonly use when logging using `tJava` (and `tJavaRow`) and `System.out.printf`, which allows a formatted string to be printed.

The `if` statement uses a sequence generated from the name to test whether this record is the first for the name (sequence is 1). If the sequence is 1, then the heading lines are printed.

The data is then formatted and printed for each line.

There's more...

Although it is fairly rare to need `tJavaRow` for logging, it does provide much more flexibility than `tLogRow`. Although it is probably even more of a rarity to produce formatted reports using Talend, the exercise above is a good one for demonstrating the flexibility of `tJavaRow` over other methods.

> If you use tJavaRow within a flow, then make sure that you remember to propagate the data using the **Generate code** option.

Note also that, if you simply want to capture the value of, say a `globalMap` field, you could just add a temporary field to the schema, and then use `tLogRow`, but remember to delete the temporary fields once your testing is over.

Using tJava to display status messages and variables

`tJava` is a very useful component for logging purposes, because it can be used in its own sub job. This enables `tJava` to be used to print job status information at given points in the process. The following recipe demonstrates this.

Getting ready

Open the `jo_cook_ch10_0070_loggingWithtJava` job.

How to do it...

The steps for using tJava to display status messages and variables are as follows:

1. Open `tJava_1` and add the following code:

```
System.out.println("\n\nSearching directory "+context.
cookbookData+"chapter10 for files matching wildcard *jo*\n\n");
```

2. Open `tJava_2` and add the following code:

```
System.out.println("Processing file: "+((String)globalMap.
get("tFileList_1_CURRENT_FILE")));
```

3. Open `tJava_3` and add the following code:

```
System.out.println("\n\nCompleted......"+((Integer)globalMap.
get("tFileList_1_NB_FILE"))+" files found\n\n");
```

How it works...

`tJava_1` and `tJava_3` simply print out process status information (starting process and process end). `tJava_2` however, it is more interesting.

The `tFileList` component uses an **iterator** link to enable the components following it to be executed multiple times. This means `tJava_2` is called once for each file found in the source directory that matches the wildcard expression.

Thus `tJava_2` is used to log information regarding each of the files being processed, which is a very useful piece of log information.

Printing out the context

This recipe here is for completeness rather than because it is in any way complex.

Getting ready

Open the `jo_cook_ch10_0080_tContextDump` job.

How to do it...

The steps for printing out the context are as follows:

1. Open the **Context** tab, and you will see a set of context variables.

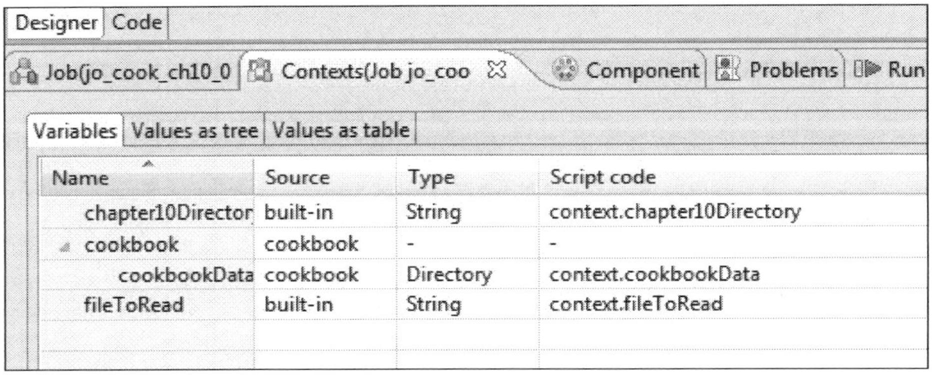

2. Drag a `tContextDump` component from the palette.
3. Attach a `tLogRow` component.
4. Run the job.

How it works...

`tContextDump` simply dumps all the context variables defined within the job into a flow that can then be logged via `tLogRow`.

There's more...

This component is most useful when running code that has been deployed to a server, because the log information is usually stored in a file. This allows us to check the values of the context variables at the time of execution that would otherwise be hidden from us. This is invaluable for debugging a deployed process that has failed.

> Often, contexts contain sensitive information, such as user names and passwords to system resources. If you do not want these to be shown, then ensure that when you dump the data, you tick the **Hide Password** option.

Dumping the console output to a file from within a job

This recipe shows how you can dump all logging data to a file, while still running the job in the Studio. It is particularly useful when debugging large data sets.

Getting ready

Open the `jo_cook_ch10_0090_consoleToFile` job.

How to do it...

The steps for dumping console output to a file from within a job are as follows:

1. Run the job and view the console output.
2. Add the following code to `tJava_1`:

   ```
   // redirect the console output to a file from within studio
   System.setOut(new java.io.PrintStream(new java.
   io.BufferedOutputStream(new java.io.FileOutputStream(context.
   cookbookData+"outputData/chapter10/chapter10_jo_0090_consoleOut.
   txt"))));
   ```

3. Run the job. You will see only the job's start and end messages.
4. Open the file in the cookbook data directory under `output/chapter10` named `chapter10_jo_0090_consoleOut.txt`. You will see that the logging information has been copied to the file, as shown in the following screenshot:

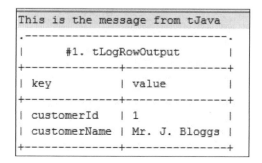

```
This is the message from tJava
.-----------------------------.
|      #1. tLogRowOutput      |
+-------------+---------------+
| key         | value         |
+-------------+---------------+
| customerId  | 1             |
| customerName | Mr. J. Bloggs |
+-------------+---------------+
```

How it works...

When the java statement is added to `tJava_1` it causes virtually everything that is normally written to the console (`System.out.println()`, `tLogRow`) to be directed to a file instead.

There's more...

The benefit of this technique is that debugging large datasets can be performed in the Studio without the massive performance hit of logging to console and without the need to export the job each time you wish to run it.

It also has added benefit over writing logging information via a `fileOutput` component, in that it retains the formatting of `tLogRow`/`tJavaRow` and `tJava` as if it was being output to the console, making the flow of the job logging information easier to understand.

Creating simple test data using tRowGenerator

This recipe shows how `tRowGenerator` allows dummy data to be created for test purposes.

Getting ready

1. Open the `jo_cook_ch10_0100_tRowGenerator` job.
2. Open the `tRowGenerator` component.

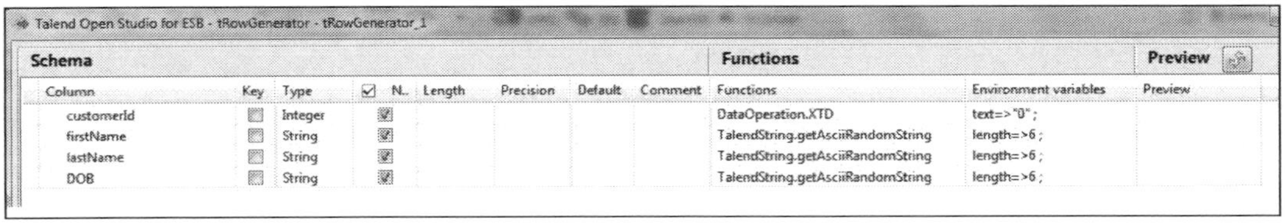

How to do it...

The steps for creating simple test data using tRowGenerator are as follows:

1. Click on the **Functions** cell for **customerId** and select **Numeric.sequence**.
2. Click on the **Functions** cell for **firstName** and select **TalendDataGenerator.getFirstName**.
3. Click on the **Functions** cell for **lastName** and select **TalendDataGenerator.getLastName**.

4. Click on the **Functions** cell for **DOB** and select **TalendDate.getRandomDate**. Your `tRowGenerator` should be as shown in the following screenshot:

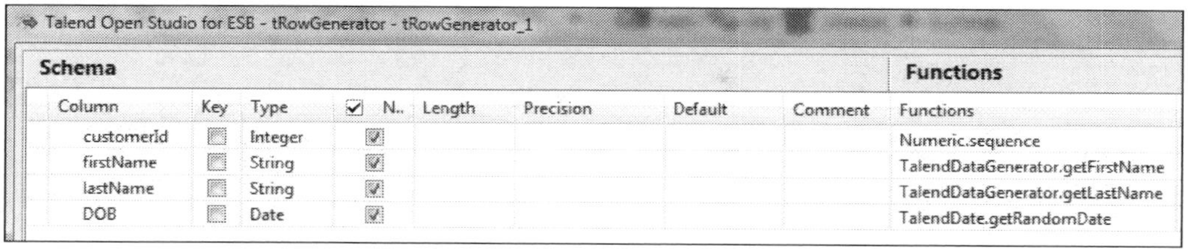

5. Exit the `tRowGenerator` component ,and run the job.

How it works...

Talend provides a set of random generators for different field types to enable test data to be created very easily. So, as you can see, we are using a sequence to create sequential customer key, random first names and last names, and a random date of birth.

There's more...

If you wish to add in a fixed values or Java/Talend method calls, then use the **Functions** option "**...**", that allows you to add in values manually in the bottom section of the screen.

If you have created any custom code routines, you will see that these also appear in the list, along with the Talend-provided data generation routines. It is therefore possible to create your own routines to generate data, such as UK postcodes in the same way as Talend does, and make them available to `tRowGenerator`.

Creating complex test data using tRowGenerator, tFlowToIterate, tMap, and sequences

This recipe shows how a more complex set of test data can be created. In this example, we will build a set of CSV data ready to be loaded into a database which has the following structure:

- Customer has 1 or more orders
- Order has 1 or more order items

Getting ready

1. Open the `jo_cook_ch10_0110_complexTestData` job.
2. You will see a section of code that has been deactivated. Do not activate this code until later in the exercise.
3. Run the job, and you will see that the customer file is created.

How to do it...

The steps for creating complex test data using tRowGenerator, tFlowToIterate, tMap, and sequences are as follows:

1. Activate components `tFixedFlowInput_2`, `tMap_2`, and `tFileOutputDelimited_2`. These are exact copies of the customer create components.
2. Change these newly activated components detailed as follows:
    1. Open `tFixedFlowInput_2` and change **Number of rows** to `Numeric.random(1,5)`.
    2. Open `tMap_2`. Change the name of the variable to `orderId`, and the name of the sequence to order.
    3. Add a new column to the output named `orderId`, and copy the variable `var.orderId` to it.
    4. Delete the **customerName** output column.
    5. In the customer expression field, press *CTRL + SPACE*, and select the `tFlowToIterate` value for `customerId`. It will populate as `((Integer)globalMap.get("row3.customerId"))`.
    6. Change the name of the file in `tFileOutputDelimited` to `context.cookbookData+"outputData/chapter10/chapter10_jo_0110_order.csv"` and tick the **Append** option.
3. Run the job. You will see that the order file has been created with between 1 and 5 orders for each customer.
4. Activate the rest of the components and run the job. You will see that the order item file has been created with between 1 and 5 items per order.

How it works...

The `tFlowToIterate` components and the `Numeric.sequence` commands are the key to this method. The `tFlowToIterate` component allows us to cascade the key information down from the highest level (customer) to the lowest level (order item), and the uniquely named sequences enable us to generate unique keys for each type (customer, order, order item).

The `Numeric.random` commands are also useful, in that they make the data "interesting". It allows us to generate a random number of orders per customer and items per order.

Note also the use of the lookup and the random function again to assign products to each item randomly. This is described in more detail in the next exercise.

Also note the deletes at the beginning. They have been set to delete the created files prior to execution, and you may also notice that they are set to never fail. The former is due to the fact that we are appending to the order and order item files; failure to do this will result in continually growing files. The latter ensures that when we first run the job, it does not fail because the files aren't found in the directory, which they will not be.

There's more...

Using all the test data generation techniques detailed in this chapter, it is possible to create varied but referentially accurate data, which will provide a platform for testing of Talend jobs.

It is also possible to use these as a basis for generating Excel files that can then be hand-cranked with additional data to make the tests even more realistic.

> Warning: This method uses random values to create data, so will probably never create the same data twice. Once you are happy with a test data set, then copy it to another directory to avoid it being overwritten. If you want repeatable tests, then use actual numbers rather than random numbers.

Creating random test data using lookups

This simple technique shows how we can randomly assign values using lookups.

Getting ready

Open the `jo_cook_ch10_0120_randomTestDataLookups` job.

How to do it...

The steps for creating random test data using lookups are as follows:

1. Open `tMap`.
2. Open the `tMap` settings for the `productData` input flow.
3. Change the **Match Model** to **First Match**.
4. For the **Expr. key** for **productData**, add the code:

   ```
   Numeric.random(1,15)
   ```

5. Drag all columns from both inputs to the output.
6. Your `tMap` should now look like this:

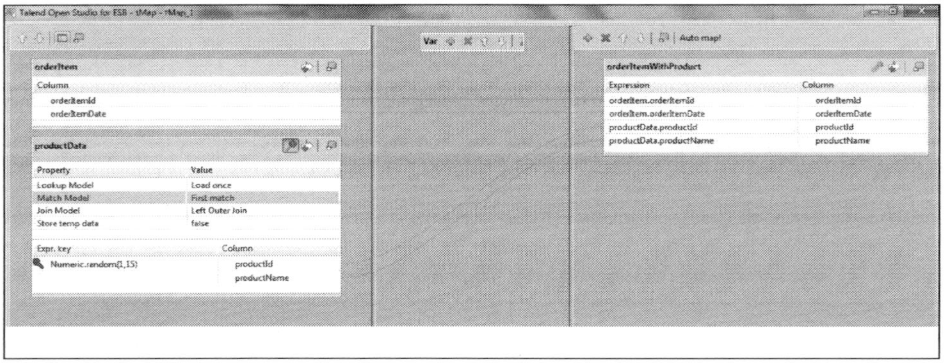

7. Exit `tMap` and run the job.

How it works...

As you will see from the output, the job will add a random product ID and product description to each order item row.

The match model of **First Match** ensures that only one match is returned for each order item line.

The `Numeric.random(1,15)` function returns a value from 1 through to 15, which is the number of products in the products list CSV file.

Thus the process will generate a random number for each order line and then use this random number as a key to look up against the product list and assign a product to the order line.

There's more...

Although the data in the previous example is technically correct, it is fairly uninteresting, because there is no deviation in the products held in the order item. This technique can be used to enhance the data further to ensure that a more realistic test set is created. This is because it uses genuine data but in a random manner, which is usually more reflective of actual order data. It is possible to use one `tMap` to reference many lookups, so a fairly small job can create rich and realistic data rows for testing.

> Be aware, though, that random data cannot be reproduced. Thus, it is usually wise to only run this job once during testing and store the results in tables or files that will be copied into the tables you will be using for the tests. This ensures that the tests are repeatable.

Creating test data using Excel

Another useful method of creating test data is to define the data in MS Excel, and then create a job to convert the Excel worksheets into the format required by the application, such as a CSV file or database table.

Getting ready

Open the Excel workbook `chapter10_jo_0130_ExcelTestData.xlsx` that can be found in the data directory. You will see two worksheets: customer and item.

How to do it...

The steps for creating test data using Excel are as follows:

1. Highlight the first two rows in the customer table and drag them down to create two more customers.
2. Copy the first 4 lines from the order workbook and change the customers to be 3 for the first two new rows and 4 for the final two. Ensure that order ids are contiguous.
3. Open the `jo_cook_ch10_0130_excelTestDataLoad` job. You will see that the customer Excel file is being copied to an equivalent XML file.

4. Drag the order Excel object from the repository location, shown as follows:

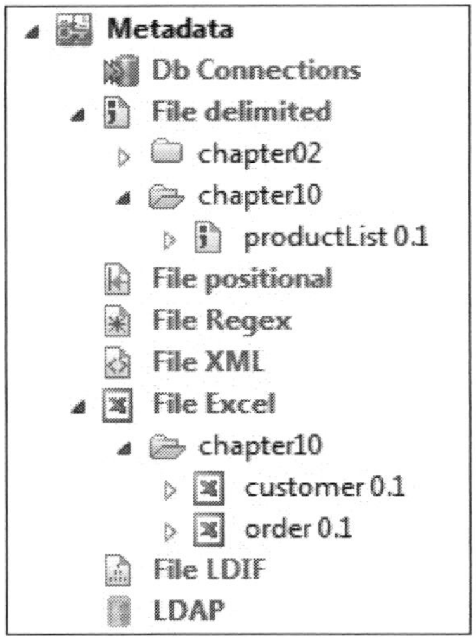

5. Drag a `tXMLOutput` component and link it to `tFileInputExcel`.
6. Open `tFileOutputXML` and change the **File Name** to `context.cookbookData+"/outputData/chapter10/order.xml"`.
7. Change the **Row Tag to** order.
8. Create an `onSubjobOk` link from the customer Excel to the order Excel components.
9. Run the job. You will see that the two XML files have been populated.

How it works...

This exercise shows how MS Excel can be used to create test data quickly. Because Talend is able to read MS Excel files directly, our test data created in the Excel spreadsheet can be transformed into any other format, such as a CSV file, a database table, or an XML file that can be consumed by a downstream process.

In this example, the inputs to our process to be tested are a customer XML file and an order XML.

There's more...

This is a great technique for creating test data, because Excel allows columns of data to be viewed, created and managed much more easily than say a set of XML files.

This technique is usually popular with testers, because they are usually very familiar and productive with Excel.

Testing logic – the most-used pattern

This is probably the most-used job design in Talend programming, and is used to ensure that a snippet of new code is not influenced by external factors within a large and complex job. This simple recipe shows how this can easily be achieved.

Getting ready

Open the `jo_cook_ch10_0140_logicTest` job.

How to do it...

The steps for testing logic are as follows:

1. In **tFixedFlowInput,** tick the box labeled **Use Inline Table**.
2. Add the values, as shown in the following screenshot:

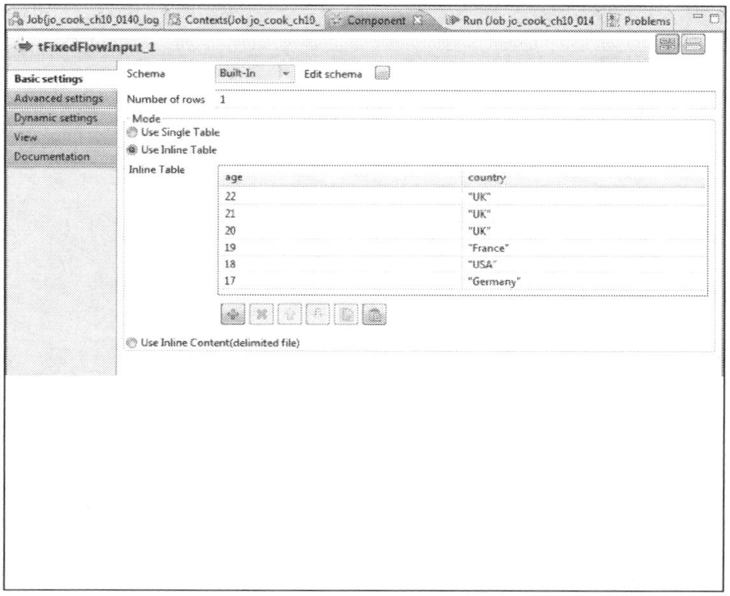

3. In the tMap, add a new field to the output named ageCheckValid, and populate it with the following code:

```
customer.age >= 21 && customer.country.equals("UK") ? true :
customer.age >= 18 && !customer.country.equals("UK") ? true : false
```

4. Run the job to see the results of the test.

How it works...

In this example, we are testing an age limit; 21 or over is valid for the UK, 18 or over valid for the rest of the world.

In `tFixedFlowInput`, we defined a set of test values that would prove that the logic test in `tMap` is working correctly.

The `tLogRow` component then allows us to see the inputs and corresponding results.

There's more...

This example is great for testing new rules, and especially for testing new code routines prior to adding to a complex job. It is quick to create, and the `tFixedFlowInput` component allows us to build a controlled set of test data that should test all return values, thus giving us confidence in the correctness of the new code or code routine.

Killing a job from within tJavaRow

Most jobs at some point require validation and will often need to be stopped if the data is found to be in error. In most cases, you can use `tDie`, however, if your error is found in a `tJavaRow` or `tJava`, then using `tDie` becomes quite convoluted. This exercise shows how the same results can be achieved using simple Java functionality.

Getting ready

Open the `jo_cook_ch10_0150_killingJobtJavaRow` job.

How to do it...

The steps for killing a job from within tJavaRow are as follows:

1. Run the job. You will see that it fails with a null pointer exception.
2. Change the line `output_row.age = input_row.age;` to the following code:

```
if (input.age == null) {
  System.out.println("Fatal Error: age is null");
  System.exit(99);
} else {
  output_row.age = input_row.age;
}
```

3. Run the job again. You will see that the job has been killed in a much more elegant fashion, as shown in the following screenshot:

```
Starting job
jo_cook_ch10_0150_killingJobtJavaRowCompleted at 22:
29/04/2013.


[statistics] connecting to socket on port 4047
[statistics] connected
Fatal Error: age is null
Job jo_cook_ch10_0150_killingJobtJavaRowCompleted
ended at 22:51 29/04/2013. [exit code=99]
```

How it works...

`System.exit` is a Java kill command and as such will cause an immediate exit from the Talend code. The value of `99` is the user-defined return code for the process.

11
Deploying and Scheduling Talend Code

In this chapter we will cover the following recipes:

- Creating compiled executables
- Using a different context
- Adding command line context parameters
- Managing job dependencies
- Capturing and acting on different return codes
- Returning codes from a child job without tDie
- Passing parameters to a child job
- Executing non-Talend objects and operating system commands

Introduction

Now, we are really down to the business end of using Talend Open Studio. All the coding techniques described in all the other chapters count for nothing if we cannot execute the jobs we create in the real world on real data.

So, this chapter shows the methods used to deploy and schedule your Talend code once you have fully coded and tested it.

This, chapter covers two main topics required to execute our Talend jobs in real-world environments; how to generate executable code that can be used within a scheduling tool or script, and how to create schedules within Talend if we wish to use Talend for scheduling.

Whichever method you choose, Talend can easily call or be called by a variety of other tools.

But first, there are a few points of note that you should read before continuing on to the recipes.

Context Variables

Some of these exercises will make reference to the context variables. It is recommended that you first complete *Chapter 6, Managing Context Variables* prior to tackling these exercises. There is also a detailed discussion on managing contexts in *Appendix B, Management of Contexts*.

Executable code

The code generated by Talend Open Studio is fully functional Java code that can be deployed as an executable jar file, the same as any other Java code.

This means that the code, once compiled, can be called via a command line, which means that it can be scheduled, just like any other Java code via any normal scheduling method, such as an enterprise scheduling tool, Quartz, cron, or Windows scheduler. It is even possible to write scheduling scripts via Linux bash scripts or Windows PowerShell.

Because Talend code is compiled into JAR files, pretty much any scheduler will be able to execute a Talend object within a schedule.

Managing job dependencies within Talend

If you choose to, it is also possible to manage complex job dependencies within Talend Open Studio, because it is possible to build a job that can call one or many other jobs. Along with a variety of trigger possibilities, it is possible to create complex sequences and dependencies.

You should be aware, however, that it can become quite complex, and additional work may be required to implement features that would be out of the box for a normal scheduling system. A good example of this would be restartability of a schedule should it fail in the middle. This feature can be added to Talend, but is given for most scheduling tools.

Creating compiled executables

This recipe shows how we create compiled code from the job we have created. First, we will export the code into a compiled executable, and then we will execute it via the command line.

How to do it...

1. Open the folder `chapter11` in the metadata repository.
2. Right-click on the job `jo_cook_ch10_0010_helloWorld`, and select the option to **Export Job**.

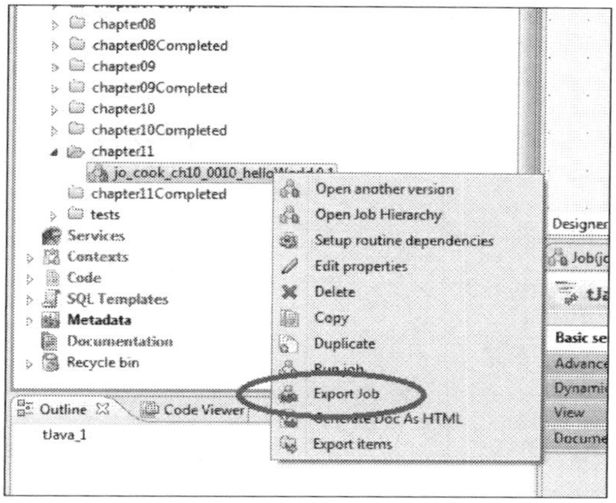

3. Click on **Browse** to navigate to the folder `compiledCode` within the cookbook directory.
4. Ensure the **Export type** is **Autonomous Job**, and tick **Extract the zip file**.
5. In the options tick **Shell launcher** and **Context Scripts**, and tick **Apply Context to children Jobs**.
6. Your dialog should look like the one in the next screenshot:

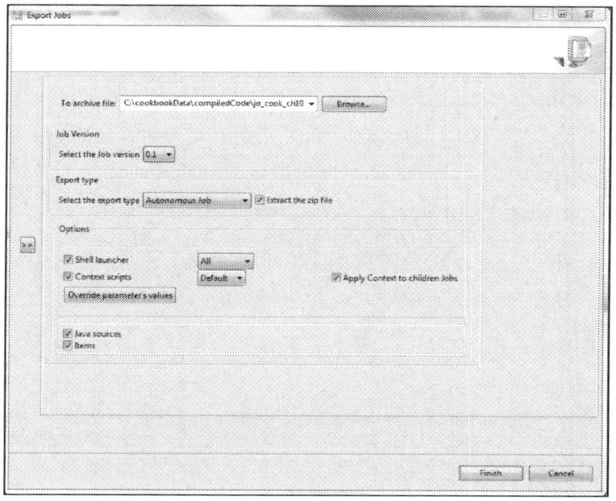

7. Click on **Finish** to compile the job.
8. Navigate to the `compiledCode` folder, and you will see a zip file and a directory for the compiled job.

   Executing the job

9. Open a command window within Windows or a shell window in Linux.
10. Navigate to the cookbook `compiledCode\jo_cook_ch10_0010_helloWorld` directory, and execute the `.bat` file for Windows or the `.sh` file for Linux.
11. The output will contain the words **Hello World** as expected.

How it works...

The export dialog exports the Talend job as a ZIP file that contains everything required to execute the Talend job.

Because we chose to unzip the ZIP file, and to create scripts and launchers, Talend unpacks the ZIP file into a directory and creates the job launcher scripts for the environment to enable us to run the Talend jobs easily manually.

Using a different context

If you have decided to use multiple contexts as a means of defining your runtime properties, then they can be selected at runtime using the following method.

Getting ready

Export the job `jo_cook_ch11_0020_differentContext`, as shown in the previous recipe.

How to do it...

1. Open a command window, navigate to the job directory, and execute the shell launcher for your environment (see previous exercise).
2. You will see that the output contains the text **Value = ABC**.
3. Open the shell launcher, and scroll to the very end of the command line.
4. Change the context from `--context=development` to `-context=test` as shown in the next screenshot:

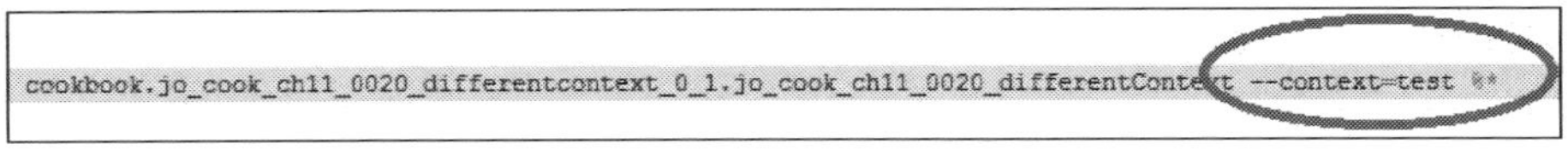

cookbook.jo_cook_ch11_0020_differentcontext_0_1.jo_cook_ch11_0020_differentContext --context=test

5. Save the change, and then rerun the shell launcher.
6. You will see that the output contains the text **Value = DEF**.

How it works...

The launcher file contains the command line used to execute the Talend job, one of whose parameters is the context being used by the job.

By setting the context variable to point to a different context, then the job will run using the different variables defined for that context.

There's more...

In addition to being able to select a different context, the context files can be amended in situ, thus allowing parameters to be changed within the deployed environment.

These files can be found in the directories below the main `compiledCode` folder. It is best to perform a search for `.properties` to find the files.

This is a reasonably good way of protecting an environment, because the context variables and launchers in production are usually available only to operational personnel, so the values available to a job in production, for example, passwords, can be set in production by operation staff, and will never be known by other personnel.

> Great care must be taken when using this method to ensure that after the first deployment of the context variables and launchers in production, that they are not accidentally copied over when deploying a new version, or that the support staff remember to update them if the new version of the code is copied to different folder.

Adding command-line context parameters

Often, it is required that one or more parameters are passed at runtime to a process to affect its behavior, such as a schedule identifier, or for instance, if the process is common for many different sources, a file identifier. This recipe shows how parameters can be passed into a job via the command line.

Getting ready

Export the job `jo_cook_ch11_0030_differentContextVariable`.

How to do it...

1. Run the exported job.
2. You will see the output contains **Hello World**.
3. Open the launcher.
4. Scroll to the end of the line, and add the line `--context_param name=Dave`.
5. Run the job again. You will see that the output now contains **Hello Dave**.

How it works...

Adding the new value to the command line instructs Talend to override any value that has been set within the job context, regardless of the environment.

There's more...

> You can add as many parameters to the command line as there are in your context simply by appending them to the end of the command line, one after the other. Remember, though, to use the exact name that is used in the context.

This method is great for creating utility jobs that can be called via the command line. This can be achieved by wrapping the launcher in another `.bat/.sh` file, and mapping the calling parameters to context parameters.

Managing job dependencies

This recipe shows how simple, serial job dependencies can be managed using Talend.

Getting ready

Open the job `jo_cook_ch11_0040_simpleSchedule`.

How to do it...

1. Drag the job `jo_cook_ch11_0040_task1` onto the canvas.
2. Drag the job `jo_cook_ch11_0040_task2` onto the canvas, and link from task 1 using an **OnSubjobOk** trigger link.

3. Drag the job `jo_cook_ch11_0040_task3` onto the canvas, and link from task 1 using an **OnSubjobOk** trigger link.
4. Your job should now look like the one in the next screenshot below:

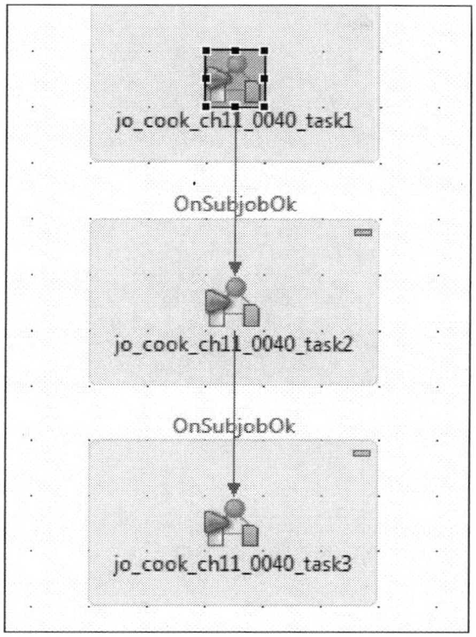

5. Run the job to see the output of the three tasks.

How it works...

Dragging each of the jobs onto the canvas automatically creates a `tRunjob` component.

Each `tRunjob` is a subjob in its own right, so testing for **onSubjobOk** will result in the jobs executing serially, assuming that they all run without error.

There's more...

The following are some additional points to be noted regarding job dependencies.

Die on error

The `tRunJob` components will die if an error occurs, because they are by default set to **Die on error**.

If you wish to allow jobs to fail, but the schedule to continue, then uncheck the **Die on child error** boxes for each of the `tRunJob` components.

Adding error checks to the schedule

If you wish to perform an error-check process, should one of the process fail, then ensure that **Die on child error** is unchecked, and then add an **OnSubJobError** trigger link from the child job to the error job.

Restartability

If you wish to add restartability to your job, then it is necessary to hold the runtime status of each step of a job in a persistent store, and add a status test to each step of the schedule before processing.

The status test can be performed using an **If** trigger, which is demonstrated in the next exercise.

Capturing and acting on different return codes

This recipe shows how we can use the return codes from a child job to control the process flow in a schedule more effectively.

Getting ready

Open the job `jo_cook_ch11_0050_ChildReturnCodes`. You will see that it is a simpler version of the job from the previous exercise.

How to do it...

We will begin by printing the return code from a child job.

Printing return code

1. Add a `tJava` component with the following code:

```
System.out.println("Return code is: "+((Integer)
  globalMap.get("tRunJob_1_CHILD_RETURN_CODE")));
```

2. Link from the task to the `tJava` component using **OnSubjobOk**.
3. Run the job—you will see that the return code is `0`.

Setting the return code

4. Double-click on the child job to open it.
5. Add a `tDie` component, and link it to the `tJava` component using **OnSubjobOk**.
6. Open the `tDie` component, and change the code to `4` . Now return to the calling (parent) job.

7. Open the component tab for the task, and untick **Die on error**.
8. Run the job—you will see that the return code is `4`.

Routing using the return code

9. Add the jobs `jo_cook_ch11_0050_task2` and `jo_cook_ch11_0050_errorHandler` to the canvas.
10. Right-click on the `tJava` component, and select **Trigger**, then select **Run If**.
11. Join it to task 2.
12. Repeat for the `errorHandler` task, as shown in the next screenshot:

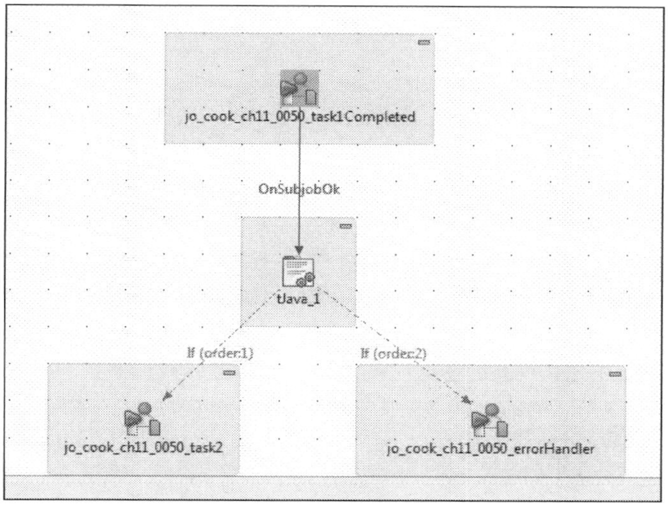

13. Click on the task 2 **If** link, and in the **Component** tab, add the the code `((Integer) globalMap.get("tRunJob_1_CHILD_RETURN_CODE")).equals(0)`, as shown in the next screenshot:

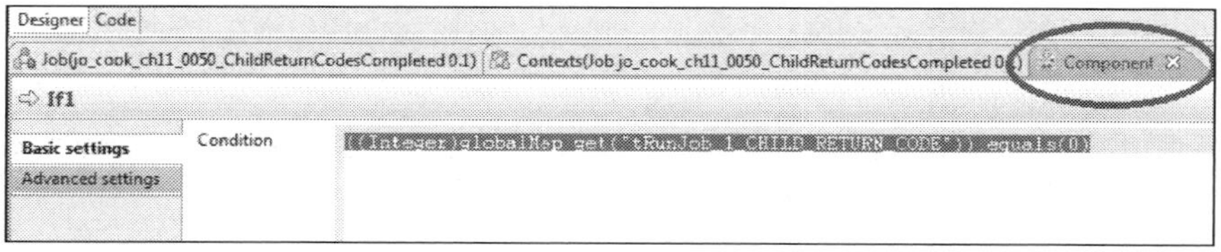

14. Repeat for the `errorHandler` if link, but this time, check for value of 4.
15. Run the job, and you will see that the error handler child job is executed.

How it works...

In the child job, we can change the return code by using a `tDie` component.

It is then necessary to ensure that the parent job does not die on error, otherwise the job will terminate immediately, and we won't be able to test the return codes.

In the parent, we then use an **If** Trigger for a return code of 0, and an **If** trigger for a return code of 4 to route the schedule to the appropriate next stage.

There's more...

This method relies on the use of `tDie` components, meaning that this method can only be used when the child job fails.

To return codes without killing the job, see the next section, *Returning codes from a child job without tDie*.

Returning codes from a child job without tDie

In this recipe we will show how return codes can be set in a child job and used in a parent, without having to kill the child process.

Getting ready

Open the job `jo_cook_ch11_0060_childReturnCodesNoDie`. This job is the end state of the previous recipe.

How to do it...

The first thing we need to do is add the return code value to a buffer for the parent job to pick up.

Buffering the return code

1. Open `task_1` and replace the `tDie` component with a `tFixedFlowInput` component.
2. Add an `Integer` column to the `tFixedFlowInput` component called `returnCode`.
3. Set the value to `4`.
4. Add a `tBufferOutput` component and add a flow from the `tFixedFlowInput` component to it.

Capturing and storing the return code in the parent

5. Return to the parent job.
6. Add a `tJavaRow` component to the job.
7. Create a flow from the `tRunJob` component for task 1 to the `tJavaRow` component.
8. Open the `tRunJob` component, and click on **Copy Child JobSchema**, as shown in the next screenshot:

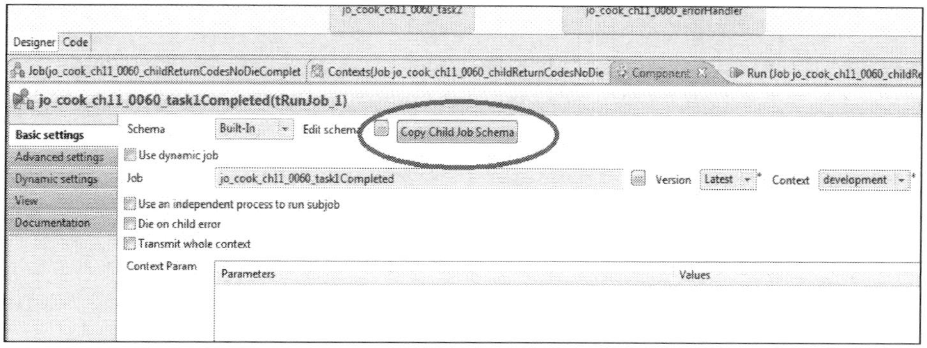

9. Open the `tJavaRow` component, and insert the following code:

```
globalMap.put("returnCode", input_row.returnCode);
```

10. Change the the `tJava` component and the two **If** links to use `returnCode` instead of `tRunJob_1_CHILD_RETURN_CODE`.
11. Run the job.

How it works...

The `tBufferOut` component is used to transmit data from a child job to a parent, and we can easily access the schema of the child job (as set in the `tBufferOut` component) using the **Copy Child Job Schema** option in the `tRunJob` component.

When the parent picks up the code, it stores it in a `globalMap` variable for use by the **If** conditions.

There's more...

Even though this method takes slightly more effort, it does mean that we aren't forced to kill a child job to return a non-zero return code, which does make it more flexible.

This method has the benefit of allowing us to return warning messages or even to return codes that will allow us to process different legs of a schedule, depending upon the returned value.

Passing parameters to a child job

In this recipe, we will show how parameters can be passed to a common child job.

Getting ready

Open the job `jo_cook_ch11_0070_childParameters`. This job simply executes a child job. If you examine the child job, you will see that it prints the value of the context parameter `inputParameter`.

How to do it...

1. Run the parent job.
2. You will see that the value for `inputParameter` is `fromChild`.
3. Open the `tRun` component tab, and click on **+** to add a **Context Param** option.
4. Untick **Transmit whole context**.
5. Select `inputParameter` in the **Parameters** column, and set the **Value** `to fromParent`, as shown in the next screenshot:

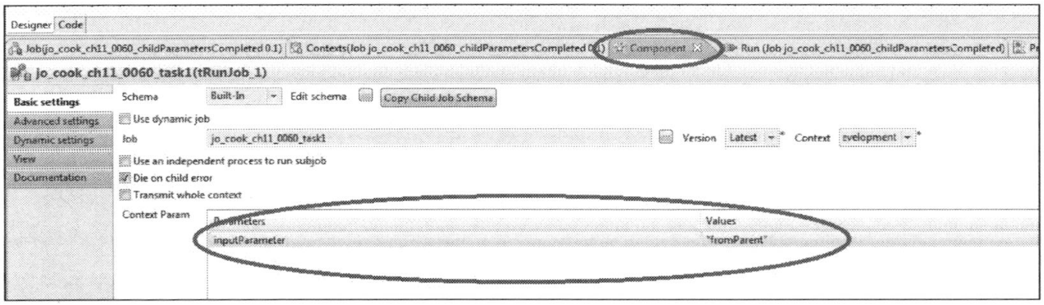

6. Run the job, and you will see that the value for `inputParameter` has changed to `fromParent`.

How it works...

All context variables defined for a child process are made available to a calling parent job via the `tRunJob` component, as we saw previously.

There's more

In this exercise, we chose to send selected context variables to the child. This is generally a good practice because it forces us to think about what data we wish to communicate from parent to child. That said, if there are many context variables, this method becomes unwieldy, or if we wish to send them all, then we can use the option **Transmit whole context**.

Executing non-Talend objects and operating system commands

Often, when running a schedule, it is necessary to execute a mixture of Talend and non-Talend objects, such as database scripts, batch files, or shell scripts. This exercise shows how this is easily achieved using Talend.

> Note that this exercise is for Windows only.

Getting ready

Open the job `jo_cook_ch11_0080_systemCalls`.

How to do it...

1. Drag a `tSystem` component onto the canvas.
2. Set the Command to the following:

```
"cmd /c"+context.cookbookData+"/batchFiles
  /jo_cook_ch11_0080_batchFile.bat"
```

3. Add a `tJava` component, and add the following code:

```
System.out.println("Return code"+
  ((Integer)globalMap.get("tSystem_1_EXIT_VALUE")));
```

4. Link the two components using and `onSubjobOk` trigger and then run the job.

How it works...

The `tSystem` component sends a call to the operating system to execute a native command. In our case, the command is to execute a `.bat` file that we have coded.

When the `.bat` file completes, the return code can be accessed using the `EXIT_VALUE` global map variable.

There's more...

Although this exercise is for Windows, the same principle applies for Linux. The only difference being that `cmd /c` is not required on the command line.

12

Common Mistakes and Other Useful Hints and Tips

This chapter contains a collection of useful tips and information that should help resolve some common issues and answer some common questions.

- My tab is missing
- Finding code routine
- Finding a new context variable
- Missing reload at each row global variable
- Dragging component globalMap variables
- Some complex date formats
- Capturing tMap rejects
- Adding job name, project name, and other job-specific information
- Printing tMap variables
- Stopping memory errors in Talend

Introduction

This chapter is unlike any of the other chapters, because it doesn't contain a set of exercises, rather it is a collection of useful information and techniques that don't really fit into the earlier chapters.

It is impossible to include everything that is missing from the previous chapters, so we have tried to incorporate hints and tips that we believe will prove most useful.

My tab is missing

If you find that, say, your `Run` job or context tab has gone missing, perhaps as a result of you accidentally closing them, then there are two options for getting them back.

How to do it...

The first option will restore a tab, the second will reset your whole UI.

Show view:

This method allows you to simply restore a missing tab.

1. In `show view` method, Click on **Window** then click on **Show view**.

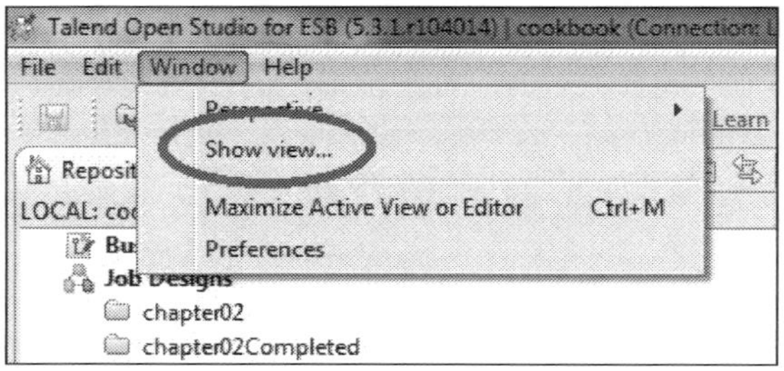

2. Open the `Talend` folder if it isn't already open then click on the tab that you are missing.

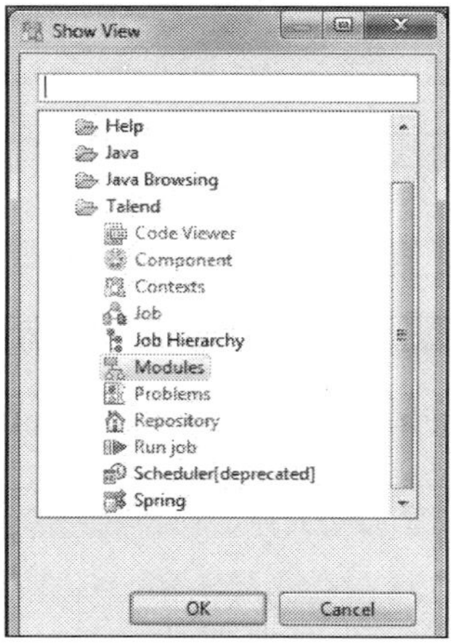

Reset the perspective

This option allows you to reset the UI to its original format, so is more disruptive than the previous method.

1. In reset the perspective method, at the top right-hand side of the Studio is a list of perspectives.
2. Click the **integration perspective** option.
3. Right-click then click, on **Reset**, as shown in the next screenshot:

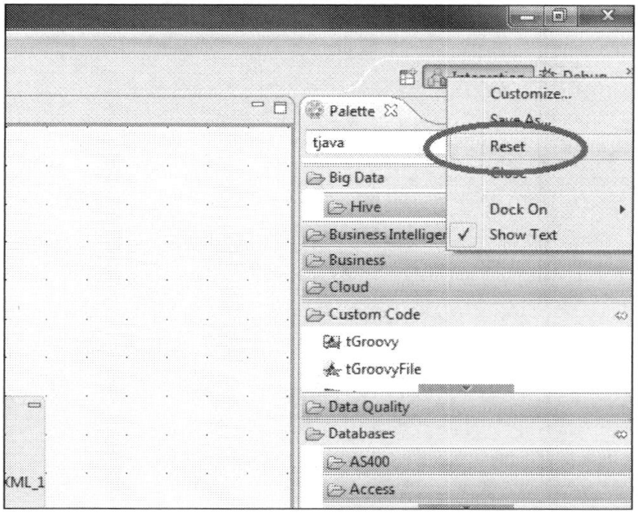

4. Click on **OK** on the dialog and your whole **Integration** view will be reset to the default, which will return your missing tabs.

Finding the code routine

Occasionally, when you call a Talend function or a function that you have created in a code routine, you will receive a compilation error message about your routine, such as: **myRoutines cannot be resolved**.

This is usually because the link between the code routine and the job has been lost. This can easily be re-established.

How to do it...

1. Close the job on which you are working.

2. Right-click the job in the **Repository** panel, and click **Setup routine dependencies**.

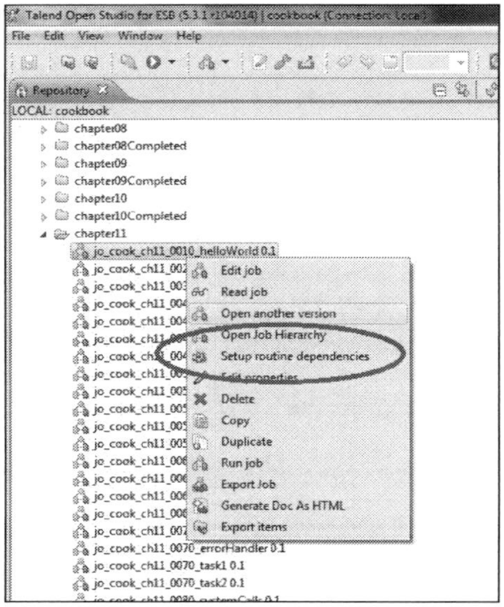

3. You should find that your routine is missing from the list that is displayed in the following dialogue. (Note we do not have any attached routines here).

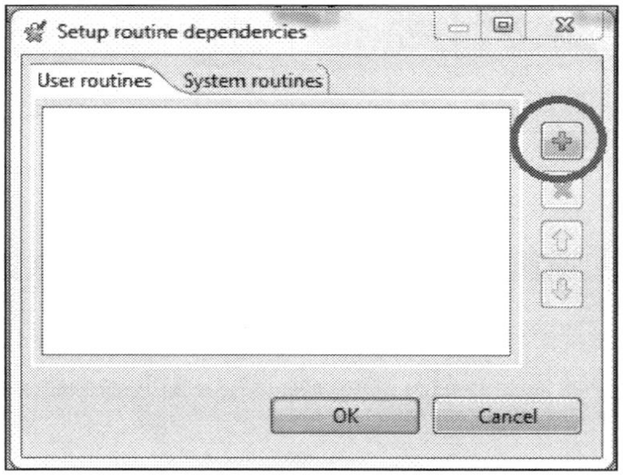

4. Click on **+,** then select your routine from the list that is then displayed. You should then see your routine in the User routines tab.

Finding a new context variable

If you add a new variable to a context group in the Repository while you have a job open (which is a normal thing to do), then Talend will not automatically add it to your job.

This means that when you run your job, expecting your new context variable to be present, you will get a compile error.

How to do it...

1. Open the context tab in your job.
2. Click the group you have just changed, then the  button.
3. You will see that the tick box is a blob, not a tick.
4. If you expand the context, you will see your new variable, but it will not be ticked.
5. Tick your variable to include it in your job, and exit the context tab.

Reloads going missing at each row global variable

When using reload at each row with **globalMap Key** (as seen in the next screenshot), Talend allows you to cut and paste expressions into the `globalMap` variable, but when you go out of the `tMap` component and come back in again, you will see that it hasn't changed.

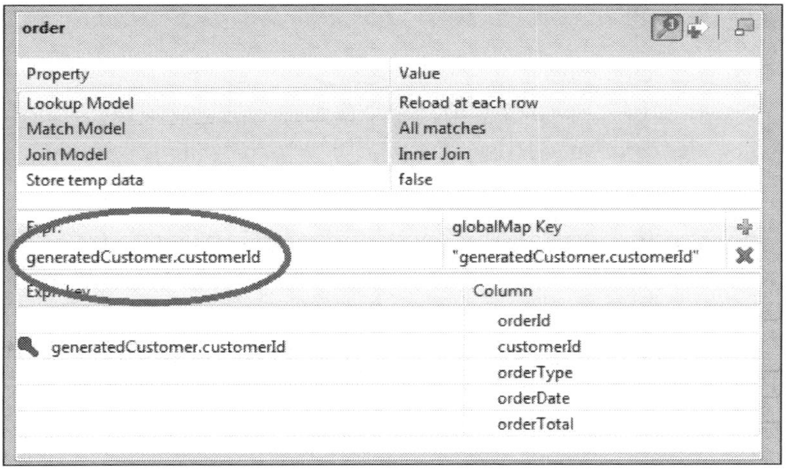

How to do it...

To get around this, you have one of two options:

1. Drag the field from an input source. This option is limited, in that the expression will be just the field name, so you cannot apply any other logic to the variable, such as substring or uppercase.
2. The second (and preferred option) is to edit the expression in the **Expression editor** tab. This method allows any expression to be coded to ensure that the variable is set correctly, as shown in the next screenshot:

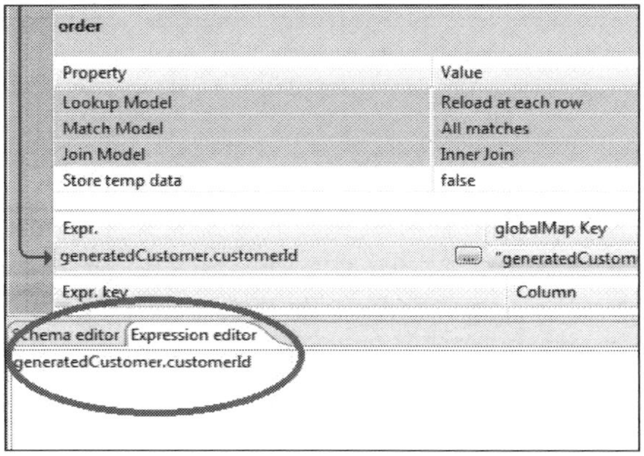

Dragging component globalMap variables

All components produce one or more `globalMap` variables that can be used within other components, such as `tJavaRow`.

If you do have lots of components, then using *Ctrl* + *Space* to locate your specific `globalMap` variable may be difficult.

A simpler method is to open the component tab for the component, ensuring that it is in panel mode, and that you can see the outline view in the bottom right-hand side of the studio.

You can then simply expand the given component and drag the variables from the outline panel into your code panel, as shown in the next screenshot:

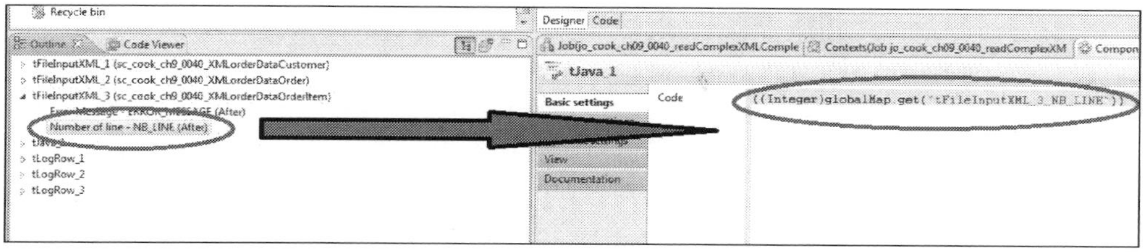

Some complex date formats

Java provides a wide range of date options that can be used to define date formats, but sometimes the options to choose for a particular date time string aren't immediately obvious.

Some date formats that may prove useful are as follows:

- **ISO 8601 with offset standard**: This format contains date, time, and the offset from UTC, as well as the `T` character that designates the start of the time, for example, `2007-04-05T12:30:22-02:00`.

  The pattern for this date and time format is `yyyy-MM-dd'T'HH:mm:ssXXX`.

- **Mtime pattern**: The `tFileProperties` component returns a field named `mtime_string` that is a string representation of a date and time format, for example, `Wed Mar 13 23:53:07 GMT 2013`.

  The pattern for this date and time format is `EEE MMM dd HH:mm:ss z yyyy`.

Capturing tMap rejects

The `tMap` component is the most powerful and flexible of the Talend components, but unless you know where to look, some of the options available aren't immediately obvious. Take for example, the **Die on error** flag.

For most components, this is in the main component panel, but for `tMap`, it is in the `tMap` configurations dialog, as shown in the next screenshot:

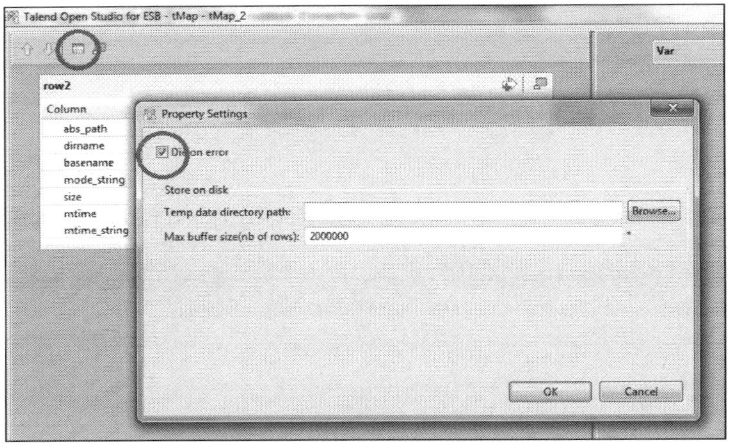

Unchecking the **Die on error** box will create a new output error flow called `ErrorReject`, containing a message and a stack trace. Additional fields may be added if required, as shown in the next screenshot:

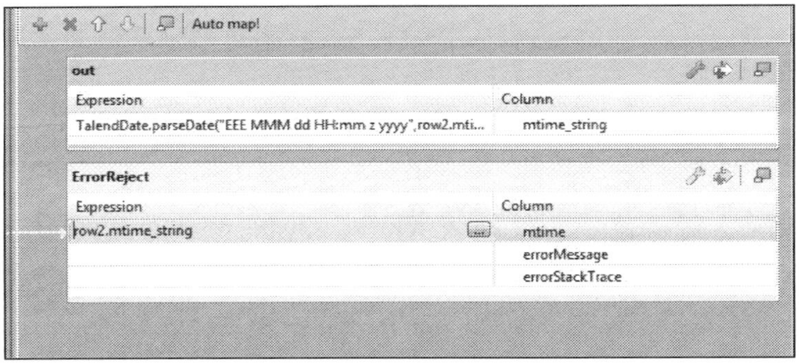

Adding job name, project name, and other job specific information

Often, for logging or error messaging purposes it is required to capture information about the job, such as the job name or the project name.

Three common values that can be used in a job are shown in the following table:

Job version	`jobVersion`
Job name	`jobName`
Talend project name	`projectName`

Talend also stores a host of other variables, such as parent and child process IDs that can be easily found by opening an empty job and inspecting the Java code.

Printing tMap variables

If you inspect code generated from a `tMap` variable, you will see that each of the expressions are converted into a line of the following format:`output column = expression;`.

This suggests that the expression is limited to one line of Java code.

Although this is how we would normally treat `tMap` expressions (in order to avoid confusion), this isn't strictly true, and there is one scenario where breaking this rule may be useful.

The scenario in question relates to `tMap` variables. If a `tMap` variable fails due to an exception in a variable expression that is itself a result of a variable expression, then the job can become quite difficult to debug.

To make it easier to see what is happening in each step, we can add a `System.out.println` code to an expression to print the state prior to execution of the failing step.

In this case, we simply force the expression logic in the generated code to become: `output column = expression; System.out.println(output column);`

This is how it looks in the expression editor in Talend:

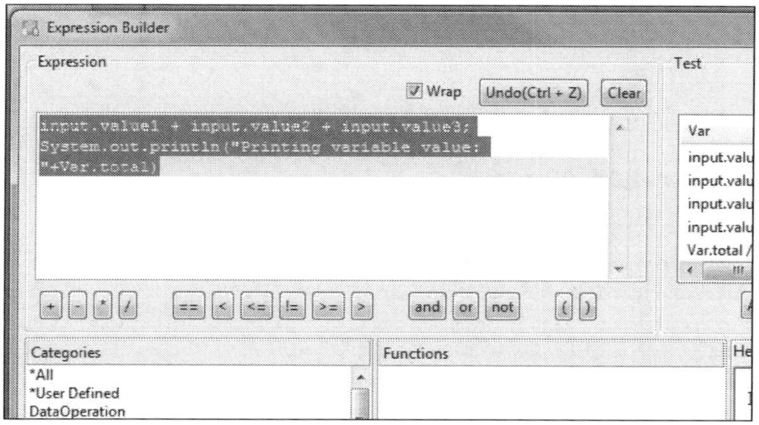

Stopping memory errors in Talend

When dealing with large amounts of data, there is often a trade-off between performance and memory usage, so it is likely that at some point in your Talend career, you will encounter a problem which is memory related.

This section will cover many of the actions that can be taken to ensure that you are able to deal with your memory errors quickly and efficiently.

Increasing the memory allocated to a job

If you have enough memory and yet your job is failing, then it is worth increasing the amount of memory available to the job you are running. You can do this by changing the value of the Java `Xmx` setting.

This setting is available via the **Advanced Settings** option from the **Run** tab, as shown in the next screenshot. Simply tick the box for **Use specific JVM arguments,** and change the value to suit your needs. Note that you can use `g` for gigabytes, for example, `-Xmx3g`.

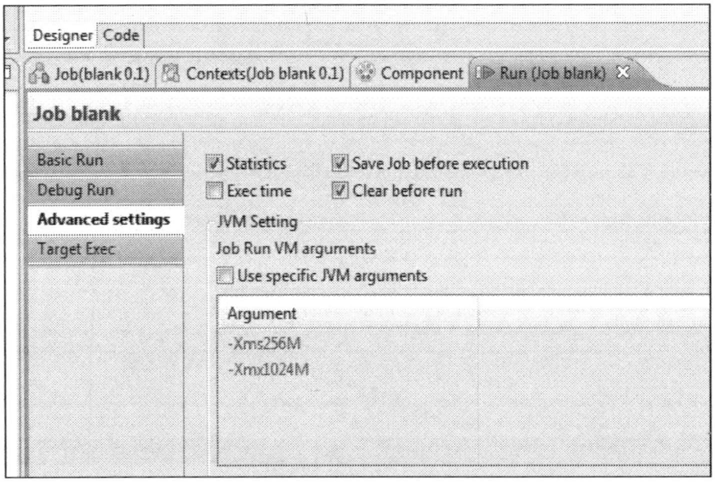

Reducing lookup data

The `tMap` lookup data is by default stored in memory, so large lookups will consume large amounts of memory. Wherever possible, ensure the following:

- You only keep columns in a lookup that you need within the `tMap`. Drop all other columns prior to the `tMap`.

- You only keep rows that you need; filter out any extraneous or duplicate rows prior to the `tMap`.

This should be best practice for any lookup, regardless of size, but for large lookups the removal of just a couple of columns for every row can sometimes reduce the memory requirement significantly.

Using hashMap/in-memory tables

If you need to read the same lookup data multiple times in a job, then it is wise to load only one copy of the data into either a `tHashOutput` component or an in-memory table at the start of the job, and then read the lookups directly from the in-memory constructs.

This technique will also ensure that your job start-up time is lower, since there will be no requirement to load multiple versions of the same data from a file or a database.

Splitting the job

You may also consider splitting the job into multiple jobs, assuming that the process can be split. This enables the memory to be freed at the end of each job, meaning that each individual job can have access to the whole of the memory available.

Be aware that this method will require one or more temporary tables to be created to hold the data between jobs.

Dropping data to disk

1. The `tMap` does allow the option to dump lookup data to disk. This method is useful when you have one or more large lookups that take up more memory than the input data would. First, you need to define the properties for the files. The `tMap` configurations options allow you to define a folder and the size of the temporary files that will be stored, as shown in the next screenshot:

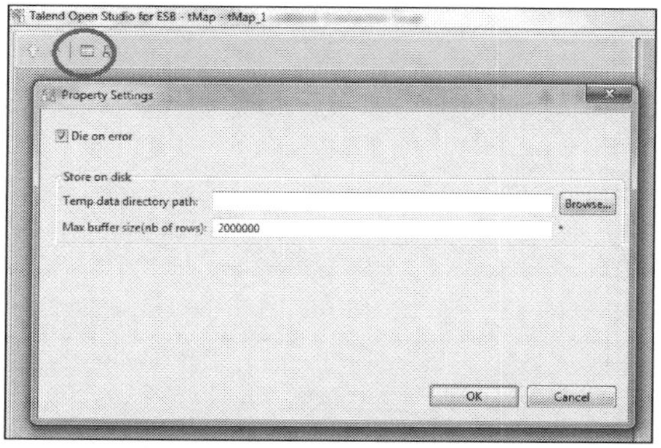

2. Note that if you choose not to do this, Talend will write to a default folder.
3. Next, select the lookups that you wish to drop to disk, as shown in the next screenshot:

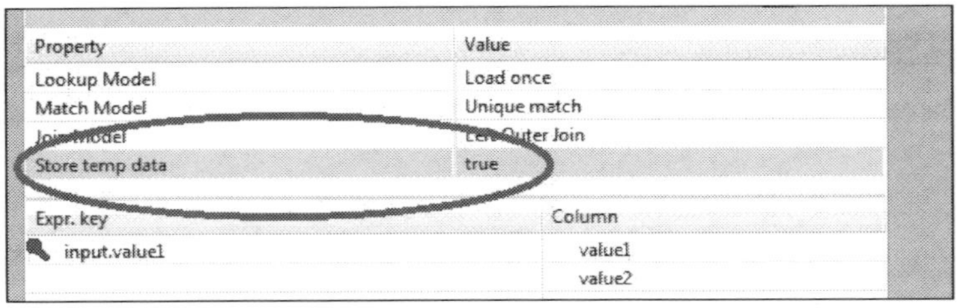

When Talend executes a `tMap` where this method is used it will write the lookups to disk, and then read the input data into memory prior to processing.

If you choose to use this method, then you must ensure that the input data to be processed takes less memory than the lookup, and you should also be aware that the order of the input records is not maintained.

Split the files

If the disk method would struggle because the input is too large, then you could consider using the same method but splitting the input into a number of files and processing them individually.

While this may affect your processing time, it will stop you from running out of memory.

Hardware solutions

As a last resort, or if an increase in the time to process is not acceptable, then consider adding more memory to your server.

It would also be possible to add additional servers and processing subsets of the input data on different servers at the same time, and then recombining the output data in a final stage.

A
Common Type Conversions

The following table is a set of Java and Talend methods that allow conversion between different data types. This is by no means an exhaustive list, but will cover many of type conversions that you will encounter.

From Type	To Type	Example
String	Integer	`Integer.parseInt(row1.myString)`
String	Date	`TalendDate.parseDate("dd-MM-yyyy",row1.myString)`
String	BigDecimal	`new BigDecimal(row1.myString)` where myString can include decimal places. For example, 99.00
String	Float	`Float.parseFloat(row1.myString)`
String	Long	`Long.parseLong(row1.myString)`
Integer	String	variable+"" or `variable.toString()`
Date	String	`TalendDate.formatDate("yy-MM-dd", row1.myDate)`
BigDecimal	String	`row1.myBigDecimal.toString()`
Float	String	`row1.myFloat.toString()`
Long	String	`row1.myLong.toString()`
Integer	Long	`row1.myInteger.longValue()`
Integer	BigDecimal	`new BigDecimal(row1.myInteger)`
Integer	Float	`new Float(row1.myInteger)`

From Type	To Type	Example
Float	Integer	To do this conversion you need to decide on a rounding methods such as `Math.round()`, `Math.ceil()`, `Math.floor()` and then cast the result to Integer.
BigDecimal	Integer	As with Float, BigDecimal can have decimal places, so will need to be rounded prior to casting to Integer.
Float	BigDecimal	`new BigDecimal(Float.toString(row1.myFloat))`

B
Management of Contexts

Context variables are very important within Talend for managing code through environments from development to production. This appendix describes different approaches for managing context variables and context groups within a project in terms of their pros and cons.

Introduction

The methods described here are all different in approach from each other and are all viable for use within a Talend project.

Which method you choose to use should be dependent upon the nature of your Talend project and the skills within the team.

It is recommended that before making any decision on contexts for your project, you should first perform a small trial of each method to understand the pros and cons more completely and then decide which one most closely suits your requirements.

Manipulating contexts in Talend Open Studio

Creating contexts in the studio is described in the recipe *Adding contexts to a context group* in *Chapter 6, Managing Context Variables*.

Pros

This is the simplest method of managing contexts. It all takes place in the Studio and is very visible to the developer.

It is also is a reasonably good way of protecting an environment, because when the code has been deployed, the context variables and launchers in production are usually available only to operational personnel. This means that the values available to a job in production, for example, passwords, can only be set in production by operation staff and will never be known by other personnel.

Cons

The number of contexts can easily get out of hand and become unmanageable, especially when multiple developers are working on the same project. Each will usually require a copy of the context, uniquely named, containing their information for their test environment.

Another downside is that it is very easy to create different context groups with different contexts, so that you end up with a variety of flavors or development, for instance, dev, DEV, Dev, and so on.

However, great care must be taken when using this method to ensure that after the first deployment of the context variables and launchers in production, they are not accidentally copied over when deploying a new version, or that the support staff remembers to update them if the new version of the code is copied to different folder.

Conclusion

If the processes surrounding this method are robust, then this can be a reasonable method for deployment in a small environment.

Understanding implicit context loading

The implicit context load method as described in the recipe *Using implicit context load to load contexts in Chapter 6, Managing Context Variables*.

Pros

The implicit context load technique is centrally managed, thus ensuring consistent use across a project. Developers do not need to remember to set context variables, because they will be set automatically.

The use of external files is good practice for managing contexts, as they are less likely to be overwritten during deployment.

Cons

This method provides the option to fail if a context variable is not present or does not contain data, which is great for validating your parameters. Unfortunately this option checks against the whole context of a job, including context variables that are only used locally within the job and will fail if the local job variables are not present in the external file. Thus we have a choice; we can add single use variables to our shared context, potentially making it very messy, or we have to turn off the option to fail the job if we find problems with the context variables, thus removing a level of validation that we may prefer to keep.

Conclusion

The implicit context load method provides a consistent method for loading contexts and requires the least effort to set up and maintain, but it does suffer from a lack of fine grain since the context variables are applied to every job in a project.

It is good for projects where there is high degree of commonality in the processing and the resources.

Understanding tContextLoad

The `tContextLoad` method as described in the recipe *Using tContextLoad to load contexts* in *Chapter 6, Managing Context Variables*.

Pros

`tContextLoad` is more fine-grained than the other methods described previously, which means that context values could be set up for individual jobs within a project.

As with the implicit context load, use of external files is good practice for managing contexts, because they are less likely to be overwritten during deployment.

Cons

`tContextLoad` suffers from the same failings as implicit context load; that is, the context variable checks are against all variables or none of them. The fine grain can also be a weakness, because this method does allow much more freedom to developers and could become unmanageable.

Conclusion

The `tContextLoad` method provides a more fine-grained approach to contexts, giving choice to the developer as to which files and which variables within the files are required for a particular task.

Unfortunately, it does suffer from not being able to check context variables individually, which is a liability; however, if this is not so important, it does mean only a small amount of additional coding is required per job to give you the fine grain context loading.

Manually checking and setting contexts

This method is very similar to the `tContextLoad`; however, instead of using `tContextLoad` to select the file and load and validate the key value pairs, this is performed by custom Java code, within a `tJavaRow` component, as described in the recipe *Setting context variables and globalMap variables using tJava* in *Chapter 5*, Using Java in Talend.

Pros

This method allows the finest grain selection and setting of context variables.

As with the implicit context load and `tContextLoad`, use of external files is a good practice for managing contexts, because they are less likely to be overwritten during deployment.

This method provides the developer with the ability to validate individual values and kill the job if they are invalid, without having to worry about local context variables.

Cons

The fine grain can also be a weakness. This method does give much more freedom to developers and could become unmanageable.

More manual code is required to manage this method than for managing any of the other methods.

Conclusion

Despite being the most complex method, it is a very good method for managing contexts in a project, so long as the processes are well defined, and the developers are diligent in following the processes.

It provides a high degree of control and is not hampered by the fact that single use context variables may exist within the jobs in the project.

Index

A

D

E

F

G

H

I

J

U

V

W

X

Thank you for buying

Talend Open Studio Cookbook

About Packt Publishing

Packt, pronounced 'packed', published its first book "*Mastering phpMyAdmin for Effective MySQL Management*" in April 2004 and subsequently continued to specialize in publishing highly focused books on specific technologies and solutions.

Our books and publications share the experiences of your fellow IT professionals in adapting and customizing today's systems, applications, and frameworks. Our solution based books give you the knowledge and power to customize the software and technologies you're using to get the job done. Packt books are more specific and less general than the IT books you have seen in the past. Our unique business model allows us to bring you more focused information, giving you more of what you need to know, and less of what you don't.

Packt is a modern, yet unique publishing company, which focuses on producing quality, cutting-edge books for communities of developers, administrators, and newbies alike. For more information, please visit our website: `www.packtpub.com`.

About Packt Open Source

In 2010, Packt launched two new brands, Packt Open Source and Packt Enterprise, in order to continue its focus on specialization. This book is part of the Packt Open Source brand, home to books published on software built around Open Source licences, and offering information to anybody from advanced developers to budding web designers. The Open Source brand also runs Packt's Open Source Royalty Scheme, by which Packt gives a royalty to each Open Source project about whose software a book is sold.

Writing for Packt

We welcome all inquiries from people who are interested in authoring. Book proposals should be sent to author@packtpub.com. If your book idea is still at an early stage and you would like to discuss it first before writing a formal book proposal, contact us; one of our commissioning editors will get in touch with you.

We're not just looking for published authors; if you have strong technical skills but no writing experience, our experienced editors can help you develop a writing career, or simply get some additional reward for your expertise.

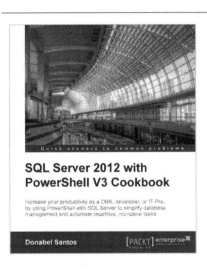

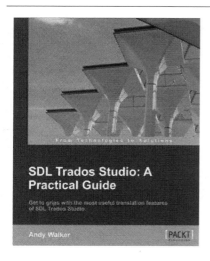

82235627R00150

Made in the USA
Middletown, DE
02 August 2018